Don't Believe Everything You Think

The 6 Basic Mistakes We Make in Thinking

Advance Praise

"This appeal to rational judgment and decision making couldn't come at a more opportune time. With relativism blurring the distinctions between valid and invalid arguments and values, pseudoscience and superstition are on the march. Credence is given to faith healing, alien abductions, extrasensory perception, astrology, communication with the dead, clairvoyance, and a host of other unfounded notions. In his engaging work, Professor Kida explains the psychological biases that produce errors in reasoning and provides the reader with the tools to debunk these and other myths. It is essential reading for anybody interested in making valid judgments and sound decisions in everyday life."

—Icek Ajzen, author of *Attitudes, Personality, and Behavior*

"The study of human cognition has provided many fascinating findings that help explain fallacies in thinking and memory. Kida has written a very nice, lively, and readable introduction to this material, and has managed to include a useful introduction to the scientific method as well."

—Arnold D. Well, professor emeritus of psychology,
University of Massachusetts, Amherst

"Kida does a succinct and entertaining job of presenting . . . mental shortcuts and their resulting biases in our own thought processes."

—Robyn M. Dawes, Charles J. Queenan Jr. Professor,
Department of Social and Decision Sciences,
Carnegie Mellon University

Don't Believe Everything You Think

The 6 Basic Mistakes We Make in Thinking

Thomas Kida

Prometheus Books
Amherst, New York 14228-2197

Published 2006 by Prometheus Books

Inquiries should be addressed to
Prometheus Books
59 John Glenn Drive
Amherst, New York 14228–2197
VOICE: 716–691–0133, ext. 207
FAX: 716–564–2711
WWW.PROMETHEUSBOOKS.COM

10 09 08 07 06 5 4 3 2 1

Library of Congress Cataloging-in-Publication Data

Kida, Thomas E. (Thomas Edward), 1951–

Don't believe everything you think : the 6 basic mistakes we make in thinking / by Thomas Kida.

p. cm.

Includes bibliographical references (p.) and index.

ISBN 1-59102-408-0 (pbk. : alk. paper)

ISBN 978-1-59102-408-8

1. Thought and thinking. 2. Error. I. Title.

BF441.K45 2006

153.4'2—dc22

2006003366

Printed in the United States on acid-free paper

To my family

CONTENTS

ACKNOWLEDGMENTS

As with most works, this book was not written in a vacuum. Rather, it's based upon the research and writing of many creative thinkers who have come before. I've tried to write the book in an easygoing, conversational style to make the topics readable and interesting to a wide audience. In fact, it's written to be a simple introduction to how we think and how our thinking can go wrong. If the topics discussed here pique your interest, I heartily recommend the following authors and researchers for a more in-depth discussion of specific issues.

The work of Carl Sagan and Michael Shermer provide the foundation for much of the discussion on science and pseudoscience, and the importance of skeptical and critical thinking. Carl Sagan's superb book *The Demon Haunted World: Science as a Candle in the Dark* is must reading for anyone interested in critical thinking. Michael Shermer wrote the excellent book *Why People Believe Weird Things* and is the publisher of the magazine *Skeptic*. The world would be a better place if every household received a copy of *Skeptic* and *Skeptical Inquirer*, a similar publication produced by the Committee for the Scientific Investigation of Claims of the Paranormal. I've also drawn on the excellent work of Theodore Schick and Lewis Vaughn's *How to Think about Weird Things*, Keith Stanovich's *How to Think Straight about Psychology*, and Stuart Vyse's *Believing in Magic: The Psychology of Superstition*.

In the area of decision making, I owe a debt to Scott Plous's superb book *The Psychology of Judgment and Decision Making*, Tom Gilovich's *How We Know What Isn't So*, and Stuart Sutherland's *Irrationality: Why We Don't Think Straight*. Specifically relating to memory, Daniel Schacter's *The Seven Sins of Memory* and the work of Elizabeth Loftus (e.g., *The Myth of Repressed Memory*, with Katherine Ketcham) were essential. William Sherden's *The Fortune Sellers*, Barry Glassner's *The Culture of Fear*, and Burton Malkiel's *A Random Walk Down Wall Street* are also fascinating books that were used in various chapters. Much of the discussion of how we make decisions is based upon the research of psychologists such as Amos Tversky, Daniel Kahneman, as well as innumerable others. My debt to these researchers and others referenced throughout cannot be overestimated.

On a more personal note, I'm grateful to many people who have helped in the development of the book. Linda Regan, my editor, believed in the book from the first time she saw the idea, and was the kind of insightful editor I had hoped to work with. Jim Smith and Kathie Sullivan provided many valuable comments that improved the manuscript, and were always there to discuss the never-ending issues that came up. In addition, I would like to thank Chris and Alicia Agoglia, Erin Moore, Ken Ryack, Tracey Riley, Ben Luippold, Steve Gill, Bill Wooldridge, Ron Karren, Lou Wigdor, Dave and Joe Goulet, and Gene Myer for their comments and assistance. Thanks also to my friends who were the inspiration for many of the stories that have livened up the book, especially the Ingari clan and the Thursday afternoon "happy hour" crew. And, of course, thanks to Charlie—for being Charlie. I'd also like to thank my colleagues at the University of Massachusetts, especially Dennis Hanno, Ron Mannino, and Tom O'Brien, for providing an atmosphere that allowed me to pursue my interest in critical thinking and decision making.

Finally, I thank my family, to whom this book is dedicated—Kathie, Elaine, Gene, Doug, Roland, Jimmy, Dave, Joe, and, of course, Mom and Dad. Our Saturday night "bull" sessions, which provided many ideas for the book, have been a constant joy. I'm glad we're going through this life together. I'd especially like to thank Kathie—for everything.

INTRODUCTION: A SIX PACK OF PROBLEMS

You are what you think . . . geez, that's frightening.
—Lily Tomlin

I saw a ghost. It was the middle of the night, and I had just woken up to get a drink of water. Before getting out of bed, I looked over to my right where Kathy was sleeping, and there, floating about a foot above her, was a glowing vision of an old woman staring back at me. The apparition was lying over Kathy as if she wanted to be near her. She looked to be about ninety, with long white hair and a deeply wrinkled face. There was a definite family resemblance; she looked like she could have been Kathy's great-grandmother or some other distant relative. Of course, this startled the hell out of me. I looked away, shook my head a couple of times, and looked back. The old woman was still there, staring right back at me. Our eyes were locked on one another for what seemed to be an hour, although it was probably just a few moments. Her face was expressionless—no smile, no warmth, just a penetrating stare. Once again, I looked away, shook my head, and then looked back. This time she was gone. A bit unnerved, I got up to get some water and then went back to bed. When we woke the next morning I told Kathy what I had seen. She remembered hearing me get up and leave the room, so we thought it wasn't just a dream. Also, what I had experienced seemed so real. It was as if I could reach out and touch the old woman.

Now, I don't believe in ghosts. While the experience was very compelling, I thought that my mind was just playing tricks on me. However, an amazing thing happened when I began to tell my story to other people. Many of them immediately took the experience as proof that ghosts exist. They often would say, "What else could explain it? Just look at the facts. You were awake; Kathy heard you get up. You saw it, and we don't see things that aren't there. It was floating and it disappeared mysteriously. That's what ghosts do. And, the woman resembled Kathy, so it was probably one of her deceased relatives watching over her." Clearly, all the evidence leads to one conclusion. I had seen a ghost! It just makes sense. Doesn't it?

It turns out that there is another, more prosaic, explanation for my "ghostly" encounter. Research has documented that we can experience hypnopompic hallucinations, which occur as we're coming out of sleep. Individuals have reported seeing all kinds of visions in this state, including alien creatures, departed relatives, and monsters. There's also a strong sense of being awake during these hallucinations. Since they occur just before waking, Kathy could have heard me get up, because I eventually did wake and leave the room. As for the family resemblance, for all I know I was just projecting what I thought Kathy would look like when she got very old. And so, my experience can easily be explained by what we know from scientific research on human perception (and misperception)—without the need to evoke supernatural phenomena. Nevertheless, those individuals who were predisposed to believe in ghosts immediately interpreted my story as proof that ghosts exist. We are often willing to form very extraordinary beliefs on the basis of very flimsy evidence.

Maybe you don't believe in things as "far-fetched" as ghosts, especially given such evidence. However, most of us hold some beliefs that have very little evidence to support them (and have considerable evidence against them). Do you think that some alternative medicines, like homeopathic remedies, cure disease, or that some people have extrasensory perception (ESP), or that near death experiences provide evidence of an afterlife? Don't believe everything you think. Why? We often believe things because we *want* to believe them, not because of the evidence. Even if we don't have a preconceived notion of what we want to believe, we can still believe things that are not true. Do you think that silicon breast implants cause major disease, that low self-esteem is a cause of aggression, or that crime in America is steadily increasing? Many people hold such beliefs, but research indicates that they're not true. As we will see, we form many incorrect beliefs because we have natural tendencies to evaluate evidence in a biased and faulty manner.

The beliefs we hold are closely tied to the decisions we make. In effect, what we believe affects what we decide. My good friend Chris thinks that he can beat the stock market. He believes that, if he puts enough time into learning the ins and outs of the market, he'll earn substantially more on his stock picks than what the average market return will give him. He once told me that a friend of his bought a couple of stocks and later sold them for a profit of over $30,000. Chris reasoned that he could do the same. He even went so far as to talk about paying off his mortgage from his stock proceeds. When I asked about the other stocks his friend bought, Chris was a little more evasive. When pressed, he said that some were losers, but he continued to focus on the winners.

My friend Chris is a very smart person. Many intelligent people believe they can beat the market if they put in the time and energy. This belief is fueled by a number of books written by "experts" who say that, if you use their method, you too can make a killing in the market. The Internet is replete with such claims. However, research has shown that it is very difficult, if not impossible, to analyze a firm's financial condition and consistently pick stocks that outperform the market at a given risk level. Experienced fund managers, who are so-called experts at picking stocks, can't consistently beat the market. In fact, a monkey throwing darts at a Wall Street Journal stock listing can usually pick stocks as well as the experts![1] Of course, you may get lucky and pick a stock that really takes off. By the same token, you could put $20,000 on red at a Vegas roulette wheel and win—but that's a very risky proposition, and you won't be able to win consistently.

A wealth of research demonstrates that it's better to put your money in a general index fund, like the Standard & Poor's 500, rather than bet on just a few stock picks. Still, people want to believe that they can beat the market. Chris's belief led him to invest a significant amount of cash in a few select stocks, which caused him to lose over $20,000 in a period when the overall market rose by about 25 percent. Erroneously held beliefs can be dangerous to your wealth!

WHAT IT'S ALL ABOUT

We humans are amazing creatures. We have the capacity to think creatively and solve complex problems. We've made technological advances that have made our lives easier and more enjoyable. We've built machines that allow us to explore the outer reaches of space and the depths of the oceans. We've made medical advancements that have significantly extended our life spans. We've built sophisticated civilizations. And yet, despite all we have achieved, we still fall prey to flawed thinking.

This book is about how we form our beliefs and make our decisions. More important, it's about the many ways that our beliefs and decisions can go wrong. A belief is essentially a point of view that we hold to be true. We can arrive at our beliefs in different ways. Sometimes, they come from a quick "gut" reaction. In other cases, we spend considerable time and effort thinking about a topic before we form a belief. In addition, variables such as parental predilections; sibling influences; peer pressures; and educational, social, and cultural influences can affect the beliefs we form.[2] Irrespective of how we arrive at a belief, if we accept a viewpoint to be true, the belief we hold can have a major impact on the decisions we make.

We obviously make many very good decisions every day of our lives. If not, we wouldn't survive very long. However, we also make many mistakes, and we're often not even aware that we make them. And yet, those mistakes can have significant consequences for our well-being. They can result in spending considerable time and money on things that don't work, and worse, they can lead us to make decisions that negatively affect our health and even our lives.

If we believe in the ability of psychics, fortunetellers, and astrologers, we're more likely to lay down our hard-earned money to find out if Uncle Harry is still mad at us from his grave, or if we should marry the person we just met last night. When the Reagans were in the White House, Nancy Reagan's belief in astrology led her to consult an astrologist when deciding President Reagan's schedule.[3] If we believe that an alternative medicine treatment works, we're likely to spend considerable money on the treatment, even if there's little reliable evidence to support it. In fact, a number of people who have avoided traditional medicine could have easily been cured by it. Instead, they embraced alternative healing techniques, and because of this, many died.[4]

Faulty beliefs and decisions affect not only our everyday personal lives, but also societal decisions that have an impact on us all. Public officials set policy, pass laws, and spend our money. Many of these decisions are based upon faulty beliefs, which can result in allocating billions of our tax dollars to solve a problem that has little impact on society's welfare, while neglecting, or actually causing, more serious problems. As an example, US cities spent around $10 billion in the 1990s to eliminate asbestos from public buildings. While asbestos may be dangerous if inhaled, its presence in most buildings was not a serious health hazard. In fact, its removal is often more dangerous than leaving it in place.[5]

So why do we fall prey to erroneous thinking? Are we stupid? It certainly doesn't seem so! All of us make the kinds of mistakes in thinking and deciding that are discussed in this book, including highly trained professionals such as doctors, lawyers, and CEOs of major corporations. Instead, two basic reasons come to mind. First, we all have natural tendencies to search for and evaluate evidence in a faulty manner. The reasons for these tendencies range from evolutionary considerations to just wanting to simplify the thinking process. Second, critical thinking and decision-making skills, which could counteract our natural tendencies to err, are typically not taught in our schools. Our education system requires courses in English, history, math, and the sciences, but not in critical thinking and decision making. Yet such courses would develop skills that could have a significant impact on the decisions we face every day of our lives.

Most of the topics discussed here come from two fascinating areas. One concerns the psychology of judgment and decision making, which has uncovered a wealth of information on how we think, and how our thinking can go wrong. The other concerns the difference between science and pseudoscience. Much of what is reported on TV and other media outlets is actually pseudo or junk science, which is not real science, but is passed off as such. You can surf the channels on any night and find so-called scientific investigators reporting on such things as ESP, alien encounters, Bigfoot, and the search for Atlantis. Given the proliferation of pseudoscientific thinking that permeates the media, we are increasingly susceptible to thinking like a pseudoscientist—which contributes profoundly to errors in our beliefs and decisions.

The essence behind many of the ideas in this book relate to being a skeptical thinker. The term *skeptic* has received a bad rap in our society. People often think of a skeptic as someone who's cynical, always looking for the fault in things. However, a skeptic is just a person who wants to see and evaluate the evidence before believing. In its truest sense, a skeptic is someone who keeps an open mind, but requires rigorous investigation before choosing to believe something. It's the quality of our reasons for believing that make us intelligent and thoughtful individuals, and the more important or extraordinary the belief, the more compelling the evidence should be before we believe it. If that's how you form your beliefs, then you're a skeptic. In essence, a skeptic follows the motto of Missouri, the "show me" state—if you've got a claim, show me the evidence.

A SIX PACK OF PROBLEMS

We make too many wrong mistakes.
—Yogi Berra

When reading any book, the details seem to fall away from memory over time. At this stage of my life, I'm lucky to remember just a few of the main points. So I think it would be a good idea to start off by listing the key points of this book. It is my hope that you'll find the rest of the book full of interesting examples of these main ideas. I've narrowed them down to six—I call them our six pack of problems.

- We prefer stories to statistics.
- We seek to confirm.
- We rarely appreciate the role of chance and coincidence in life.
- We can misperceive our world.
- We oversimplify.
- We have faulty memories.

1) We prefer stories to statistics.

We have evolved as storytelling creatures. From our very beginnings, our history and knowledge have been passed from one generation to the next by means of personal stories. In evolutionary terms, it's only recently that we recorded and stored our knowledge in forms that are easily accessible. As a consequence, we have a penchant to pay close attention to information that comes to us in the form of a story or personal account.[6]

Stories are wonderful. They add enjoyment to our lives, they engage our imagination, they move us. We are social animals, so we're particularly interested in the personal stories of others. As we will see, however, relying on this anecdotal evidence to form our beliefs and decisions can be fraught with errors. Why? It means that we ignore other more relevant information. For example, we shy away from statistics. The mere word can cause otherwise intelligent individuals' eyes to glaze over. At our core, we are storytellers, not statisticians. But statistics often provide us with the best and most reliable information with which to make our decisions. In many cases, unfortunately, our knowledge of even simple statistics is rudimentary. Former president Dwight Eisenhower was appalled to learn that about half of our children had below average intelligence, thinking that something had to be done about such poor performance. But, of course, about half of our children will be below (and half above) average intelligence.[7] In other cases, we ignore statistics because they seem abstract and boring. As a result, even if we know the statistics, we let personal stories affect us more.

Consider the following. You're thinking about buying a new car, so you check *Consumer Reports* to investigate its reliability. The statistics from prior years' models indicate that the car is very reliable. Happy with your research, you go to a party where a friend informs you that he recently bought that very same car. "It's been nothing but trouble!" he exclaims. "It's in the shop every few months. I've replaced the clutch, there were brake problems, and it keeps stalling out on me." How do you react to this information? For many of us, learning of our friend's plight would make us question our decision and possibly not buy the car. However, it's better to rely on the frequency of repairs, as summarized in *Consumer Reports*. That data is based upon a large sample of similar cars, while our friend's experience is based on only one car. There's variance in everything—there can be lemons with any model of car. Your friend may have just been unlucky to get one of the few problem cars. The point is, if you listen to your friend, you're basing your decision upon anecdotal evidence that is much less relevant. And yet, most of us have a tendency to give considerable attention to such personal experiences when making our decisions.

2) We seek to confirm.

If you support gun control, do you give more credence to information that supports a ban on guns? If you have a favorite presidential candidate, do you pay more attention to information that's favorable to the candidate? If you believe in the ability of psychics to predict the future, do you remember the few times they were right, and forget the vast majority of times they were wrong? It turns out that this is how we think. We have a natural tendency to use "confirming" decision strategies. That is, we place greater importance on information that supports our existing beliefs and expectations, or what we want to believe, and less importance on information that is contradictory to those beliefs. In effect, we remember the hits and forget the misses.

Our penchant to attend to confirming evidence is so deeply ingrained in our thinking processes that we'll often seek out supporting data even when we don't have a strong belief or expectation. To see what I mean, think of someone you know and try to decide if the person is charitable. More likely than not, you will think of instances when the person exhibited charitable behavior, such as donating money, helping others, etc. You won't think of all the times the person wasn't charitable but could have been. Why is that? We seem to find it easier to think in terms of those instances that support whatever notion we're testing. The problem is, by selectively focusing on supporting information, we ignore contradictory information that may be very relevant to the decisions we make.

3) We rarely appreciate the role of chance and coincidence in life.

Suppose you see an ad in the *Wall Street Journal* touting the performance of the "Super-growth" mutual fund. "This fund has earned more than the average of all other funds over the past five years!" the ad proclaims. A photo of its big-name manager is also prominently displayed, leading you to believe that the fund's earnings are directly related to the manager's stock-picking prowess. Sounds convincing, but does that performance demonstrate superior knowledge of the stock market? Should you invest in the fund? Before deciding, you have to ask yourself, Could this superior performance be due to just chance? If you flip a coin five times, it will sometimes come up heads five times in a row simply due to chance. As we'll see later, the evidence suggests that the long-term performance of mutual funds is similar to flipping a coin. Thus, the so-called experts typically don't achieve superior returns over the long run. In fact, it may be prudent *not* to invest in a fund that has outperformed the average recently because it will likely drop in the future due to a phenomenon called regression to the mean.

Why are we so quick to believe that superior knowledge led to the fund's above average performance? We generally don't appreciate the role that chance and coincidence play in our lives. While chance affects many aspects of our world, we don't like to think that things happen by chance. Instead, we want to believe that things happen for a reason. We are causal-seeking animals—we have an ingrained desire to find cause and effect relationships in the world. This desire to look for causes likely arose because of our evolutionary development. Our early ancestors who discovered the causes for things survived and passed on their genes; for example, those who noticed that a spark starts a fire began using fire and were more likely to survive. This preference to seek out causes usually serves us well. The problem is, the tendency is so central to our cognitive makeup and thought processes that we overapply it. We start seeing causes for things that are simply the result of chance occurrences.

4) We can misperceive our world.

We like to think that we perceive the world as it actually is. How many times have we heard someone say, "I know what I saw." However, our senses can be deceived. Sometimes the problem is selective perception, where we don't see certain things because our focus is elsewhere. In other cases, we can actually see things that aren't there. Remember my ghostly encounter? Well, studies show that a significant number of us have hallucinated at some point in our lives. Of course, problems are likely to arise when we use these inaccurate perceptions in our thinking. Two factors have a particularly important effect on how we perceive the world: our expectations and our desires. That is, our perceptions are greatly influenced by what we expect to see and what we want to see. Consider the following events.

A newsflash just reported that a large and dangerous bear has escaped from the city zoo. What happens? The 911 switchboard lights up. The bear has been spotted in a tree, running across the park, and rummaging in a dumpster down a back alley. People report seeing the bear all over town. But it turns out the bear never wandered more than 100 yards from the zoo.[8] Our expectations create perceptions. Suppose we're at a football game when our favorite team is playing its archrival. Chances are we'll notice many more infractions committed by the other team than by our team. Of course, those rooting for the other team will likely see more penalties committed by our side.[9] We see what we want to see.

Our faulty perceptions have led to a number of bizarre occurrences throughout human history. Every now and then, a collective delusion occurs that causes mass hysteria in some segment of society. A "monkey man" scare recently occurred in India, where people reported seeing a half monkey–half human creature with razor-sharp fingernails and superhuman strength. Outbreaks of "penis shrinking" panics occur in various parts of Asia, where people perceive their genitalia shriveling up into their bodies.[10] And, of course, in this country there are the numerous reports of alien abduction. Clearly, our perception of reality can be unreliable, which should make us wary of beliefs that are based only on our personal experiences, especially if those beliefs are extraordinary.

5) We oversimplify.

Life can be very complex. We often have to juggle many different things just to get through the day. This also happens when we make decisions. Sometimes the amount of information available is overwhelming. In fact, if we paid attention to all of it, we'd spend most of our time just gathering and evaluating information. To avoid this "analysis paralysis," we use a number of simplifying strategies. For example, we often base our decisions upon information that can easily be brought to mind. If we're deciding whether a sport, like downhill skiing, is risky, we don't conduct an exhaustive search of the ways a person could get hurt skiing, or search out the number of skiing injuries per year. Instead, we often simplify the task by thinking about our friends' skiing experiences or about skiing accidents we heard reported on TV. We may remember, for example, that both Sonny Bono and Michael Kennedy were killed while skiing in the same year and conclude that skiing is a very dangerous sport (even though there are more injuries in many other recreational activities, such as boating and bike riding).

Simplifying strategies can be quite beneficial. They save time and effort, and allow us to make a decision quickly and move on to something else. Fortunately, they often result in reasonably good decisions. While they may not give us the best decision, they often are "good enough." However, when we use these simplifying strategies we don't pay attention to all the information that's relevant to a decision, which can get us into trouble.

What if you went to your doctor and got tested for a debilitating viral disease. The test comes back positive—it says you have the virus! How worried should you be? The doctor tells you, "The test is 100 percent accurate in indicating a person has the virus when they actually have it, but it also says a person has the virus when they don't have it 5 percent of the time." You also learn that about one in five hundred people have the virus. So, what's the probability you have the virus if the test says you do? Most people say it's around 95 percent. In fact, the correct answer is only 4 percent! As we will see, our use of simplifying strategies results in ignoring very important information, which can lead to grossly inaccurate judgments.

6) We have faulty memories.

Imagine that you're having a relaxing evening watching TV when you hear a knock at the door. As you open it, a policeman slaps a pair of handcuffs on you and states, "You're under arrest for sexual assault." Amazingly, you find out that your daughter has just accused you of sexually molesting her when she was a little girl, some twenty years ago. You can't believe it because you've always had a great relationship with your daughter, and you know that you never abused her. However, to resolve some emotional problems, she recently saw a therapist who thought that her problems could be the result of childhood sexual abuse. After several sessions of hypnosis, your daughter started to remember a number of instances in which you sexually assaulted her. Based on these repressed memories, you're convicted and sent to prison, even with a complete lack of physical evidence for the abuse.

Sounds crazy? You don't think it could happen? Well, it has happened in a number of cases in the United States.[11] Why is that? Many of us—including those who testify as witnesses—think that our memory is a permanent record of past experiences. Of course, we know that we can't remember everything, but many of us think that if we use special techniques, like hypnosis, we'll be able to recall previously inaccessible events. In fact, surveys indicate that most Americans hold this view of memory.[12] And when we're confident in our memory, we believe that we remember things as they actually occurred.

However, considerable research indicates that our memories can change. We can even create new memories for events that never actually happened! In effect, our memory is not a literal snapshot of events which we later retrieve from our album of past experiences. Instead, memory is constructive. Current beliefs, expectations, environment, and even suggestive questioning can influence our memory of past events. It's more accurate to think of memory as a reconstruction of the past—and with each successive reconstruction, our memories can get further and further from the truth. Memories thus change over time, even when we're confident that they haven't, and those memories can have a significant influence on the beliefs we form and the decisions we make.

SUMMING UP

As you can see, we have a number of tendencies that can lead to faulty beliefs and decisions. Some of them are deeply rooted in our cognitive processes because of our evolutionary development, as in our preference for stories over statistics. Others are there to simplify our complex lives and decision making. Of course, we don't always fall prey to these problems. While we often seek out confirming data, we sometimes pay attention to disconfirming information. In addition, these cognitive characteristics can serve us very well in many instances. If we didn't use simplifying strategies, we would often become overloaded with information, making it difficult to reach any decision. However, these tendencies also cause us a number of problems when we form our beliefs and make our decisions.

One other thing must be kept in mind. Don't feel bad if you find yourself making the kinds of errors in thinking that are discussed in this book. I've made them, my friends have made them, and everyone I've ever known has made them. That's how ingrained they are in our cognitive makeup. Since we're typically not even aware they exist, the first step in making better decisions is to identify the pitfalls in our thinking. So let's take a look at where and why we can go wrong.

CHAPTER 1: WEIRD BELIEFS AND PSEUDOSCIENTIFIC THINKING

It is not disbelief that is dangerous to our society, it is belief.

—George Bernard Shaw

On a popular local radio station, three morning show personalities were talking with a frequent guest. "Unbelievable!" "Amazing!" That's how they described their guest's incredible ability. In fact, they urged their audience to get to one of her seminars as soon as possible. Why? Because she can talk with the dead. Now these talk-show hosts are critical of many things; they often try to uncover the folly in what other people say or do. However, they were completely taken with the psychic. So were their listeners. Caller after caller was amazed by what she said—some even cried upon hearing what they thought were the words of their deceased loved ones.

You're at the hospital with severe abdominal pain. While lying on the examination table, a nurse enters the room, places her hands several inches above your body, and begins moving them in a gentle, wavelike motion, starting at your head and progressing slowly down your torso. "What are you doing?" you ask. "I'm driving the negative energy from your body," she says. "It's what's causing your pain." Sound a bit crazy? That wouldn't happen, would it? Well, it could. The nurse is practicing a technique called therapeutic touch. More than forty thousand nurses have been trained in this technique, and more than twenty thousand actively practice it today. In fact, it's taught at more than one hundred colleges and universities worldwide, including major medical schools at respected universities like NYU, and it's used in at least eighty hospitals in the United States alone.[1]

My good friend Joe is a geologist. He runs a water exploration company and travels the world finding drinkable water for towns, cities, and even small countries. He uses the most advanced technology, from complex computer models to satellite imagery, to locate high-output wells. Joe is very successful at what he does. In some areas of the Caribbean he has achieved an almost godlike status for his ability to find water where no one else could. Joe is one of the most intelligent individuals I know. And yet, at one point in his career, he used dowsing in his water exploration. Dowsing is a technique in which an individual holds an object, like a Y-shaped tree branch, and walks around the land in search of water. When the branch twitches, it's taken as a sign that water is below. Joe met a "professional" dowser while working in New England and became convinced that it works. In fact, many years ago when I bought some land to build a house he came over, dowsed the land, and told me where to drill.

What do these cases have in common? Very bright, capable, highly trained people are holding extraordinary beliefs that have little or no credible supporting evidence. In fact, the evidence indicates the reverse—talking with the dead, therapeutic touch, and dowsing don't work (my well has never yielded much water), but smart people continue to believe.[2] It happens to medical professionals, successful businesspeople, scientists, and to you and me. Now you may say, "I wouldn't believe in such bizarre things." But what about other beliefs that may, on the surface, seem more plausible? Consider the case of "facilitated communication."

SOUNDS REASONABLE, DON'T YOU THINK?

Your friend has an autistic child. Autism is a medical condition in which children can be unresponsive, aloof, and seem incapable of forming relationships with others. One's heart goes out to the children and parents affected by such a debilitating condition. Then there appears to be something that can help. Your friend recently told you of a fantastic new discovery that has enabled him to talk with his child. He says the technique, called facilitated communication, has demonstrated that autistic children are quite intelligent, and that their main problem centers simply around their inability to communicate. Delighted for your friend and intrigued by this breakthrough, you decide to learn more about the technique.

You find that facilitated communication has been used since the 1970s, when a teacher discovered that if you provide physical assistance to a severely autistic child, by holding their hand or arm to a typewriter or computer keyboard, the child will type out coherent, intelligent thoughts. Apparently, hidden beneath the impaired exterior of an autistic child lay a very capable mind that would demonstrate considerable intellect if put in a situation enabling him to communicate. In effect, facilitated communication demonstrated that severely autistic children have communication problems that are primarily caused by physical, rather than mental, limitations.

Based on this amazing discovery, the Dignity Through Education and Language Center was opened in 1986 to promote facilitated communication, and since then other centers have been established at major American universities. At Syracuse University, the Facilitated Communication Institute was established, which has trained thousands of therapists, and programs have been developed at other schools.

As time went by, the usefulness of facilitated communication gained support. Numerous reports were published indicating that facilitated communication was effective even for people with severe autism. Thousands of children throughout the world have been communicating with their parents and others using the technique. In fact, autistic children have been attending regular schools and progressing quite well with the help of facilitated communication.

The evidence seems compelling, doesn't it? Research centers are set up at major universities. Numerous personal testimonials indicate that parents can now communicate with their children. Severely autistic children are succeeding in school. And, there's "research" to support it. Pretty convincing stuff. Or is it?

It turns out that when controlled scientific studies were conducted, facilitated communication was shown to be worthless. In one very dramatic example, a researcher put headphones on both the facilitator and the child and asked a series of questions. When both received the same question, the child answered correctly. But when the child and facilitator were asked different questions, the child typed the answer to the facilitator's question.[3] In another compelling study, a thin wall was erected between the child and facilitator. Each was then shown different items and asked to identify them. The item identified by the child was what the facilitator saw, not what the child saw. These studies clearly demonstrate that it is the facilitator, and not the child, who is responding during facilitated communication. The facilitator is simply guiding the child's hand, likely without even knowing it.[4]

All it takes to test the claims of facilitated communication are a few simple experiments. Yet, people are willing to accept the belief that it works on the basis of unscientific evidence. Why? We often believe what we want to believe. Parents desperately want to communicate with their children. Facilitators also want to help the children. They may also be motivated by professional prestige and greater funding opportunities. Unfortunately, when such motivations are not held in check by rigorous scientific testing, we can believe things that just aren't true. This desire to believe is so strong that many of the proponents of facilitated communication are still defending it, even in the face of compelling contradictory data.

THE PERVASIVENESS OF WEIRD AND ERRONEOUS BELIEFS

Man is a credulous animal, and must believe something; in the absence of good grounds for belief, he will be satisfied with bad ones.

—Bertrand Russell

The variety of strange things that people believe seemingly knows no bounds. Many people believe that aliens have visited the earth, psychics can foretell the future, astrology works, crystals can heal sickness, Bigfoot exists, the Bermuda triangle swallows up ships and planes, people can levitate, houses can be haunted, near death experiences prove that there's an afterlife, and psychic detectives can find murderers. In fact, a Gallup poll conducted in June 2005 indicates that the majority of us (73 percent) hold at least one paranormal belief.

Table 1[5]

Percent of People Holding Various Beliefs

41%	extrasensory perception
37%	houses can be haunted
42%	people are sometimes possessed by the devil
31%	telepathy, or communication between minds without the five senses
24%	extraterrestrial beings have visited the earth
26%	clairvoyance, or perceiving things not present to the senses
21%	people can communicate with the dead
25%	astrology
20%	reincarnation

From a Gallup poll, June 2005.

We believe even though there is little or no credible evidence to support these beliefs; in fact, many are contradicted by hard evidence. Take, for instance, the so-called Bermuda Triangle. We have all probably seen or read something about the mystery surrounding the triangle. It's commonly believed that an extraordinary number of ships and planes have disappeared there, apparently because of paranormal or alien forces. However, a close examination reveals that these losses can be explained by a variety of normal causes. In fact, when you consider the increased rate of traffic in the area, there are actually a smaller proportion of losses in the Bermuda Triangle as compared to the surrounding areas.[6]

Weird beliefs are found in every segment of our society. Our federal government, for example, has made a number of costly decisions based on faulty beliefs. The Pentagon has spent millions trying to develop weapons based on ESP and psychokinesis (the ability to affect physical objects simply by thinking about them). The Defense Intelligence Agency and CIA has spent $20 million on the Stargate program alone, investigating psychics' supposed ability to view objects that are hundreds of miles away. And our government continues to give large grants to investigate such bizarre claims. This money is spent even though belief in these phenomena contradicts many of our well-established principles of science.[7] Might this money be spent better elsewhere?

Corporations make similar errors in judgment. Major companies in Europe and the United States have used graphologists when making their hiring decisions. A graphologist analyzes a job applicant's handwriting to determine what kind of person he is—not by the content of what he writes, but by how he loops his letters and cross his Ts. Research shows that graphology is totally useless, but you may have been denied a job in the past if a graphologist said your handwriting indicated you're not trustworthy.[8]

What about our leaders? Does it trouble you to learn that the actions of one of our presidents, arguably the most powerful person in the world, were guided by astrology? As noted earlier, and as reported by Donald Regan, White House chief of staff for President Reagan, "every major move and decision the Reagan's made during [his] time as White House Chief of Staff was cleared in advance with a woman in San Francisco who drew up horoscopes to make certain that the planets were in a favorable alignment for the enterprise."[9] It probably shouldn't be too surprising, since an American living in the twenty-first century is more likely to take astrology seriously than a person who lived during the Middle Ages.[10] We live in an era that has witnessed a rise of so-called New Age thinking, which rejects much of western science, and has given us "channelers" who speak with the dead, crystals possessing the power to heal, and the books (and lives) of Shirley McLaine (more than eight million sold).

Influential writers are also not immune to believing weird things. Sir Arthur Conan Doyle, the celebrated author of the Sherlock Holmes series, created a character known for his ability to solve crimes by using a superior capacity for reason and logic. You might expect that the creator of such a rational character would value critical thinking above all else. However, Sir Arthur also believed in fairies. In 1917 and 1920 two girls from Cottingley, England, took five photographs of fairies that, they claimed, played with them. When Doyle saw the pictures, he became convinced that fairies actually exist. Years later the girls admitted that the pictures were a hoax—the fairies were simply cut out from a children's book.

Figure 1. Picture of a little girl with "fairies" that Sir Arthur Conan Doyle accepted as good evidence for the existence of fairies (reprinted by permission of the Granger Collection, New York).

University professors can be believers in the weird as well. Harvard professor and psychiatrist, John Mack, wrote a book in 1994 titled *Abduction* in which he argued that several hundred thousand, and possibly as many as several million, people may have been abducted by aliens or had related experiences, oftentimes without even knowing.[11] Dr. Mack believed this because of the stories he heard from a number of people about their abduction experiences. No hard physical evidence exists to support these abductions, only stories.

So, is there any credible evidence to support these extraordinary claims? Numerous scientific investigations reveal that when such claims are put to close scrutiny, the evidence falls away.[12] In fact, the James Randi Educational Foundation has offered $1 million to anyone who can demonstrate a true psychic or paranormal phenomenon under well-controlled conditions. To date, no one has won the prize.

We also believe many things that, on the surface seem reasonable, but just aren't true. Research has shown that many commonly held beliefs turn out to be false when put to empirical test. For example, many people believe we only use 10 percent of our brains, but there's no basis in neuroscience to support this claim. What about the supersensitive hearing that the blind are said to develop? Not the case. How often have you thought that crime and drugs are out of control in the United States? Data show that violent crime rates have dropped 33 percent over a ten-year period ending in 2003, and the number of drug users is also down.[13] While many people think that low self-esteem is a cause of aggression, empirical research indicates no connection.[14] How about the perception that religious individuals are more altruistic than less religious people? Once again, a closer look reveals that religious people are no more likely to be charitable or help their fellow man than people who say they're atheists. Do opposites attract? Not according to the research. If you're happy in your job, will you be more productive? Not necessarily.[15] But that would seem like "common sense," wouldn't it? We all believe in common sense. As psychologist Keith Stanovich notes, however, 150 years ago it was a matter of common sense that women shouldn't be allowed to vote and that blacks shouldn't be taught to read.[16] Faulty thinking can lead us to hold many unfounded beliefs.

THE IMPACT OF THE MEDIA ON WEIRD AND ERRONEOUS BELIEFS

Television programs on Atlantis, Bigfoot, psychic powers, the existence of ghosts, as well as a variety of other equally weird topics appear every week on cable TV channels like The Learning Channel (TLC), Discovery Channel, History Channel, and the Travel Channel. For example, a recent TLC show reported on psychics who used remote viewing to pinpoint unknown military installations in the Soviet Union during the cold war, and who correctly predicted movements in the silver markets nine times in a row (allegedly proof of psychic powers).[17] Shows on such extraordinary topics are even aired on the national networks. ABC ran a program called the "World's Scariest Ghosts," which was filled with personal accounts of ghostly encounters. My favorite quote from the show was, "I knew right away it was a ghost because there was no other way to explain it."

These shows typically provide only a one-sided view. Rarely do they report on scientific data that refutes the claim, or interview one of the many competent skeptics, such as James Randi, Michael Shermer, or Joe Nickell, who might provide other plausible explanations for the phenomena. For example, the TLC show failed to report on the scientific evidence that demonstrates remote viewing doesn't work. Why? The sensational sells, so viewers are typically not made aware that extraordinary claims have been tested by legitimate science and found to be false. Nor did the show interview a skeptic who might have pointed out that the psychic's ability to predict the silver markets could easily be explained by probability theory. If skeptics are interviewed, their comments are often limited to a few choice sentences, which are quickly dismissed with comments such as, "Could the skeptics be wrong? There appears to be something the skeptics can't explain."

The fact is, the phenomena reported in these shows can usually be explained by scientific knowledge—but *that information* is not reported. Why is this important? Failing to report the scientific evidence can have a significant impact on the beliefs we hold. Research has demonstrated that shows about paranormal phenomena, such as UFOs, are more likely to foster belief in the paranormal if they don't carry disclaimers than if they do.[18] To see the power of the media on our beliefs, just consider one of the greatest accomplishments of the twentieth century—man walking on the moon. With all the evidence to support a successful landing, a poll in July 1999 revealed that 11 percent of Americans thought the lunar landing was a hoax. Incredible—but more striking was the fact that the percent *doubled* after Fox televised "Conspiracy Theory: Did We Land on the Moon?"[19] Simply reporting a number of fantastic and unsubstantiated claims changed the views of millions.

My intent is not to uniformly bash TV or the popular press. They report on many well-researched topics that provide us with valuable information. Unfortunately, they also provide us with a great deal of misinformation, so distinguishing between the two is not always easy. One reporter, who often wrote stories about psychic abilities, was asked if he believed those stories. He replied, "I don't have to believe in it. All I need is two Ph.D.'s who will tell me it's so and I have a story."[20] Since there are many people who hold strange beliefs, and among them some have doctorates, the media can often report bizarre things with "expert" testimony.

In fact, budding reporters often hold extraordinary beliefs themselves. A recent poll of students at Columbia's graduate school of journalism revealed that 57 percent believe in ESP, 57 percent believe in dowsing, 47 percent believe that you can read a person's aura, or energy field, and 25 percent believe in the lost continent of Atlantis.[21] With Columbia's journalism students holding such beliefs, their future articles written on these subjects are likely to be slanted. In fact, articles in the popular press supporting topics like ESP, ghosts, and astrology outnumber skeptical articles on these issues by about two to one.[22] Whatever people find interesting will find its way to TV and the print media, no matter how bizarre.

The media not only fosters beliefs in the weird, they can also affect our beliefs concerning things that are not bizarre. Studies reveal that the amount of media coverage of various health dangers is often inversely proportional to those dangers.[23] Drug use is one of the lowest ranking risk factors for serious illness and death, yet it receives about the same amount of coverage as the second ranked risk factor, diet and exercise. Over a period when our country's murder rate dropped by 20 percent, the number of murder stories on network newscasts soared by 600 percent.[24] Such biased reporting can affect the beliefs we hold. One study analyzed the number of stories that contained the words "drug crisis" as well as the changes in public opinion over a ten-year period. At times, nearly two out of three Americans thought that drugs were our most important problem, while at other times only one out of twenty believed drugs were most important. Not surprising, changes in public opinion coincided with changes in media coverage.[25]

The media often distort the facts by focusing on personal accounts rather than scientific or statistical data. In 1994 stories about flesh-eating bacteria gobbled the media's attention, replete with graphic videos of disfigured patients. Even though medical authorities pointed out that you're fifty-five times more likely to be struck by lightning than to die from flesh-eating bacteria, the media dismissed that fact. As stated on ABC's *20/20*, "Whatever the statistics, it's devastating to the victims."[26] Flesh-eating bacteria is, no doubt, devastating to its victims. However, these vivid personal accounts make us worry about an event that has almost no chance of occurring. Similarly, during the summer of 2001, the cry was

"Stay out of the water!" out of a heightened fear of shark attacks, and in 2002, thc hot media story was child abduction. In each case, the facts did not warrant a greater concern, as there was little or no change in the frequency of these events as compared to previous years. But media coverage led many of us to conclude they were on the increase. With such biased reporting, it's no wonder that we form incorrect beliefs. While crime rates were actually dropping throughout the 1990s, two-thirds of Americans thought they were climbing. The number of drug users was cut in half by the late 1990s compared to a decade earlier, but nine out of ten people thought the drug problem was out of control.[27]

These incorrect beliefs can affect the decisions we make. For example, in a year when the number of deaths from violence in our nation's schools was at a record low, and only one out of ten public schools reported any serious crime, *Time* and *U.S. News & World Report* ran stories with headlines like "Teenage Time Bombs." As sociologist Barry Glassner indicates, these media accounts heighten public awareness, and result in spending considerable money to protect children from dangers that only a very few will experience. At the same time, about 12 million American children are malnourished and 11 million have no health insurance.[28]

And so, media coverage can affect our individual beliefs and our society's public policy decisions. Television producers, and newspaper and magazine editors often gravitate toward the sensational stories that grab their audiences' attention. Unfortunately, many of the most sensational reports concern weird and erroneous beliefs. Therefore, we have to be vigilant in how we think to counteract the media barrage. We would be less likely to be taken in by such reporting if we didn't naturally make errors in how we think. A main problem lies in our tendency to rely on anecdotal evidence.

TELL ME YOUR STORY—OUR BIAS FOR ANECDOTAL EVIDENCE

A few years back, women started reporting a variety of major illnesses after getting silicon breast implants. The women went on national shows to talk about how breast implants caused all sorts of diseases, from rheumatoid arthritis to chronic fatigue and breast cancer. As the number of women with such stories grew, the talk shows began interviewing some doctors who also said that implants could cause such serious health problems. How did the doctors know this? They had patients who developed serious illness after getting the implants, and when the implants were removed, the patients got better. On the basis of such stories, Congressional hearings were held, and, in 1992, the US Food and Drug Administration banned the use of silicon breast implants for the general public.

The media continued to play up the risk. Lawsuits were filed and juries awarded women up to $25 million for illnesses caused by their implants. In 1994 a federal court granted $4.25 billion to plaintiffs in the largest product liability settlement to that date, compensating women for illnesses caused by leaking implants. Dow Corning, the manufacturer of the implants, was forced into bankruptcy proceedings.[29]

So, do silicon breast implants cause serious illness? The evidence seems quite compelling, but it isn't based on science. Very intelligent women and doctors were making a very serious, yet common, decision error. They were relying on anecdotal evidence, such as personal stories and individual accounts, to prove that implants cause chronic disease. Not being considered here is that there are other plausible explanations for the women's problems. Just because women recently had implants and then got sick doesn't mean the implants caused the disease. The illness and the implants could have happened coincidentally.

So what should we do to determine if there's an implant-illness link? We need to compare a sample of women who did not have breast implants to a sample of women who did to see if the two groups differ in their incidence of major disease. That is, we need a scientific study to determine if women with implants have a significantly higher occurrence of serious illness. If they do, then there's reason to believe that the implants cause problems. If they don't, then implants are not causing the problems, and the women are erroneously attributing their problems to the implants.

One of the first scientific studies examined the records of over seven hundred women with, and over fourteen hundred women without, implants. The study found no difference in the rate of connective tissue disease between the two groups, which implants were accused of causing.[30] Of course, we shouldn't rely solely on the results of one study, especially on such an important issue as this. In science, a study has to be replicated before we can place much confidence in its conclusion. Over subsequent years, a number of other studies were conducted, and the evidence suggests that implants do not cause breast cancer or other chronic, major disease.[31] Of course, there can be complications from the surgery (as with any surgery), including infection and hemorrhage, and pain may occur from hardening of the breast tissue, but these complications are not major connective tissue diseases, the basis for most of the million-dollar lawsuits. To explain why so many women and doctors were erroneously concluding that implants cause serious disease, Marcia Angell, the executive editor of the *New England Journal of Medicine*, observed that the evidence they were depending on was exclusively anecdotal—the personal stories of individuals.[32]

Research demonstrates that we prefer to rely on stories instead of statistics. As an example, one study had people view a taped interview with a prison guard. Some saw an interview with a guard who was humane, while others saw a guard who was extremely inhumane. Half of the subjects then received information indicating that the guard was either typical, or not typical, of the majority of prison guards. It turned out that the information concerning how representative the guard was of guards in general had little effect on individuals' opinions. Instead, people relied more on the information conveyed in the single interview, and ignored how unreliable or unrepresentative that interview might be.[33] Even experienced doctors are affected by anecdotal data. Research shows that doctors who deal with the effects of smoking (e.g., chest physicians) are more likely to quit smoking than are doctors in general practice.[34] All doctors surely realize the health hazards of smoking, but those that see the personal effects in their patients are affected the most. While statistical information is typically the most relevant evidence to consider, we respond more to personal accounts.

Interestingly, the news media recognizes our penchant to rely on anecdotal evidence. Most of the television news magazines, such as *Dateline* and *20/20*, report on personal stories. Even *60 Minutes*, the show with a no-nonsense reputation for getting to the facts of an issue, doesn't report a lot of data and statistics. In fact, Don Hewitt, the producer of the show, says that he wouldn't accept a segment from Mike Wallace, Lesley Stahl, or any other reporter unless it had a story to tell. In effect, Hewitt implicitly recognizes our desire for a good story. As a result, the media plays up personal stories and downplays the science and statistics. While this may be good for TV ratings, personal accounts can lead us to believe things that science has shown to be false.

Relying on personal testimonials is particularly troubling because they can be easily manipulated. A few years ago, magician and renowned skeptic James (The Amazing) Randi demonstrated just how easy it is to create bizarre testimonials. While on a New York talk show, Randi told the audience that he saw a number of orange V-shaped objects flying overhead when he was driving in from New Jersey. Within minutes, the station switchboard lit up with a number of eyewitnesses confirming the sightings. These calls actually contained many details that Randi didn't mention, including a report that the objects made more than one pass. Great talk radio, but Randi made up the whole story—there were never any V-shaped flying objects! With this simple example, he clearly demonstrated how worthless personal testimonials can be. It's possible to generate testimonials to support just about any bogus claim.[35]

So what can we take away from all this? Our cognitive makeup naturally gravitates toward anecdotal evidence when we form our beliefs and make our decisions.[36] We like to hear, and respond more strongly to, stories. However, this doesn't mean we should set our beliefs on the basis of such evidence. Anecdotes are just stories told by potentially biased human storytellers. As such, fifty anecdotes are no better than one. Instead, what we need are rigorous scientific studies to determine if breast implants cause serious illness or if facilitated communication actually works. Before we believe that humans are being abducted by extraterrestrials, we should ask to see some physical evidence, some tangible proof of this extraordinary event, as opposed to relying solely on personal abduction accounts. If not, we will fall into the trap of thinking like a pseudoscientist.

PSEUDOSCIENCE

We live in an age of science, but as we've seen, many of us hold unscientific and pseudoscientific beliefs. Pseudoscience refers to "claims presented so that they appear scientific even though they lack sufficient supporting evidence and plausibility."[37] Some refer to it as junk science, or voodoo science. Essentially, pseudoscience is an endeavor that pretends to be a science, but lacks the rigor of science. The conclusions of junk science are typically drawn from low-quality data, such as anecdotal evidence and personal testimonials, as opposed to carefully controlled studies. Most fields of science have a corresponding pseudoscience. For example, some may view the investigation of ancient astronauts to be archeology, tinkering with perpetual motion machines might seem to be physics, and the shared study of stars and planets links astronomy and astrology in some people's minds. And, of course, there is the science of psychology and the pseudoscience parapsychology.[38]

Claims made in the pseudosciences have a couple of common features. First, the claim is controversial because, while people can point to some supporting evidence, the evidence is typically of dubious quality. Second, the claim is often at odds with current well-established scientific principles. As an example, consider the case for levitation. There are people who claim to have levitated, and some photographs show people apparently floating in midair. Supporters point to this evidence, but the quality of the evidence is quite flimsy, especially considering how extraordinary the claim is. Personal testimonials can be wrong and photographs can be tampered with. In fact, if levitation works, our entire understanding of how gravity operates would have to change.[39]

One of the foremost examples of pseudoscience is parapsychology. Parapsychologists test a range of phenomena that supposedly occur due to extrasensory perception, such as telepathy (reading another's mind), clairvoyance (perceiving things not present to the senses) and precognition (seeing the future).[40] J. B. Rhine began investigating these phenomena at Duke University in the 1930s, using what are called Zener cards—five cards with different symbols on the back, such as a plus sign, square, or wavy lines. In a typical experiment, an assistant would select and observe a card, and a subject would try to identify the card by reading the assistant's mind. Rhine found greater than chance accuracy in identifying the cards, and coined the term extrasensory perception. However, a review of his methods revealed many other potential explanations for the accuracy achieved. In some cases, the subjects could get subtle cues from the experimenter. In other cases, the cards were printed with such pressure that the subjects could actually see or feel the indentations on the backs of the cards. While the evidence appeared to support ESP, the experiments were not tightly controlled, and so the credibility of the evidence is questionable.

Numerous ESP studies conducted over the years point to one overriding conclusion. Studies supporting ESP consistently lack proper controls, and studies with proper controls consistently find no support for ESP. This has led prominent psychologist and parapsychologist Susan Blackmore, who has worked in the field of parapsychology for nearly thirty years, to reluctantly conclude that psi does not exist. After analyzing a recent series of experiments that were said to have found evidence of ESP, she stated, "These experiments, which looked so beautifully designed in print, were in fact open to fraud or error in several ways . . . the results could not be relied upon as evidence for psi."[41] The fact is, decades of ESP research has not produced a single example in which an ESP phenomenon has been replicated under tightly controlled conditions. The main reason ESP is not investigated by mainstream psychology today is that it has been examined over a number of years and nothing has come of it.[42] And yet, 41 percent of the people recently surveyed by Gallup believe in the power of ESP.

PSEUDOSCIENTIFIC THINKING

Why do we hold many pseudoscientific beliefs? Probably the main reason is that we *want* to believe in them. As the noted astronomer Carl Sagan observed, pseudoscience and other weird beliefs often meet our emotional needs.[43] They make us feel good; they're comforting. They may make us feel more in control of our lives. They even may give us hope that our diseases will be cured. We want simplicity in our lives, and belief in superstition, fate, the supernatural, and other pseudoscientific beliefs often provide simple explanations for life's events.

Pseudoscience also has many of the trappings of science, and so we have a hard time distinguishing pseudoscience from real science. For example, Edgar Cayce's Association for Research and Enlightenment, where ESP research is conducted, occupies a big, modern building, with professionally appointed offices and a research library. It appears official and authoritative, and so we're more likely to accept what the organization says, even though it may say some pretty weird stuff.[44]

Many of us also find the topics of pseudoscience interesting and intriguing, and we all want to be entertained. It's fascinating to think that ancient astronauts created the pyramids or that someone has the power to read other people's minds. Finally, pseudoscience is everywhere in our popular culture, while skeptical treatments are harder to find. There are hundreds of books and countless TV shows on the Lost Continent of Atlantis, but it's typically not reported that plate tectonics indicates there couldn't have been a continent between Europe and America ten thousand years ago.[45] Atlantis remains lost while belief in pseudoscience abounds.

Table 2

Characteristics of Pseudoscientific Thinking

(1) Preconceived notion of what to believe.
(2) Search for evidence to support a preconceived belief.
(3) Ignore evidence that would falsify a claim or belief.
(4) Disregard alternative explanations for a phenomenon.
(5) Hold extraordinary beliefs.
(6) Accept flimsy evidence to support an extraordinary claim.
(7) Rely heavily on anecdotal evidence.
(8) Lack of tightly controlled experiments to test a claim.
(9) Employ very little skepticism.

With such powerful desires at work, we have to be careful in how we form our beliefs. How do pseudoscientists arrive at their erroneous beliefs? Table 2 lists some of the more common faults of pseudoscientific thinking. In general, pseudoscientists have a preconceived notion of what they want to believe. This creates a strong motivation to search for evidence that supports the belief, and to ignore evidence that falsifies the claim. Pseudoscientists typically focus on only one explanation for a phenomenon, quickly brushing aside alternative explanations. And, in their desire to support their belief, they are willing to accept flimsy, oftentimes anecdotal, evidence.

Before you start thinking that these pseudoscientists are a pretty lame lot, you should realize that many of these same characteristics are evident in our everyday thinking. Like pseudoscientists, we also make these errors when shaping our beliefs. Why? We're all human, and our general cognitive characteristics follow very similar patterns. So this type of thinking isn't limited to just bizarre topics—it affects how we form beliefs and make decisions in every aspect of our lives.

PROBLEMS WITH PSEUDOSCIENTIFIC THINKING

As we've seen, pseudoscientific thinking can lead to poor public policy decisions, inappropriate lawsuits, and wasteful spending: Things we all want to avoid. However, some may ask, What's the harm in holding a few pseudoscientific beliefs? If you believe in facilitated communication, psychic ability, fringe alternative therapies, or talking with the dead, you're not hurting anyone, and they can, at times, provide you with a great deal of comfort. The problem is, they often have insidious negative effects that we're not even aware of.

Consider the case of facilitated communication. Parents certainly find solace in thinking they can communicate with their autistic child. However, they are being misled because it's the facilitator, and not their child, who is interacting with them. In addition, considerable money is spent to have a facilitator sit with a child at school, when it turns out the facilitator is actually the one taking and passing exams. The negative effects are even more dramatic—children have accused their parents of sexual abuse during facilitated communication.[46] Of course, the facilitator was making the claim, but if you believe in facilitated communication, you would likely believe that the claim was true. In fact, people have been imprisoned because of child molestation charges obtained from facilitated communication. Our desire to believe can ruin lives.

What harm is there to believing in things like astrology, psychic readings, and fringe alternative therapies? Most psychics on television charge about $4 per minute, or a whopping $240 an hour. That's about twice the fee of a professional psychiatrist! Some people have spent thousands on phone bills because of psychic hot lines. Hundreds of millions are spent each year on questionable medical practices, including homeopathy, magnetic therapy, urine therapy, reflexology, iridology, therapeutic touch—the list goes on and on. And worse, many of us have eschewed proven drug remedies in favor of these fringe alternatives, negatively affecting our health and even our lives.

Pseudoscientific thinking can also affect us in a variety of more subtle ways. We're more inclined, for example, to develop erroneous stereotypes. Many of us believe that homosexuals are more likely to be pedophiles. Numerous studies of pedophiles refute that belief. In fact, one study found that a child is one hundred times more likely to be molested by the heterosexual partner of a close relative than by a homosexual. Nonetheless, the stereotype persists and represents the pernicious effects of pseudoscientific thinking.[47]

Pseudoscientific thinking can also lead to misplaced fears. We have been sensitized to murder in the workplace, listening to stories of disgruntled employees with guns and office massacres. But did you know that, out of approximately 121 million people who work, only about one thousand are murdered on the job each year, and that includes high-risk jobs like police and taxi drivers. Furthermore, about 90 percent of these murders are committed by people attempting robbery. The chance of being murdered by someone you work with is less than one in two million. You're several times more likely to be hit by lightning than to be done in by Frank in shipping. In fact, the often-used term *going postal* is a misnomer. Postal employees are actually two and a half times less likely to be killed on the job than the average worker.

Perhaps you're afraid that one of your children will eat poisoned candy or an apple containing a razor blade on Halloween. You're not alone. An *ABC News/Washington Post* poll in 1985 revealed that 60 percent of parents were afraid that their children could be victims of a Halloween treat gone bad. Why? They heard stories. However, a study investigating all of the reported incidents up to that time found that not a single death or serious injury occurred from Halloween candy received from strangers. In the two instances in which children died, apparently from eating poisoned candy, it turned out that family members deliberately spiked the candy.

As sociologist Barry Glassner states in *The Culture of Fear*, "We waste tens of billions of dollars and person hours every year on largely mythical hazards like road rage, on prison cells occupied by people who pose little or no danger to others, on programs designed to protect young people from dangers that few of them ever face, [and] on compensation for victims of metaphorical illnesses."[48]

So what harm can be caused by pseudoscientific thinking? Plenty! It leads to a decline in critical thinking and scientific literacy, it decreases our ability to make well-informed decisions, it diverts resources that could be spent on more productive activities, and it leads to monetary losses and even death. Clearly, we should be looking for ways to improve our thinking processes so that we can avoid such problems.

CHAPTER 2: A GREMLIN ON MY SHOULDER

Keeping an open mind is a virtue, but not so open that your brains fall out.

—Bertrand Russell, James Oberg

I have a little gremlin on my shoulder. He's about seven inches tall, and usually dresses in dark green or red clothing. He's invisible to you, but I can see and hear him. He sits there, twenty-four hours a day, and tells me what to do. All of my thoughts and conversation originate with him. He whispers into my ear and tells me what I should think, what I should say, and how I should act. In fact, all of my actions are the result of his prodding. Now, you may say that the idea of an invisible gremlin is ridiculous. Nobody would believe in that—where's the evidence? It's just my word that I'm experiencing him. But the fact is, some of the beliefs that we hold have about as much credible evidence to support them as my gremlin. Yet, we continue to believe.

As we've seen, many people believe that houses can be haunted, extraterrestrials have visited the earth, people can be possessed by the devil, and psychics can predict the future. These claims are all very extraordinary, yet the evidence to support them is quite ordinary—and flimsy. And to make matters worse, other competing, more plausible explanations for these experiences exist and are being ignored. Not all evidence is created equal. When forming our beliefs, we need to assess both the quality of the evidence and the reasonableness of the belief. In effect, the more extraordinary the belief, the more compelling the evidence should be to support it.

EXTRAORDINARY CLAIMS REQUIRE EXTRAORDINARY EVIDENCE

The Discovery Channel recently reported on proof for the existence of ghosts—paranormal researchers actually recorded voices of the dead! How did they do it? They taped sounds in a cemetery, and after enhancing the recordings with a number of audio techniques, it sounded like someone was saying "I'd love to find me stone." The ghost hunters then went to "haunted" Brookdale Lodge in California, asked questions as they walked from room to room, and recorded any sounds in reply. Once again, the responses were inaudible to human ears, but the researchers massaged the very low frequencies of the recordings until you could hear "help me" and "stand over here." So there you have it. Not only do people report seeing ghosts, physical evidence indicates that their voices can actually be recorded. Seems pretty convincing, doesn't it?

Do you remember the "Paul is dead" phenomenon of the 1960s? It was thought by many that Paul McCartney, one of the Beatles, had died. A simple rumor took hold and quickly gained a life of its own. People began looking for clues of Paul's death in all sorts of places. They analyzed album covers and noticed that Paul was the only one barefoot on the cover of *Abbey Road*. The most compelling evidence, however, came from an analysis of the Beatles' songs. When some songs were played backward, or were slowed down, people heard phrases like "Paul is dead." Of course, Paul McCartney is alive and still making great music.

So what can we take away from this? If we have enough data, and massage it hard enough, we can find just about anything we're looking for. From the hundreds of Beatles' songs played backward and slowed down, there's bound to emerge some sound that resembles "Paul is dead." No one ever said those words in the music, but thousands, if not millions, of people believed it. So it is with the detailed massaging of tapes from haunted houses. By manipulating the recordings, stretching, and condensing the different sounds, we'll be able to occasionally produce a sound that appears to be a ghost speaking to us.

When we evaluate evidence and set our beliefs, we need to keep in mind a simple idea—extraordinary claims require extraordinary evidence. The concept of a ghost is quite extraordinary. We have to believe that some form of "energy" from our former selves exists, decides to hang around this world for a while, and then decides to communicate or interact with us every now and again. We should have extremely compelling evidence before we accept such an extraordinary belief. Do the tape recordings provide such evidence? We already know from the "Paul is dead" phenomenon that recordings can be easily manipulated to make them sound like all sorts of things. Should we accept such evidence as proof that ghosts exist? Hardly! The quality of that evidence is quite poor.

Of course, paranormal researchers say that such recordings are only one type of evidence. They also point to temperature changes in haunted houses, or the presence of bright lights and ghostly images on photographs. But these phenomena are easily attributed to natural causes. Cold drafts are likely to occur in old houses, and overexposures or reflected light on photographs can look like a ghostly image.[1] What about personal sightings? As we'll later explore, there's considerable evidence to indicate that we can misperceive our world, often seeing things that aren't there. This especially occurs when we expect or want to see something. As a result, personal stories do not offer compelling evidence for the existence of ghosts. We need something more tangible.

What about all those other mysterious experiences that yield physical evidence? It turns out that when these experiences are carefully investigated, reasonable explanations typically prevail. For example, my friend Shawn once thought that the spirit of his deceased grandfather was visiting his condo. Why? The door to the downstairs, where his grandfather used to spend a lot of time, was mysteriously locking. This particular type of door could only be locked from the inside, and to do so, you had to push and turn the button on the door handle. How could that happen with no one in the room? The only explanation was a ghostly visitor. Intrigued, I went to examine the door. It turned out that the lock button was sticking, so it just had to be pushed in, but not turned, to set the lock. And, since there was no door stop to prevent the door from hitting the wall when opened, the button was depressed and locked by the wall when the door was thrown open. Time after time, when critically examined, supernatural explanations give way to natural ones.

So does this mean that ghosts don't exist? Not necessarily. It just means that we don't have strong evidence to support that they do exist. But without such evidence, doesn't it make sense to withhold our belief in ghosts at this time? The point is, we have to examine the quality of the evidence for a claim before accepting it. On first glance, there may appear to be considerable evidence to support the existence of ghosts. After all, we have tape recordings, pictures, and personal experiences. But a lot of bad evidence is still bad evidence—sheer volume cannot make the evidence any better.[2]

Unfortunately, when we form our beliefs, we often give too much importance to the amount of evidence and too little to its quality. Remember the silicon breast implant controversy discussed earlier? People became convinced that implants cause major disease because thousands of women reported serious illness after receiving implants. But a link was not established between the implants and the illnesses. It seemed that there was a lot of evidence, but it was all low-quality, anecdotal data. The volume of evidence in support of a claim should not be the primary factor when setting our beliefs. With evidence, quality is king. As we saw earlier with the case of facilitated communication, a single rigorously controlled study provided much more compelling evidence on the technique's usefulness than did a thousand personal stories.

And yet, we are quick to believe extraordinary claims on the basis of rather thin evidence. We believe in alien encounters and talking with the dead just because some people report they had a personal experience. But if someone makes such an extraordinary claim, they should have some pretty extraordinary evidence, especially if the claim goes against many of the well-supported physical laws of our universe. Some followers of transcendental meditation believe that they can levitate their bodies several inches off the ground during meditation. Should we accept their word for it? If we do, we would have to reject what we already know about gravity. What if we saw it for ourselves? Remember, magicians like David Blaine amaze people by levitating right on the sidewalks of New York. We can be fooled into believing something that isn't actually happening. The entire world of magic depends on it. It's worth remembering that virtually all of the phenomena that paranormal researchers point to as evidence of supernatural or mystical occurrences can be replicated by magicians, most of whom readily admit they're illusionists and they're performing a trick. Doesn't that tell us something?

And so, I have a little gremlin I want you to meet. My gremlin may sound bizarre, but that's because gremlin stories aren't prevalent in this day and age. Since gremlins aren't part of our culture, it's easy to see that we need extraordinary evidence before we believe such a claim. My word isn't good enough. On the other hand, things like alien encounters, Bigfoot sightings, and ghostly experiences are everywhere in our popular media, so belief in them seems more reasonable, even without extraordinary evidence. Don't forget though, at one time people believed in gremlins and fairies.

A look through history reveals an interesting pattern. As Carl Sagan noted, in ancient times, when people thought that gods came down to earth, people saw gods. When fairies were widely accepted, people saw fairies. In an age of spiritualism, people saw spirits. When we began to think that extraterrestrials were plausible, people began seeing aliens.[3] You have to ask, are things like aliens the gremlins of today? Why do people who report seeing aliens say they have a humanoid body with a large head and eyes? If an alien from another planet came to Earth, it would likely look very different from a humanoid. Just look at the diversity of life on this planet. Only a few species have two arms and two legs. Imagine the differences that would arise if life formed on an entirely different planet. Yet, we see aliens that look remarkably like ourselves. Why is that? Aliens are typically depicted as humanoid in magazines, on TV, and in the movies. When science fiction accounts in the 1920s and 30s showed small hairless beings with big heads and eyes, people started seeing such creatures. Alien abduction accounts were rare until around 1975, when a TV show depicting an abduction aired. We don't hear much about gremlins and fairies these days. I wonder where they've gone. Abducted by aliens, perhaps?

It Could Be!

Do you remember the movie *Animal House*? At one point in the film a young freshman, nicknamed Pinto, is smoking pot for the first time with one of his professors. While under the influence, they have a deep philosophical discussion about the true nature of the universe. With the professor's urgings, Pinto says, "OK—So that means that our whole solar system could be, like, one tiny atom in the fingernail of some other giant being?" Looking down at his own finger he then says, "That means that one tiny atom in my fingernail could be one little tiny universe?" When the professor nods in agreement, Pinto asks, "Could I buy some pot from you?"

We often hear people say, "It could be." Aliens could be visiting us from other planets. We don't know for sure. The problem with this line of reasoning is that it implies that one belief is as good as another. And if that's the case, then there's no such thing as objective truth—reality is just what we believe it to be. However, as Theodore Schick and Louis Vaughn point out, if we believe that all truth is subjective, then no statement is worthy of belief or commitment because every belief is arbitrary. As a result, there can be no such thing as knowledge, because if nothing is true, there can be nothing to know (So why bother going to school?). But while many people believe that anything is possible, that claim can't be true. Some things can't be false and other things can't be true. For example, 2 + 2 = 4, and all bachelors are unmarried, are necessary truths, while 2 + 2 = 5, and all bachelors are married, are necessary falsehoods. In effect, some things are logically impossible. Other things are physically impossible. It's logically possible for a cow to jump over the moon, but it's physically impossible.[4]

So what's the upshot? Not all beliefs are created equal. Saying, "It could be" doesn't get us anywhere. It's just not a sound argument to use when forming our beliefs. Instead, we have to evaluate the reasonableness of the belief—consider the plausibility of the claim—then evaluate the degree of credible, verifiable evidence in its favor.[5]

How we think affects what we believe, and what we believe affects what we decide. When our beliefs go beyond the available evidence, they're more likely to be wrong. And, if we base our decisions on those erroneous beliefs, those decisions are more likely to be in error. We therefore need to apply a considerable degree of skepticism when forming beliefs and making decisions.

THE IMPORTANCE OF SKEPTICAL THINKING

If you would be a real seeker after truth, it is necessary that at least once in your life you doubt, as far as possible, all things.

—Descartes

Many people think, as noted earlier, that a skeptic is a cynic—someone who just wants to find the fault in everything. But that's not what a skeptic is. A skeptic is someone who simply wants to evaluate the evidence for a claim before he believes it.[6] Skepticism is a method, not a position. A true skeptic doesn't take a strong position until considerable credible evidence is available for believing or disbelieving a claim. In effect, skeptics proportion the extent of their belief by the extent of the evidence for or against a belief. And, of course, a skeptic's mantra is "extraordinary beliefs require extraordinary evidence."

The hallmark of skepticism is science. People often criticize scientists and skeptics for being too close-minded. They say that skeptics don't believe in things like ESP and ghosts because they just don't fit with their theories of how the world works. But scientists are constantly trying to find support for new, and sometimes bizarre, theories. In fact, a scientist who develops a new theory that is substantiated by the evidence achieves great fame and fortune. We don't remember the scientist who just plugs along testing someone else's ideas, we remember scientists like Darwin and Einstein, who proposed new, earth-shattering concepts. So what's the difference between skeptics and believers in the paranormal and other bizarre claims? Skeptics and scientists require considerable, repeatable evidence before they accept a claim. Don't you think that any scientist would love to find compelling evidence for the existence of extraterrestrials or ESP? He would achieve considerable status and be remembered throughout history.[7]

And so, one of the goals of skeptics and scientists is to keep an open mind. In fact, true skeptics perform a delicate balancing act, best described by Carl Sagan as follows:

> It seems to me what is called for is an exquisite balance between two conflicting needs: the most skeptical scrutiny of all hypotheses that are served up to us and at the same time a great openness to new ideas. If

> you . . . have not an ounce of skeptical sense in you, then you cannot distinguish useful ideas from the worthless ones. If all ideas have equal validity then you are lost, because, then . . . no ideas have any validity at all.[8]

As we opened this chapter, philosopher Bertrand Russell and NASA scientist James Oberg said, "Keeping an open mind is a virtue, but not so open that your brains fall out." If this metaphorically describes skeptics, doesn't it make sense to take a skeptical position when forming our beliefs? So why don't we do it more often? Why don't we like to be skeptical? Perhaps it's because we don't like uncertainty and ambiguity, and being a skeptic means we have to accept uncertainty as a major part of life. Skeptics choose not to believe something until there's adequate data supporting that belief. This is a problem for many people, because we typically abhor uncertainty and have a low tolerance for ambiguity. As a result, we want to believe things, even in a world full of ambiguity. However, wanting something to be true doesn't make it true, and wanting to believe is no basis for accepting a belief.

As a skeptic, you have to be comfortable saying, "I don't know." This makes sense because, in many cases, nobody knows. Some things are inherently unknowable, and other things we just don't know with our current state of knowledge. Given the size of the universe, it's possible that other life-forms exist, but we don't currently know if they do because credible evidence has not emerged to support that belief. A skeptic, therefore, suspends belief in extraterrestrial life for the time being. However, if the SETI (Search for Extraterrestrial Intelligence) project, which is scanning the skies for radio signals emanating from other planets, finds compelling evidence of aliens, a skeptic would reassess her position. With skepticism, we have to accept the uncertainty of life—but isn't that better than filling our lives with a number of unsubstantiated, sometimes silly, and potentially dangerous beliefs?

In essence, we should look on our belief as a continuum, ranging from strong disbelief to strong belief, as in figure 2. Importantly, the midpoint of the continuum is "I don't know."

Given our desire to believe things, we all too quickly end up on the right end of the scale, strongly believing in something despite little credible evidence. However, we need to start at the midpoint, embrace the notion that "I

Strong Disbelief ⇐ **Moderate Disbelief** ⇐ **Slight Disbelief** ⇐ **I Don't Know** ⇒ **Slight Belief** ⇒ **Moderate Belief** ⇒ **Strong Belief**

Figure 2. A continuum of belief: As we move from the midpoint, we hold a progressively stronger belief or disbelief.

don't know," and then examine the evidence for or against something. As we evaluate the evidence and plausibility of a claim, we can move farther out on the continuum, either toward strong disbelief or strong belief.[9] In that way, we're likely to be more open to different ideas and more likely to set informed beliefs. Of course, the question arises, what's the best approach to take to guide our movement along the belief continuum?

A FIRST-RATE BELIEF GENERATING TECHNIQUE

> *Man's most valuable trait is a judicious sense of what not to believe.*
>
> —Euripides

As we've noted, it's not only extraordinary beliefs that we have to be skeptical about. We also hold a number of erroneous beliefs that, on the surface, may appear to be plausible. As a result, we have to employ skepticism when forming any belief. So what's a good approach to take when we shape our beliefs? Theodore Schick and Lewis Vaughn proposed the following four-step method that can be quite useful:[10]

1) State the claim.
2) Examine the evidence for the claim.
3) Consider alternative hypotheses.
4) Evaluate the reasonableness of each hypothesis.

State the claim

When deciding whether to believe something, we need to state the belief as clearly and specifically as possible. We can't be ambiguous—ambiguous claims have too many loopholes that can make them essentially untestable. For example, many people hold the superstition that things come in threes—such as deaths of celebrities—but they don't state a time horizon for the three events. Is it one week, one month, or five years? Without a time horizon, we can be misled into believing the superstition because, sooner or later, similar events will happen in the future.

Examine the evidence

Remember that not all evidence is created equal. As we've seen, anecdotal evidence can lead us astray; human perception and memory can be distorted, and so personal stories can be misleading. Ambiguous data are very difficult to evaluate, and even scientific studies can have errors. And so, we have to proportion our belief not only to the amount of evidence for and against a claim, but to the quality of that evidence.

Consider alternative hypotheses

There are often many possible explanations for phenomena. However, we're not naturally inclined, or taught, to look for competing alternatives, so we often focus on a single explanation (and it's usually the one that we want to believe). Since we also have a tendency to pay attention to information that supports our belief, we start to think it has considerable support. But there's often equally compelling evidence to support other competing explanations, if we simply look for it. We therefore have to make a conscious effort to consider alternative hypotheses and evaluate the evidence for them all. The importance of this step cannot be overemphasized. One of the most critical factors in improving how we form beliefs and make decisions is to be on the lookout for competing explanations.

Evaluate the reasonableness of each hypothesis

After we bring to mind other competing explanations for a phenomenon, we need to evaluate their reasonableness. There are a number of criteria that can be used to evaluate whether one hypothesis is better than another. As a start, here are three important questions to ask:

1) Is it testable?
2) Is it the simplest explanation for the phenomenon?
3) Does it conflict with other well-established knowledge?

Is it testable? When evaluating any hypothesis, the first question to ask is, Can it be tested? Many hypotheses can't be tested. This often happens when we examine extraordinary phenomenon. The inability to test doesn't mean that the hypothesis is false, but it does mean it's worthless from a scientific point of view. Why? If a hypothesis can't be tested, we'll never be able to determine its truth or falsehood. As Karl Popper indicated, a hypothesis has to be "falsifiable"; that is, we must be able to try to prove it wrong.[11] If there's no way to falsify a hypothesis, we'll never be able to assess if it's true or false.

As an example, consider my little gremlin. Can we test the hypothesis that I have a gremlin on my shoulder and he's responsible for all my actions? If you say, "Let's see him," I say, "He's invisible." If you say, "Let's hear him," I say, "He only talks to me." "Ask him to leave so I can see if you still function normally," you suggest. "Sorry, but I can't—he's there all the time," I sigh. In effect, for every test proposed, there's a reason why it can't be used to detect my gremlin. As a consequence, the gremlin hypothesis is worthless. As Carl Sagan has noted, "Claims that cannot be tested, assertions immune to disproof are veridically worthless, whatever value they may have in inspiring us or in exciting our sense of wonder."[12]

Is it the simplest explanation? Many people learn how to walk over a bed of hot coals with their bare feet. In fact, you can take seminars on how to accomplish that feat from fire-walking gurus—for a few thousand dollars! Firewalkers often maintain that some mental or psychic energy protects them from getting burned, and that they can teach you how to harness that energy. But there's nothing mystical or spiritual about fire walking—it's just the physics of heat capacity and conductivity of the coals. You may have noticed that different materials can be the same temperature, and yet some will burn you while others won't. If you stick your hand into a 350° oven, it feels hot, but it won't burn. If you place your hand on top of a cake in the oven, it still won't burn. But if you touch the metal pan holding the cake, you'll burn instantly. Why? The heat capacity and conductivity of these things are different. The air and cake have low capacity and conductivity, while the metal is high. Even though the coals in firewalking have been heated to 1,200° F, they have low capacity and conductivity, and therefore won't burn your feet—unless you linger too long. So some people are paying thousands to learn how to walk quickly.

What does this mean for setting our beliefs? All other things equal, we should choose the simpler of two different explanations for a phenomenon. By that I mean the explanation that makes the fewest untenable assumptions. The simpler the hypothesis, the less likely it is to be false since there are fewer ways for it to go wrong.[13] To accept many of the firewalkers' explanations, you have to assume that some extraordinary psychic or mystical power exists. But you don't need to believe in such mystical power to explain firewalking. The laws of physics offer a simpler explanation.[14] This guiding rule of science—choosing the simplest explanation—is called Occam's razor, after the fourteenth-century English philosopher William of Occam. As a general rule, we should always apply Occam's razor to cut away unnecessary and unsupported assumptions when setting our own beliefs.

Does it conflict with other well-established knowledge? I was in Australia awhile back and caught some type of flu. I went to the pharmacy and, as I was searching through the traditional cold and flu remedies, the pharmacist suggested that I try a homeopathic cure. Just to the right of the traditional medicine was a large display containing numerous homeopathic remedies. "Do they work?" I asked. "Definitely, I use them all the time," he exclaimed.

So what is homeopathy? Homeopathic medicine is based on the belief that very small amounts of substances that cause illness in healthy people can cure a sick person. A fundamental proposition of homeopathy is the law of infinitesimals, which states that the smaller a dose is, the more powerful it is. Doses are diluted to such an extent in homeopathic remedies that, in some cases, not even a single molecule of the active agent is left in the treatment. But that's okay, because as German physician Samuel Hahneman, the creator of homeopathic medicine, believed, a "spirit like" essence was left in the small doses that cured people.[15]

Homeopathic medicine would certainly not survive Occam's razor. It requires belief in unsubstantiated, unproven "spirit like" essences. In addition, it conflicts with other well-established knowledge that we have about how the world works. There's no other instance in science where a smaller dose of something leads to a greater effect. And yet, homeopathic medicine is based upon that premise. Other things being equal, we should prefer a hypothesis that doesn't disagree with well-established knowledge, since if it does, it's more likely to be wrong. Homeopathic medicine has been tested and shown to be bogus, but millions of people still pay good money for homeopathic treatments.[16]

CHOOSE THE HYPOTHESIS

It is the mark of an educated mind to be able to entertain a thought without accepting it.

—Aristotle

Let's take a look at a couple of the beliefs mentioned earlier and apply the approach outlined above for forming reasoned beliefs. [17]

Therapeutic Touch

Therapeutic touch rests on the idea that we have an energy field emanating from our body and that we can cure disease by detecting and manipulating this energy. A practitioner of therapeutic touch moves her hands a couple of inches above a patient's body to detect and push away any negative energy causing illness. Therapeutic touch is thought by many to be a valid and accepted medical practice. As previously mentioned, it's used in at least eighty hospitals in the United States, and is taught in more than one hundred colleges and universities worldwide. Over forty thousand healthcare professionals have been trained in the technique and about half actively use it. In addition, our government has spent thousands to investigate the usefulness of the technique.[18]

So, does it make sense to believe in therapeutic touch? Let's begin by stating a specific, testable hypothesis.

Hypothesis 1: People have an energy field that emanates from their bodies that can be detected and manipulated to cure disease.

The next step is to examine the evidence for our hypothesis. Practitioners of therapeutic touch point to thousands of individuals who got better after undergoing their treatment. What could be more compelling evidence? People are sick, they get the treatment, they get better. And, this happens in thousands of cases. But these are all anecdotal cases, and we must remember that personal experiences can be misleading. What is needed are controlled experiments. So we continue digging through the evidence in search of some rigorous experimental data.

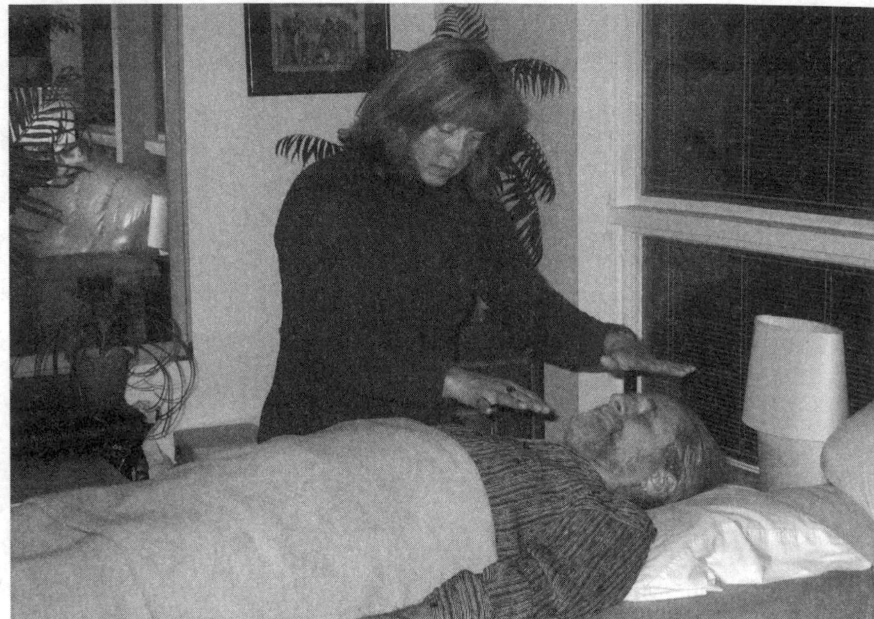

Figure 3. An illustration of therapeutic touch, where a person waves her hands above a patient's body to drive out negative energy that supposedly causes illness (photograph taken by the author).

A basic foundation of therapeutic touch, that we have an energy field coming from our bodies that can be detected, was tested in a controlled experiment involving twenty-one therapeutic touch practitioners. The design of the study was quite simple, yet elegant. In fact, it was designed by a nine-year-old girl by the name of Emily Rosa for her fourth grade science fair project![19] The practitioners put their hands, palms up, on a flat surface twenty-five to thirty centimeters apart. Emily, who was on the other side of a screen so the practitioners couldn't see her, put her hand eight to ten centimeters above one of the subject's hands and asked them to identify which hand she was above. If the practitioners could detect a human energy field, they should be able to accurately indicate which hand Emily was hovering over. Each subject had ten trials, and the position of Emily's hand was randomly determined each time. Of course, we would expect the practitioners to be right about 50 percent of the time simply by chance alone. Over the course of two different experiments, the average accuracy of the therapeutic touch practitioners was 44 percent—worse than just guessing!

And so, a basic proposition of therapeutic touch, that an energy field can be detected by the practitioners, was found to be highly questionable. But if that's the case, what accounts for all the reports of individuals getting better after undergoing therapeutic touch treatment? To have a more balanced and informed opinion about the issue, we have to consider competing explanations. Two hypotheses come to mind.

Hypothesis 2: People feel better after therapeutic touch because of the placebo effect.

Hypothesis 3: People believe that therapeutic touch cures them because they misinterpret the variability of disease.

The placebo effect is pervasive in medical science—many people feel better after receiving a given treatment, even though the treatment has no real therapeutic component.[20] In fact, since medical science has developed most of the treatments with real therapeutic effect in just the last hundred years, it's been said that, "prior to this century, the whole history of medicine was simply the history of the placebo effect."[21] Studies have shown that about 35 percent of patients with a number of different types of ailments receive benefit from placebo pills (e.g., sugar pills).[22] Placebos even help about 35 percent of patients with severe postoperative pain. Their effects are so potent that some people actually get addicted to placebo pills.[23] And so, many people can get better after a therapeutic touch treatment just because they think it's going to help them. Their "cure" has nothing to do with the technique itself.

In addition, most symptoms exhibit some degree of variability—sometimes they're better, while other times they're worse. We often seek medical help when we feel our worst, so any improvement is attributed to the treatment we receive. However, many illnesses improve on their own naturally, whether a treatment is given or not. It's been estimated that 85 percent of our illnesses are self-limiting—they'll end without any intervention. Even chronic diseases such as rheumatoid arthritis, multiple sclerosis, and cancer can have spontaneous remissions.[24] As a result, patients may get better after receiving treatment even though the treatment itself had no real therapeutic benefit.

Now that we have these three hypotheses, let's evaluate them. They are all testable. While therapeutic touch has some evidence in its support, that data is primarily anecdotal, which controlled experiments have brought into question. On the other hand, scientific studies have documented the placebo effect and the variability of illness. When we evaluate the simplicity of the hypotheses, therapeutic touch falls short. Why? Therapeutic touch requires that we believe in some unknown energy field, while placebo effects and the variability of disease do not. In addition, therapeutic touch conflicts with other scientific evidence. Controlled experiments demonstrate that therapeutic touch practitioners cannot discern an unknown energy field that they assume emanate from our bodies. Thus, it seems more reasonable to accept the placebo and variability hypotheses as contributing explanations for why people get better after therapeutic touch.

Similar analyses can be made for homeopathic medicine, magnetic therapy, and many of the other so-called alternative medicines.[25] In fact, a number of alternative practices have been tested and shown to be false. Yet, a subcommittee of the US Congress estimated that we spend around $10 billion annually on questionable medical practices; an amount considerably greater than the funds spent on actual medical research.[26] In addition, a survey of 126 medical schools in the United States found that 34 offered a course in alternative medicine. In fact, at the insistence of some congressmen on Capitol Hill, the National Institutes of Health established the Office of Alternative Medicine (later changed to the National Center for Complementary and Alternative Medicine) in 1991 to test the efficacy of alternative medical practices. While testing such practices is a good idea, many of the office's investigations have not involved accepted scientific techniques, like double-blind studies and control groups.[27] Instead, some rely on pseudoscientific arguments and anecdotal accounts. Therefore, after more than ten years and $200 million in research funding, much of the research sponsored by the office has not been able to validate or invalidate any alternative therapies.[28] As Michael Shermer, editor of *Skeptic* magazine, notes, why should we have a separate office of alternative medicine? All medical practices should be tested with the same rigor. We don't have an office of alternative airlines, which tests planes with only one wing.[29]

Talking with the Dead

Remember the radio show psychic mentioned earlier? The DJs on a local morning show were completely taken by her ability to talk with the dead. Caller after caller was amazed, and in some cases brought to tears, when they thought they were communicating with a deceased loved one. How does the psychic do it? She asks callers a number of leading questions about how their relatives died, what kind of people they were, what they liked to do, etc. In doing so, she culls information, makes a number of general statements, and then focuses on the ones that hit the mark. She inevitably ends the conversation on a positive note, saying something like, "Your father wants you to know that he's not suffering and that he loves you very much." When the listeners are asked if her comments were accurate, they typically report how amazed they were by how much she knew about their relatives. So, can the psychic talk to the dead? Let's formally examine the following hypothesis.

Hypothesis 1: Some people can uncover information about a deceased person by communicating directly with the dead.

Of course, to test this hypothesis we have to ensure that the psychic had no way of knowing information about the deceased prior to the reading. History reveals that a number of psychics have perpetrated hoaxes. In some instances, readings have been given for a confederate that was known to the psychic. In others, the psychic's assistants mingle with individuals, gather pertinent information prior to the reading, and then relay that information covertly to the psychic. There are many ways to fake psychic powers.

Since the readings were done by phone, and members of a reputable radio station chose the calls, let's assume that the psychic did not have prior information on the callers. What else could account for her accuracy? The callers definitely felt she knew a lot about their relatives. Does she really have the ability to give callers information about their deceased loved ones that she could not have known otherwise? Let's consider the following alternative hypothesis:

Hypothesis 2: Some people can uncover information about a deceased individual by using a technique known as "cold reading."

Cold reading is a technique in which the psychic asks general questions about the deceased until she gets some useful feedback from the subject. When she obtains useful information, she becomes more specific in her comments. If the listener responds positively, she continues with the line of inquiry and comment. If she's wrong, she makes it sound as if she were right. For example, statistics show that most people die of an illness somewhere in the chest area, like a heart attack. A standard technique for the psychic would be something like the following:

> Psychic: You lost a loved one. I'm getting a pain in the chest. Was it a heart attack?
> Subject: It was lung cancer.
> Psychic: Of course, that explains the pain in the chest.

The psychic got the illness wrong, but made it sound as if she was right. Is this what the radio show psychic did with her callers? Exactly! Listening closely, you begin to realize that she asks a number of rapid-fire, general questions. In many cases, the caller doesn't even have a chance to respond—instead, the psychic quickly jumps in and says something like, "You know what I mean," giving the impression that she was right. When callers respond negatively, she deflects the inaccuracies with a few common ploys. Some of the interactions that I heard went like this:

> Psychic: Your father died of a heart condition?
> Caller: No, he didn't.
> Psychic: Then it must be his sister that's coming through with him.

Or in another case:

> Psychic: Was she in a wheelchair?
> Caller: No.
> Psychic: If it's not her, it's on her mother's side of the family.

When she's wrong about the deceased with whom she's supposedly communicating, she deflects attention by saying she's picking up some other relative that's with the deceased. In some cases, she even had the audacity to suggest that the caller simply doesn't know the truth about what she's uncovering. For example:

Psychic: Who wore the pin striped suits?
Caller: No one.
Psychic: If you don't get what I'm saying, write it down and ask your other relatives.

Or in another case:

Psychic: Where are the twins?
Caller: There are no twins.
Psychic: He says there are twins. Either that or someone lost a baby very young with another one. Ask your mother.

As can be seen, the psychic's technique is to ask a number of leading questions and look for answers where she's on the right track. If she happens to hit one, she pursues it. If not, she deflects her error, attributing it to some other spirit coming through from the other side, or to the fact that the caller doesn't have the knowledge and has to ask his relatives. Invariably, she keeps it positive, with comments like, "Your father has the nicest smile," "He's with his grandmother now," and "I'm going to give you a big hug from your mother." Without fail, the deceased wants the caller to know that he's not suffering and that he loves the caller very much.

So, can cold reading really be the reason that people think they're talking with their deceased relatives? Can we be fooled so easily? A considerable amount of data says that we can. Researchers have known for years that we interpret very general comments as applying directly to ourselves. That is, we have a tendency to accept vague personality descriptions as uniquely describing ourselves, without realizing that the identical description could apply to others as well. It's called the Forer effect.[30] Also, you have to remember that people who seek out a psychic are those who desperately want to talk with their loved ones. As we will see, our perceptions can be clouded by what we want to see and believe. Cold reading works because people want it to work. They want to talk with their loved ones, and they don't want to be disappointed. And so, they are inclined to believe, and are therefore more than willing to overlook any errors in the psychic's comments as long as the end result assures them that their deceased relatives are okay and say they love them.

If we truly want to believe something, we'll remember the hits and forget the misses. As an example of this phenomenon, consider a reading that another renowned psychic did for nine people who had lost loved ones. Michael Shermer observed the readings. According to Shermer, the psychic applied a number of standard cold reading techniques, such as rubbing his chest or head and saying, "I'm getting a pain here," and looking for feedback. In the first two hours, Shermer said he counted over a hundred misses and about a dozen hits. Even with this poor hit rate, all nine people still gave the psychic a positive evaluation. If we want to believe it, we will.[31]

It's also worth noting that a good magician can do the same thing as these psychics. The difference is, the magician doesn't say he's talking with the dead—he knows it's a trick and so does the audience. In fact, there are articles on cold reading from which you can learn the technique yourself.[32] We have to ask ourselves, if psychics can really communicate with the dead, why do they have to question the living to learn about the dead? Shouldn't they just be able to sit back, contact the dead, and convey all the information they're getting directly from the deceased? Asking leading questions of the living should tip us off as to the psychics' real source of information.

So which is the more reasonable hypothesis to accept? Do some people have the ability to communicate with the dead or do they extract their information from the living through cold reading? We can certainly test the cold reading hypothesis because someone can employ the technique and we can gather data to see if people thought they were right. We can also test the communicating-with-the-dead hypothesis, although we have to be very careful in designing the study to make sure that the psychic does not have any prior knowledge about the deceased. As far as simplicity is concerned, cold reading wins out because it doesn't require us to assume that spirits exist and that some people can contact them. In addition, cold reading is consistent with what we already know about how humans form beliefs, while there is no credible scientific evidence for the existence of spirits. The cold reading hypothesis seems like the way to go.

I mentioned above that when we test a psychic's ability to communicate with the dead we have to ensure that he has no prior information about the deceased. That is, he's not conducting a "warm reading." Warm readings occur when a psychic has the opportunity to overhear or in some way get information from the subjects prior to a reading. Many people believe the psychic readings they see on TV. When watching a show, you often get the feeling that not all of what is said can be obtained by cold reading. Remember, however, you're often watching an edited show, and you don't know what went on prior to the taping. An audience member on one of these shows recently sent magician James Randi the following comment on his experiences.

> [The psychic] had a multiple guess "hit" on me that was featured on the show. However, it was edited so that my answer to another question was edited in after one of his questions. In other words, his question and my answer were deliberately mismatched. Only a fraction of what went on in the studio was actually seen in the final 30 minute show. He was wrong about a lot and was very aggressive when somebody failed to acknowledge something he said. Also, his 'production assistants' were always around while we waited to get into the studio. . . . [O]nce in the studio we had to wait around for almost two hours before the show began. Throughout that time everybody was talking about what dead relative of theirs might pop up. Remember that this occurred under microphones and with cameras already set up. . . . He also had ringers in the audience. I can tell because about 15 people arrived in a chartered van, and once inside they did not sit together.[33]

Whether that psychic is obtaining information from his audience is an open question. However, examples such as this demonstrate that there are alternative hypotheses to consider before accepting such an extraordinary claim as talking with the dead. In fact, failing to consider alternative explanations is one of the most important errors we make in forming our beliefs. If we open ourselves to entertain alternative explanations, and then select the one that's testable, simple, and consistent with well-established knowledge, we can put ourselves on the right track toward evolving more reasoned beliefs. By using such an approach, many of the weird and erroneous beliefs that we hold would simply fall away. In essence, we need to think like a scientist.

CHAPTER 3: THINKING LIKE A SCIENTIST

One thing I have learned in a long life is that all our science, measured against reality, is primitive and childlike—and yet it is the most precious thing we have.

—Albert Einstein

The ad catches your eye, "build confidence, reach peak performance in work, studies, the arts or sports . . . conquer habits like smoking, alcohol and drugs without the struggle . . . relieve stress, enhance healing . . . [achieve] effortless weight control for a lifetime."[1] You read this and think, "Sounds great—how can I do it?" Upon further reading, you learn that a newly discovered technology using subliminal tapes is the answer. The tapes play while you sleep, and since they target your unconscious, proponents claim that dramatic results can be quickly achieved. Too good to be true? Maybe, but the ad appeared in *Psychology Today*, a reputable magazine whose articles cover current developments in psychological research that influence our everyday life.

Intrigued, you search the Internet and find research reporting that subliminal tapes can enhance a person's memory, self-esteem, concentration, and word power. It seems pretty convincing, so you buy a tape to improve your memory. After playing it for a few weeks while you sleep, you notice that you actually *can* remember things better. "It's amazing!" you tell your friends, "You've got to try this tape." But does the improvement you see provide reliable evidence that the tape works? Consider the following study.

Psychologists gave one group of people a subliminal memory tape and told them it was designed to improve their memory. Another group was given a self-esteem tape and told it would improve their self-esteem.[2] Prior to each person's listening to the tape, the psychologists measured each individual's perception of his or her memory and self-esteem, and then instructed each to listen to the assigned tape every day for one month. When measured a month later, the people who used the memory tape reported improved memory, while those using the self-esteem tape reported improved self-esteem. Seems pretty convincing, doesn't it? But how good is this evidence? Although it may seem scientific, a close examination reveals that the evidence is purely anecdotal—amounting to nothing more than the personal testimonials of people who have used the tapes.

To scientifically test the credibility of these personal testimonials, the psychologists also analyzed two additional groups of people, but for these groups the tape labels were switched. That is, the "memory" tape was labeled "self-esteem," and the "self-esteem" tape labeled "memory." Amazingly, those who thought they had received the memory tape reported improved memory, despite having listened to a self-esteem tape, while the group who believed they were listening to a self-esteem tape reported higher self-esteem. To top it off, other more objective tests of memory effectiveness and self-esteem revealed no actual improvement in any of the groups. So the tapes were worthless, but they generated plenty of personal testimonials. Why? People thought their memory or self-esteem improved because they were expecting improvement. The implications are clear. We simply can't trust personal testimonials to provide us with objective, reliable evidence.

If we can't use personal testimonials to form our beliefs, what can we do? The most credible forms of evidence are those produced by scientific inquiry, and one of the more common and effective techniques used by scientists to evaluate a claim is the experimental method. With an experiment, some people receive a certain treatment (the "experimental" group), while others do not (the "control" group), and the two groups are compared to see if the treatment had any effect.

What about all those studies reported on the Web supporting the usefulness of subliminal tapes? They seemed scientific. The problem is, many studies that appear to be scientific are, in fact, the result of pseudoscience. Remember, those who practice pseudoscience often try to look "scientific," so it's sometimes difficult to tell the two apart. How can we tell the difference? First, if the study relies heavily on personal testimonials, be wary. Second, if an experiment is conducted, we need to evaluate how tightly the experiment was controlled. Good science requires extremely tight controls, while the controls in pseudoscientific experiments are often loose, opening up the possibility that alternative explanations caused the results. Not all experiments are created equal—an experiment is only as good as the tightness of its controls.

YOU HAVE TO TIGHTEN IT UP

To illustrate the importance of an experiment's controls, let's design a study to investigate whether a new drug is effective in treating a certain illness. We could simply give the drug to a group of people and see if they get better. But we already know that people sometimes get better on their own because the body has a tremendous capacity to heal itself. And, diseases have a natural variability, so even people with major illnesses can feel better at times. If people improve after taking the new drug, we might be tempted to claim that the drug cured the disease, but that's not necessarily the case. This research design doesn't rule out the other competing explanations.

So let's add a second group to the study, people who do not receive the drug treatment. Getting better in this group could only be the result of the body's ability to heal itself or the natural variability of the disease. If about the same number of people get better with and without the treatment, we can conclude that the drug did not contribute to the healing. But what if significantly more people got better in the group who received the drug? Can we conclude that the drug worked? I'm afraid not. We still have plausible alternative explanations. Remember the placebo effect—if people believe they are receiving a treatment that works, even if it's nothing more than a sugar pill, they are more likely to get better than if they receive no pill at all.

We can eliminate this problem by replacing the no treatment group with a placebo group (i.e., people who receive a sugar pill or some other treatment with no medicinal benefits). Further, we have to be sure that the people don't know whether they're receiving the actual drug or the placebo. That is, the participants have to be "blind" to the treatment they receive. Are these controls tight enough? Not yet! Studies have found that if the person giving out the pills knows who gets the drug and who gets the placebo, he can give subtle clues, even unknowingly, that tell participants what they're getting. So both the person giving the pills and the people receiving the pills must be blind to who is receiving what. The experiment is then said to be "double-blind."

Even with double-blind controls in place, other factors can come into play that may influence the results. What if there were more men in the drug treatment group, and more women in the control group? What if the people in the drug group exercised more or ate more healthy foods? These things could also affect the study's results, and may lead us to believe falsely that the drug had an effect when it didn't. To overcome these problems, we have to randomly assign people to the different groups. By randomly assigning a large number of individuals to the different groups, we should get a similar mix of subjects in each of the groups.

As you can see, if you want good evidence, many different types of controls have to be built into a study. Without adequate controls, the door is open to alternative explanations, and there's no sound basis for choosing one over the other. Since many people don't realize the importance of tight controls, they are prone to accept the results of studies when they shouldn't. This unquestioning attitude leads to beliefs in all types of pseudoscientific phenomenon. Think back to the ESP experiments reported earlier. In those studies, subjects could actually see or feel indentations of the symbols they were trying to identify on the backs of the Zener cards. The controls were very loose, and so alternative explanations abounded. Pseudoscience often gets results to support preconceived beliefs because their studies are not tightly controlled. The bottom line is, if we don't assess the quality of the test, we're more likely to form erroneous beliefs.

And so, the fundamental nature of the experimental method is manipulation and control. A scientist manipulates a variable of interest (e.g., gives a drug to one group and a placebo to another), and sees if there's a difference. At the same time, he/she attempts to control for the potential effects of all other variables (e.g., by randomization). The importance of controlled experiments in identifying the underlying causes of events cannot be overstated. In the real—uncontrolled—world, variables are often correlated. For example, people who take vitamin supplements may have different eating and exercise habits than people who don't take vitamins. As a result, if we want to study the health effects of vitamins, we can't merely observe the real world, since any of these factors (the vitamins, diet, or exercise) may affect health. Rather, we have to create a situation that doesn't actually occur in the real world. That's just what scientific experiments do. They try to separate the naturally occurring relationships in the world by manipulating one specific variable at a time, while holding everything else constant.[3] Without such a procedure, we would be doomed to believe in things like therapeutic touch and facilitated communication.

Our knowledge of science and the scientific method is crucial to our ability to form reasoned beliefs. And yet, the National Science Board estimated that two-thirds of us do not clearly understand the scientific process.[4] The sad truth is that most of us don't know enough about scientific procedures to be able to adequately evaluate the quality of data when we formulate our beliefs.

SO WHAT IS SCIENCE?

Science relies heavily on controlled experimentation, since, as we have just seen, an experiment is one of the best ways to determine if A causes B. Of course, not all of science can use controlled experiments. Many geological and astronomical hypotheses, for example, can't readily be tested in the lab. But they can be tested in the field where we can look for data that confirms or refutes a given hypothesis. So what is science?[5] The hallmark of science is the rigorous testing of hypotheses. As science writer Kendrick Frazier observes, "Science proposes explanations about the natural world and then puts those hypotheses to repeated tests using experiments, observations, and a creative and diverse array of other methods and strategies."[6]

My favorite definition of science was proposed by Michael Shermer: "Science is not the affirmation of a set of beliefs, but a process of inquiry aimed at building a testable body of knowledge constantly open to rejection or confirmation."[7] I like this definition because it emphasizes an extremely important point—science does not try to prove any specific belief. Science doesn't start with a preconceived notion of what we should believe, as some other human institutions do. Rather, science is simply the process we use to better understand our world. In fact, a true scientist never claims to know anything with absolute certainty. Instead, a scientist believes that all knowledge is open to rejection or confirmation, and that we are constantly refining and expanding our knowledge of the world. This quest for knowledge may never result in absolute truth—but it's still the best thing we've got to unravel the mysteries of life.

HOW SCIENCE OPERATES

Science generally begins with a simple question about something in our world. For example, does smoking cause health problems? Next, we form a hypothesis to specifically address the question. A hypothesis is a testable statement about the relationship between two or more variables. For our question, a testable hypothesis might be that smoking causes lung cancer. This statement identifies two specific variables that can be measured, smoking and lung cancer, predicts a causal relationship between the variables, and can be falsified. A scientist then conducts an experiment, or uses a number of other rigorous testing methods, to confirm or refute the hypothesis. Upon completion, the study is submitted for publication. But before a study is published, it's reviewed and critiqued by the scientist's peers to ensure that the research is of high-quality. And once in print, the research is open to criticism by the entire scientific community.

This process of review and criticism is one of the most important aspects of the scientific method because it provides an error-correcting mechanism that keeps science on track. In fact, this self-correcting mechanism is a main reason for the success of science over the years.[8] In science, every idea is open to criticism. When a scientist publishes a study, she must give the details of her study so others can attempt to replicate the results. If the study's results can't be replicated, they're not worth much. As you can see, you have to have pretty thick skin to be a scientist—your work is constantly under scrutiny!

Peer review and criticism are essential because scientists are human, and can make the same decision-making errors as everyone else. Some scientists may have a favorite theory they want to support, and may therefore search for supporting evidence and discount contradictory evidence. The great advantage to the scientific approach, however, is that any scientist's potential biases are scrutinized and criticized by his peers. In essence, science provides a process of checks and balances, where the errors of one scientist are rooted out and corrected by others.[9]

One study, by itself, can't tell us all that much. Even in legitimate science, the quality of studies can vary, which is one reason we sometimes get conflicting results. Confounding variables can affect the results, statistical errors can be made, and the data can even be faked. That's why others must replicate the findings of any study before we give them much credence.[10] As the preponderance of evidence from different studies converge, our confidence in a finding should rise. For example, initial research on smoking pointed to health problems. However, true experiments are difficult to perform on this issue because you can't force a random sample of people to smoke or stop smoking. As a consequence, researchers had to analyze the incidence of illness in smokers and nonsmokers. But any observed differences in one study could have been the result of some confounding variable. The smokers examined in one study might have been experiencing more stress, and it actually could have been the stress causing their health issues and not smoking. To eliminate this and other possible explanations, a number of studies needed to be conducted to ensure that other competing explanations, such as stress, diet, exercise, age, and gender, were ruled out. As more studies were conducted, the preponderance of the evidence pointed to smoking causing lung cancer and a host of other serious illnesses, so we can have a good deal of confidence in the belief that smoking causes ill effects.

To appreciate the significance of peer review, publication, and replication in the scientific process one just has to look at the cold-fusion fiasco. In the 1980s Professors Stanley Pons and Martin Fleishman of the University of Utah obtained some preliminary results that seemed to indicate they had developed a method to generate unlimited energy through a procedure called cold fusion. Rather than submit their study to a peer-reviewed journal, where their methods could be evaluated, Pons and Fleishman immediately called a press conference to announce their findings. In good science, information is typically not brought to the media until the study has gone through peer review; in fact, if a study hasn't had peer review, it's usually an indication of "bad science"—that is, poorly done science. Pons and Fleishman opted for the immediate fame of a national press conference, but paid the price. After their spectacular announcement, other researchers attempted to replicate their results—and failed. Cold fusion has since been relegated to the junk heap of pseudoscience. The bottom line is, science's greatest strength is its ability to self-correct. Bad science can and will occur, but the process of scientific inquiry should, over time, weed out the bad from the good.

HOW SCIENCE PROGRESSES

Science uses theories in its attempt to better understand our world. Many people believe that a scientific theory is nothing more than a guess or a hunch. But for a scientist, established theories are far more than simple intuition. Viable theories have considerable data in support of their predictions. This distinction between the public's perception of the term and its scientific meaning has led to a lot of misunderstanding. For example, some people say that since evolution is only a theory, we should consider creationism as an equally plausible alternative theory and teach it as such in our schools. This argument demonstrates a fundamental misinterpretation of the word *theory*. The theory of evolution is not merely someone's guess as to how we got here. Rather, it represents a conceptual structure that is supported by a large and varied set of data. No other alternative approach comes anywhere near to explaining our place in the world than evolution.[11] But remember, there are no absolute truths in science. A scientific "fact" is nothing more than a conclusion that has been confirmed to such an extent that it's reasonable to believe it at this time. In science, all knowledge is provisional.[12]

So how does science progress? An initial theory is advanced that attempts to explain part of our world. As we've seen, hypotheses based upon the theory are proposed, and researchers gather data to empirically test them. If the data support the hypotheses, we can be more confident in the correctness of the theory. As the number of studies providing support for the theory increase, it becomes established and accepted by the majority of the scientific community. A well-established theory, such as evolution, is often called a "paradigm," and has become widely accepted because the evidence from many different scientific studies supports it.[13]

If, on the other hand, the hypotheses tested are shown to be false, we must modify the theory in some way to adapt to the new evidence, or else discard it and propose a new and better theory. Whether we modify an old theory, or propose a new one, the resulting theory has to explain everything that the old theory did, as well as accommodate the anomalous evidence that has been uncovered. This incremental, adaptive process is how science progresses. Study by study, science brings us closer to a truer understanding of our world.

As an example of scientific progress, consider our early belief that the Earth was flat. A flat Earth theory was accepted because it seemed to make sense—the Earth certainly looked flat! However, some more careful observations were inconsistent with the theory. People noticed, for example, that when a ship sailed away from port, the bottom of the ship disappeared before the top, which couldn't happen if the Earth was flat. So a radical new theory had to be proposed—the Earth was round! As science developed, Sir Isaac Newton's work on gravity predicted that the Earth should not be a perfect sphere. Rather, the Earth should bulge a little at the equator and flatten out at the top and bottom, a fact that was confirmed by empirical tests years later. We now know that the Earth's diameter is 7,900 miles from North to South Pole, and 7,927 miles at the equator. Rather than perfectly round, the Earth is an oblate spheroid.

As this simple example illustrates, theories change or get refined to provide a better understanding of our world. The spherical theory was a significant advancement over the flat Earth theory, while the oblate spheroid theory is an even better refinement. As psychologist Keith Stanovich notes, when scientists argue that all knowledge is tentative, they're typically referring to this process. We're not going to suddenly discover that the Earth is, in fact, a square. But we may further refine our knowledge of the spherical nature of the world. The theory may be altered, but we're getting closer to the true nature of the Earth.[14]

Or consider the case of continental drift. Scientists originally thought that land masses on the Earth were stable, but anomalous evidence brought that theory into question. In the early 1900s, meteorologist Alfred Wegener noticed that the west coast of Africa and the east coast of South America appeared to fit neatly together, like pieces of a jigsaw puzzle. In addition, fossils of a freshwater reptile called mesosaurus were found in only two places, Brazil and West Africa, and other dinosaur remains were found separated by the vast Atlantic. Scientists first explained this data by hypothesizing that the dinosaurs must have walked across an ancient, but no longer existing, land bridge. However, as we learned more about our Earth through the study of plate tectonics, we found evidence that the Earth's rigid plates lay atop a layer of hot mantle, which would enable the continents to shift. As the evidence that our landmasses have been moving over time grew, the scientific community shifted paradigms to embrace continental drift. In this way, our knowledge progresses.

So what do we get from science if all its facts are provisional? As we saw in the last chapter, the strength of our beliefs typically follows a continuum, from strong disbelief to strong belief. Where we are on the continuum should be governed by the extent of the valid and reliable evidence in support of a belief, and science provides us with the best way to uncover that evidence. Of course, science sometimes finds conflicting evidence. Remember, individual studies can be flawed or biased (e.g., many studies finding no link between smoking and health risks were purportedly funded by tobacco companies). Since every study will not necessarily reach the same conclusion, we must consider the preponderance of the evidence gathered by scientific researchers if we're to set our beliefs in the most informed manner. In effect, we should ask ourselves if there is general consensus in the scientific community on the issue. If the answer is yes, the most informed belief would be the one that coincides with the consensus view (whether it leads to a stronger belief or disbelief in a certain phenomenon). If, on the other hand, there is no consensus in the scientific research, the most informed position would be to stay at the midpoint of the belief continuum, recognizing that we just don't know.

Can the consensus view be wrong? Of course! But it's still the best evidence we have to base our beliefs upon. And yet, people continue to disregard the findings of science because they don't fit with their own personal or political point of view. For example, when asked about global warming, a well-known conservative preacher indicated that he doesn't believe in it—that it's just a myth![15] It doesn't seem to matter that the vast majority of knowledgeable scientists now believe that substantial evidence exists for the rising of the Earth's temperature. One can only wonder what he was basing his belief upon.

SCIENCE AND THE PUBLIC'S MISPERCEPTIONS

With all that science has offered human civilization over the years, you'd think we would embrace scientific research and findings. In countless ways, science has made our lives immeasurably easier, and has contributed to even extending our life span. However, many people distrust science. Often, people believe that their own intuitive theories of how the world works are quite accurate, and so they question the value and findings of science, especially when it conflicts with their intuition. But our intuitive understanding of things is often wrong. Consider, for example, the research of Michael McCloskey on "intuitive physics."

Suppose you were twirling a ball tied to the end of a string and the string suddenly snapped. What trajectory would the ball take? When McCloskey asked this question of college students, about one third thought the ball would fly off in a curved arc. But, in fact, it would fly in a straight line. The students' intuition was off the mark.[16] Or consider this: if objects that are moving forward are dropped, such as bombs dropped from a plane, where will they land? About half of the people queried thought the object would fall straight down, indicating a basic misunderstanding of how an object's forward motion determines its trajectory.[17] Now, you may say that these questions are unfair because you'd need a physics course to answer them correctly. But we see falling objects every day, and so we have ample opportunity to observe these phenomena as they naturally occur. Despite considerable personal experience with moving and falling objects, our intuitive theories of motion can be quite inaccurate.[18]

McCloskey's findings have a parallel in the social sciences. People often hold intuitive beliefs about human behavior that they think are as good as anything that science has to offer. Essentially, they view the science of psychology as simply a matter of common sense. However, many of our intuitive beliefs about human behavior are wrong.[19] As we saw earlier, many people think that religious people are more altruistic than less religious people, that opposites attract, that happy employees are more productive employees, and so on. But when these commonsense notions are carefully studied, they are proven wrong time and time again.[20]

It's no wonder we think we're excellent judges of human behavior. We have an explanation for nearly everything that happens! For example, many people rely on short, generally accepted, sayings to explain human behavior. These pithy little proverbs also serve to guide our decisions and actions. Unfortunately, for just about every proverb, you can be sure to find another that contradicts it. It's better to be safe than sorry, isn't it? But, on the other hand, nothing ventured nothing gained. Two heads are better than one, but, of course, too many cooks spoil the broth. While a penny saved is a penny earned, it is also true that you can't take it with you. Don't forget to look before you leap, but remember, he who hesitates is lost. Sure, opposites attract, but everyone knows that birds of a feather flock together. It may be true that where there's smoke there's fire, but of course, you can't tell a book by its cover. While we all know that absence makes the heart grow fonder, we also think out of sight, out of mind. If we try, we can find some commonsense saying to explain virtually any behavior, after the fact. As a result, these aphorisms are unfalsifiable, and so they are worthless in explaining behavior or providing sound advice to guide our own behavior.[21] What's the bottom line? We need scientific inquiry to understand our world.

Some people claim that we can't trust the findings of science because scientists keep changing their minds. First, we're told, "Eggs are bad. Too much cholesterol." Then we hear, "Eggs are good. They're an important source of protein." Well, what's the story? Are eggs good or bad? Why can't scientists make up their minds? This view, however, demonstrates a basic misunderstanding of how science operates. As we've seen, science is a cumulative process, and the results of a single study tell us very little. We shouldn't form strong beliefs on the basis of one, or even a small number of studies. When evaluating scientific results, or any other evidence for that matter, we should look at the consensus view of qualified experts. Initial studies may contradict one another, and a number of studies may be needed before a consensus view emerges, but we shouldn't consider initial contradictory findings as a big problem. As Keith Stanovich observed, it's better to view the process like a projector, slowly being brought into focus. The initial blur we see on the screen could be just about anything. As the picture becomes sharper, however, a number of alternative ideas about what the picture is can be ruled out and the contents of the picture become clearer. So it is with the research process. While early contradictory evidence may blur our understanding, later work often brings the picture into sharper focus.[22]

When programs to help disadvantaged children, such as Head Start, were first studied, we saw headlines like "Early Intervention Raises IQs by Thirty Points," along with "Head Start a Failure."[23] What are we to believe from such contradictory headlines? The problem is that the headlines were premature. While they appeared to be definitive, it actually took another decade of research to give us a scientific consensus. As it turns out, while short programs of early intervention do not typically result in thirty-point IQ gains, they do have definite beneficial effects. Children who participated in Head Start were less likely to go into special education classes or to be held back a grade, and they showed improvement in later educational work.[24]

In effect, the reporting practices of the media can exacerbate the public's mistrust of science. The media typically reports the results of a single study, making it seem as if it's the consensus view. If a later study contradicts the first, we naturally tend to question what science tells us. However, the fault lies not with the science, but with the reporting and our interpretation of those reports. While scientists are noted for being conservative in interpreting a study's findings, the media and the public tend to exaggerate the implications of the results. For example, after initial research found that listening to Mozart marginally improved students' scores on one type of test, and for only a short period of time, the media played up the benefits of classical music. Before long, conscientious moms were playing Mozart symphonies to their unborn babies.

Scientists also seem to disagree on many issues because the science they currently conduct operates on the frontiers of what we know. There are obviously many things that scientists agree upon, things that are so well established from past science that they are accepted as fact. We know that the Earth revolves around the sun and that blood circulates through our bodies. Quite naturally, scientists are interested in other issues—they want to discover the unknown. Since this is where uncertainty lies, consensus is more difficult to come by. But this is also the work that will advance our knowledge.

DIFFERENCE BETWEEN SCIENCE AND PSEUDOSCIENCE

Now that we've examined what science and pseudoscience do, let's recap their differences. Science differs from pseudoscience in the evidence required before a belief is accepted, as well as in the plausibility of its arguments, the testability of its hypotheses, the amount of skepticism and criticism employed, and the benefits it has provided to us.[25]

UFO researchers claim that scientists are too closed-minded to believe in alien encounters. But are they? In fact, astronomers are extremely interested in finding what's "out there." They have built elaborate telescopes like the Hubble, sent out space probes, and listened for signs of intelligent life. In fact, the Search for Extraterrestrial Intelligence (SETI) project has been listening for radio signals from space for many years. This endeavor is science because it attempts to find hard evidence for the existence of alien civilizations. Given the immense size of the universe, it's certainly plausible that other life-forms exist somewhere in the cosmos. On the other hand, to believe that aliens are abducting individuals on this planet is to fall prey to pseudoscience. The physical evidence in support of this claim is suspect, and it's highly implausible that aliens are beaming thousands of individuals into spaceships hovering above the Earth, without detection and without anyone being reported missing. A fundamental difference between the two approaches is that science doesn't accept the existence of aliens without hard evidence. Pseudoscience does.

In science, testable hypotheses are developed so that they can be disproved. In pseudoscience, the hypotheses advanced are often not questioned even in the face of negative evidence. For example, when psychics and mediums are put in controlled situations, they fail to demonstrate any facet of extrasensory perception, beyond what you would expect from chance. Instead of accepting these results as evidence against the existence of psi phenomenon, psychics explain them away by claiming that the skeptical investigators conducting the experiments give off "negative energy," preventing them from performing better. In effect, the psychics set up a situation where they can't be tested. For every test conducted, they provide a reason why it won't work. But, as we saw, if a claim can't be tested, it's worthless.

Skepticism, a cornerstone of science, is suppressed in pseudoscience. Scientists open themselves up for criticism, while pseudoscientists are defensive and wary of opposing views. In pseudoscience, we don't see other pseudoscientists criticizing the results of a study. Why? They all want to believe the same thing. Their agenda is different than that of science. Pseudoscientists already know what they want to believe as they come into a study, and they selectively search for data to confirm their preconceived belief. Of course, science is guided by theories that may bias its search for knowledge. Also, scientists are human, so they can fall prey to human frailties. They have egos and may also want to find support for their pet theory. Fortunately, science has that built in error-correcting mechanism—criticism—to counteract the problems of human frailty. For every scientist publishing the results of a research study, a number of other scientists stand ready to find fault with the research. The end result is that useful ideas are retained, and nonuseful ideas abandoned.[26]

To appreciate the difference between real science and pseudoscience, just think about the great advancements of our civilization. We live longer, healthier, easier, and, for the most part, more fulfilling lives, primarily due to the knowledge we gained from science. Science has given us cures for a multitude of diseases, the ability to explore space, and technological marvels like the computer, television, and cell phones. On the other hand, paranormal investigators are still trying to establish the basic premise that ESP exists, and it's difficult to find a single practical benefit from that questionable research.[27] In the words of magician Penn Jillette, of Penn and Teller fame, "Being pro science is one of the oddest things you can do in show business. Which is very strange, because it was science that, oh, cured polio. I could list others—isn't that enough? Oh, Western medicine doesn't work; I'm sorry, we cured polio. . . . And guess what? It cures polio even if you don't believe in it."[28] Enough said!

THINKING LIKE A SCIENTIST

So what can we take away from our knowledge of science that would help us set more informed beliefs and make better decisions? Table 3 summarizes the major characteristics of a scientific approach to acquiring knowledge. Each of these items can be extremely useful in our everyday lives. As we've seen, we should keep an open mind to new phenomenon and explanations, but we should also be skeptical of any claim that's unsubstantiated. We have to make sure a claim or belief can be put to the test, because if it can't be tested, we'll never be able to determine its truth or falsehood.

Table 3

Characteristics of Thinking Like a Scientist

(1) Keep an open mind, but be skeptical of any unsubstantiated claim.
(2) Make sure a claim or belief can be tested.
(3) Evaluate the quality of the evidence for a belief (e.g., assess the tightness of the controls and don't rely on anecdotal evidence).
(4) Try to falsify a claim or belief (e.g., look for disconfirming evidence).
(5) Consider alternative explanations.
(6) Other things being equal, choose the claim or belief that is the simplest explanation for the phenomenon (i.e., the one that has the fewest assumptions).
(7) Other things being equal, choose the claim or belief that doesn't conflict with well-established knowledge.
(8) Proportion your belief to the amount of evidence for or against that belief.

It's extremely important to evaluate the quality of the evidence when testing any claim. We all too often simply accept anecdotal data or trust the results of a research study without evaluating the tightness of the controls. Given our underlying tendency to seek out confirming evidence, we need to be particularly vigilant in our search for disconfirming data. At the same time, we have to consider alternative explanations that may better account for the phenomenon. And, if the alternatives are equally proficient in explaining the phenomenon, we should choose the one that provides the simplest explanation and doesn't conflict with other well-established knowledge.

Finally, we have to proportion our belief to the amount of evidence for or against that belief. If the evidence doesn't strongly support a belief, a leap of faith will never establish the belief as true. We simply can't make something true just by believing it.[29] Consequently, we may have to withhold judgment on certain issues until the preponderance of the evidence indicates that it's more prudent to accept one belief over the alternatives. If we follow these basic guidelines used in science, we can all form more reasoned beliefs and make better decisions.

Chapter 4: The Role of Chance and Coincidence

Million to one odds happen eight times a day in New York.
—Penn Jillette

Do you remember the first season of *Survivor* that aired a few years back? Sixteen people were stranded on a deserted island and had to survive both their physical surroundings and social interactions. Every week, one person was voted off the island by the other members of the game, and the last person left was to receive one million dollars. In the final episode only two players, Kelly and Richard, remained. Their fate was determined by a vote of seven others who had already been eliminated. To help in their decision, the former members asked Kelly and Richard a number of questions, such as what three qualities they thought were most important to surviving the game. The results couldn't have been closer—after six votes were counted, the score was tied. The seventh and deciding vote gave Richard the million.

When the jury was asked why they voted the way they did, one of the members, Greg, said he couldn't decide, so he asked Kelly and Richard to pick a number between one and ten. Richard said seven and Kelly said three. Greg was thinking of the number nine and voted for the person who came the closest. After surviving thirty-nine days of physical, mental, and social challenges, the winner of the million-dollar prize was ultimately determined by chance! So it is in many aspects of our lives. We like to think that we can control our environment through our intellect and hard work. But the fact is, chance plays an important role in our everyday lives.

As Michael Shermer likes to say, we are causal-seeking animals.[1] We have an innate desire to find patterns in our world. Throughout our evolution, people who discovered the causes for things survived and passed on their genes. For example, those early ancestors who saw that certain rocks could be chipped and formed into spearheads were more likely to be successful hunters. They were better able to hunt prey, feed their families, and produce offspring that would survive. This inherent tendency to seek out causes has usually served us well. However, our desire to find causes is so central to the way we think that we often see causes for things that are simply random events or the result of chance occurrences.

You're driving down the street thinking about your recently deceased Uncle Jim. Lost in thought, you're driving a little slower than usual. As you approach a busy intersection, a speeding car runs a stop sign on your right—you would have crashed if you were just two seconds earlier! Instead, you drive away safely, although a little rattled. Many people attribute supernatural or divine intervention to such an event. They say, "Uncle Jim was watching out for me—that's why I slowed down." But we have to ask ourselves, does Jim's supernatural intervention offer the simplest explanation for the near miss? Remember Occam's razor—we should choose the explanation with the fewest assumptions. To accept the Jim hypothesis we have to assume that spirits of dead relatives exist, hang around this world, and watch out for our welfare—assumptions that have no hard evidence to support them. On the other hand, given the millions of cars on the road, probability theory predicts that there will be some accidents and some near misses. And so, a well-supported theory can explain the near miss without having to make untenable assumptions.

We naturally look for the reasons things happened the way they did. We want to believe that there's a reason for everything, and that if we understand what it is, we can, in some way, control the event. This even happens for the most obvious of chance events—the lottery. The lottery is certainly determined by chance, and yet, many people carefully choose their lottery numbers, thinking they can improve their odds. Entire books are written on the best way to choose winning numbers. In fact, studies show that people require more money to give up a lottery ticket if they pick their numbers than if they don't.[2] We want to, and think we can, control chance events. However, before we attribute some underlying cause for an event, we should first ask ourselves if the event can be explained by the laws of chance. If the well-established rules of probability can explain an event, there may be no reason to attribute any other cause.

THE BELL CURVE

A while back I went to the casino with my friend Tom. As we walked by the gambling tables he said, "I've got a sure-fire way to win at Roulette." When I asked him about the system he said, "Bet on either black or red, and if you win, take the money and make the same bet again. If you lose, double your bet on the next spin. Think about it. You can't lose too many times in a row—it's close to a 50/50 chance after taking out the house's edge—so you're bound to win fairly soon. And, when you finally win after a few losses, you'll recoup all of your prior losses and still win the current bet. You can't lose!" The system sounded great, so we pooled the meager resources we had at the time and went to the table with around $400. We put $5 on red and lost on the first spin. Undaunted, we doubled our bet and put $10 on red. Lost again. We then doubled the bet to $20 and lost a third time. Tom said, "We can't lose every time," so we put $40 on red—and lost. Thinking it couldn't go on much longer, we put $80 on red, and lost. Finally, we put $160 down, and watched as the ball landed on black. Losing most of our money, we walked away in disgust.

Why doesn't this system always work? It seems like it should. To understand why, we have to realize that there are distributions for most things in this world. What do I mean by a distribution? Consider the height of all the males in the United States. There are many men around 5'8" to 6', and fewer men above 6'8" or below 4'8". If we were to graph the numbers of men in various height categories, we'd see a picture something like figure 4. This is a common shape for a distribution, and it's known as the bell curve. The midpoint of the distribution is quite high, indicating more people at that height, while the two ends tail off, indicating far fewer people with those heights. Distributions like the bell

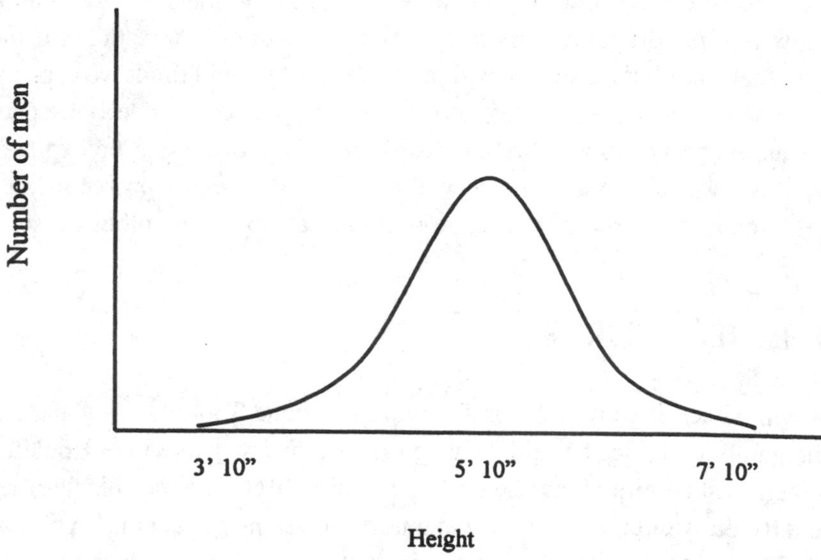

Figure 4. The bell curve: An example of a hypothetical height distribution of males in the United States.

curve are significant when we think about chance because they illustrate that there are extreme observations, called outliers, for many different types of measurements. As a result, if you observe any single case, you can get an outlier by chance alone. If you select one male from the United States, he could be seven feet tall, or only four feet tall.

What does this have to do with our miserable performance at the roulette table? Forgetting about the house's edge (the ball landing on 0 or 00), the probability of coming up red or black is similar to flipping a coin. If you flip a coin, the probability of getting a heads (or tails) is 0.5, because there are only two possible outcomes. What's the probability of getting two heads in a row? It's .5 × .5, or .25. That is, there's a 25% chance of getting two heads in a row. We can see this from the following list of possible outcomes, where H and T designates heads and tails:

HT, TH, HH, TT

Since there are four possible outcomes, HH has a one in four chance of occurring (25%). Now carry this reasoning to six flips. To calculate the probability of getting six consecutive heads, just multiply 0.5 by itself six times. The result is 1.56 percent. So, the probability of getting six heads in a row is roughly 1.5 percent for any set of six flips. While the probability is low, there are times when six coin flips will yield six heads. It's not as likely as, say, three heads and three tails, or four heads and two tails, but it can still occur for any given sequence of six flips. In fact, it's very likely to occur some of the time if we make a large number of six coin flips. For example, if we performed one thousand flip sequences, we would expect fifteen of them to be all heads by chance alone (1,000 x 1.5%). The same goes for the roulette wheel. With the thousands of spins on the roulette wheel, my friend Tom and I were just unlucky to be there when the ball landed on black six times in a row. Unfortunately, we lost our bankroll before a red number hit.

Since people think these extreme events are unlikely to occur, they frequently attribute some other, often mysterious, cause for the occurrences. They may think that the person flipping the coin or spinning the roulette wheel has some special power to control the outcome. However, before we attribute other possible causes, like psychic or mystical powers, for an event, we have to determine if those powers can make the event occur more than what we would expect from chance. As we saw, if we conducted one thousand six-coin flip sequences, we would expect around fifteen to be all heads from chance alone. Before we believe that someone's psychic power caused six heads in a row, it must be demonstrated that their power can yield significantly more than fifteen series of heads out of one thousand. If not, the six heads can be explained by chance.

The extreme occurrences that are evident in the tails of a distribution have led many people to form erroneous beliefs. Suppose your friend was just told he has a serious cancer, and that his average life expectancy is only one more year. When given such news, some patients try bizarre healing techniques, such as therapeutic touch, healing crystals, or even psychic surgery. Some of those patients may live longer than a year, and if they do, they often believe the alternative technique extended their life. But there's variability in the life span distribution—while the average life expectancy may be one year for a person with the cancer, some people may die after a month, while others may live for another five years. In essence, the tails of the distribution indicate that some people will live considerably longer than the average, a fact often ignored when forming beliefs.

The tails of a distribution are also a good reason to listen to the consensus of qualified experts rather than to a single individual. There are thousands of experts in most fields, and it's likely that some of them will believe some pretty weird things. There are outliers even among scientists, professors, and other qualified experts—something isn't true just because one expert says so. Remember the weird beliefs of John Mack from Harvard on alien abduction? If we look for the consensus view of the experts, we're more likely to get closer to the truth as we now know it.

Extrasensory Perception

Probability theory can explain many occurrences that, on the surface, seem inexplicable. Consider, for example, ESP. Michael Shermer went to Edgar Cayce's Association for Research and Enlightenment in Virginia Beach, an official-looking organization that conducts ESP experiments.[3] When he arrived, they were running an experiment in which people (receivers) tried to discern certain shapes that another individual (a sender) was viewing. The "sender" concentrated on a card which displayed either a plus sign, square, star, circle, or wavy lines. At the same time, the "receivers" were told to concentrate on the sender's forehead and attempt to discern what he was thinking. Thirty-five people participated in the experiment, which ran two trials of twenty-five cards each.

The instructor said that everyone has ESP to some degree, although some have more than others. He indicated that, on average, people should correctly identify five out of twenty-five because of chance alone (since there were five symbols). In fact, he said that probability can explain any accuracy between three and seven. However, anyone who correctly identified more than seven symbols was said to have ESP. It turned out that three people identified eight symbols in the first trial, and one identified nine in the second trial. So, according to Cayce's association, at least four people participating in the experiment demonstrated ESP without even being trained. But did they really?

Probability theory indicates that there will be variation in the subjects' accuracies because of chance alone. While three people correctly guessed eight symbols in the first trial run, there were also three people who only got two right—the other twenty-nine correctly guessed between three and seven. In the second trial, there was one person who got nine right, but three people correctly guessed only two or one (all different people than those who scored low and high in the first set), and the rest were between three to seven. Remember the bell curve? These results look remarkably like a normal bell curve distribution that has an average of around five and some deviation around that average. So by chance alone, we would expect some people to get eight or nine right. In fact, with large groups of subjects we would expect some people to score even higher. The bottom line is, probability theory predicts these types of results, and so we don't need to invoke some mysterious cause like ESP.

According to Shermer, when he mentioned the bell curve to the group, the instructor said, "Are you an engineer or one of those statisticians or something?"[4] The group laughed and the instructor went back to lecturing on how to improve their ESP. When we want to believe in something, we'll ignore, downplay, or even ridicule conflicting explanations. And, this is more likely to happen if we lack a good understanding of probability. In fact, researchers have found that people who believe in ESP do not understand probability as well as nonbelievers, and are therefore more likely to attribute paranormal explanations to extreme events.[5]

THE GAMBLERS' FALLACY

Let's go back to the roulette wheel. As you're watching the ball land on successive spins, you notice that it landed on black the last four times. If you had to put $100 on the next spin, would you put it on red, on black, or would you have no preference? Many people would choose red. Why? Because they think it's due. This is the gamblers' fallacy. If each spin is independent of the others, there's an equal chance the number will be red or black, irrespective of what happened on prior spins. But many people believe that what has recently occurred will affect what will occur next, even though the two events are independent. Every time I go to a casino

I see seasoned gamblers falling prey to this fallacy, and losing their shirts because of it![6]

The gambler's fallacy says that people will view independent events to be related in some way. In some cases, the fallacy leads people to believe that events will change, as in the case of the roulette wheel (red will come up next because black has come up a few times in a row). In other situations, however, people think that if an event has occurred, it's more likely to occur again. We can see this in the "hot hand."

The Hot Hand

You're at a basketball game watching your hometown team play for the championship. It's the last quarter and your team is down, but they're making a comeback. In fact, your favorite player, Michael J., has just made three baskets in a row. People in the crowd start screaming, "Mike's hot—give the ball to Mike!" Why? It's common knowledge that basketball players get on a roll—they get hot. They get into a zone, and seem like they can't miss. Everybody's seen it happen. In fact, a survey of basketball fans showed that 91 percent thought a player was more likely to make a basket if he just made the last two or three shots, than if he missed the last two or three. Eighty-four percent thought the ball should be passed to a player who just made a couple of shots in a row.[7]

The problem is, there's no such thing as a hot hand. Psychologists Tom Gilovich, Robert Vallone, and Amos Tversky analyzed the shooting statistics for the Philadelphia 76ers and the Boston Celtics during the 1980–1981 season, and found absolutely no evidence to support the hot-hand theory.[8] Streak shooting implies that the probability of making a basket, after having just made two or three baskets, is greater than the probability of making a basket after two or three misses. When you analyze the statistics, this just doesn't happen. For example, consider Dr. J. (Julius Irving), who typically took the most shots for the 76ers. The probability that Dr. J. would make a basket after having just made two baskets in a row was 52 percent, while the probability of his making a basket after two misses was 51 percent. If he made three baskets in a row, he sunk his next shot 48 percent of the time, while if he missed three baskets, he scored on his next shot 52 percent of the time. In short, the likelihood of him making a basket was around 50 percent, irrespective of what happened on his last few shots. Analyzing the free throws of the Boston Celtics revealed the same result. Larry Bird's chances of making a free throw were about the same (88 percent and 91 percent) whether he made the last free throw or not.

The data on a number of other players revealed similar findings. When Gilovich and his colleagues examined all the players on the 76ers, they found that the probability of a hit was actually a little lower after a hit than after a miss (average of 51 percent versus 54 percent over nine players). In addition, the probability of a hit following a hot period (three or four hits in the last four shots) was 50 percent, while a hit after a cold period (none or one hit in four shots) was 57 percent. They also analyzed the number of runs that the players had. A run is a sequence of consecutive hits or misses. For example, if X stands for a hit, and O a miss, the sequence XOOOXXO contains four runs. Streak shooting suggests that a player's hits cluster together, and so there should be fewer runs than what you would get from a random process. Only one player (Daryl Dawkins) deviated from chance, and he had more runs than expected, contrary to the hot-hand hypothesis. In fact, the analyses of twenty-three players on three different teams (the 76ers, New York Knicks, and New Jersey Nets) revealed similar results, even for players typically considered to be streak shooters, like Andrew Toney.

Gilovich and his colleagues then asked college players to shoot free throws and predict whether they would make the next basket given how they felt. According to the hot-hand theory, if they felt confident, like they were "in a zone," they should be able to sink more shots. However, there was no association between the players' predictions and their actual performance. In essence, the data indicate that there is no hot hand in basketball. Remember, there are tails to any distribution, so by chance alone we would expect a player to occasionally hit a number of baskets in a row. It's not a hot hand, it's just the vagaries of chance. And yet, when players on the 76ers team were interviewed, all of them thought it was important to pass the ball to someone who had just made a few shots in a row.[9]

So why do we believe in streak shooting when successes and failures are statistically independent of one another? We misperceive random sequences. Consider, for example, the following problem:[10]

Which of the following sequences of Xs and Os seems more like it was generated by a random process (e.g., flipping a coin)?

_____XOXXXOOOOXOXXOOOXXXOX

_____XOXOXOOOXXOXOXOOXXXOX

Most people say the second is more random. However, the Xs and Os switch 70 percent of the time in the second case (they switch on fourteen of twenty possible alternations). On the other hand, the Xs and Os switch 50 percent of the time in the first case (ten out of twenty), which is similar to what you'd expect from a 50/50 chance sequence. And yet, 62 percent of people tested thought that the first case was similar to streak shooting.[11] In effect, the first case is random, but looks streaky, while the second is not random, but is seen as such. If you said the second case looks random, you're expecting too many switches between the Xs and Os, which can lead you to see streaks in random processes. And if you see streaks in the randomness of the first case, you're likely to believe that a basketball player sometimes gets a hot hand.

Our intuitive ideas of randomness clearly don't coincide with the laws of chance. We tend to think that there shouldn't be a number of runs (e.g., a number of heads flipped or baskets made, in a row) because it doesn't seem random. However, if you flip a coin twenty times in a row, there is an 80 percent chance that at some point you'll get three heads or three tails in a row. There's a 50 percent chance you'll get four in a row, and a 25 percent chance you'll get a streak of five in a row.[12] Once again, our intuitive theories of the world can be erroneous, which is why we can't rely just on our experiences—we need systematic scientific inquiry.[13]

So what can we take away from all of this? On the one hand, we have probability theory and its well-established principles. To believe in the other, hotter hand, we would need to demonstrate that the baskets made deviate from what would be predicted by probability theory. Why? Occam's razor. If the events can already be explained by a well-established concept, we don't need another explanation, such as the hot hand. However, we are constantly on the lookout for the causes of things, and we don't appreciate the fact that many events in life are random. As a result, we start to attribute other causes for essentially random events.

COINCIDENCES

It is likely that unlikely things should happen.
—Aristotle

When I was in college one of my professors told our class about a long-shot meeting. He went on vacation to England during the summer, and, as he was walking down a street in London, he ran into one of the other professors in the department. You can imagine their surprise upon seeing one another, since they didn't tell each other they were going to vacation in England at that time. What are the chances of meeting someone you know on the streets of London during your vacation? Of all the places you can vacation, of all the times you can take your vacation, the odds are astronomically low. Isn't that proof there's something more going on?

When I was a doctoral student, I went to a casino night which the university was holding for charity. While driving to the affair, I happened to look down at the odometer and saw that my car had 55,555 miles on it. I said to myself, jokingly, "I guess five is my lucky number tonight." As soon as I walked into the casino hall I went over to the Roulette wheel and put $5 on number five. It came out on the first spin, paying me thirty-five to one! Amazed, I took my winnings to the next roulette wheel, where I again put $5 on number five. Unbelievably, it again came out on the first spin, paying me thirty-five to one!

Coincidences can be quite astounding. A man by the name of George D. Bryson was traveling by train from St. Louis to New York. At the last minute, he decided to make a stop in Louisville, Kentucky, a city he'd never seen before. He asked for a hotel and was told to go to the Brown Hotel, where he registered and was given room 307. As a joke, he asked if he had any mail. The clerk handed him a letter addressed to Mr. George D. Bryson, Room 307. The prior occupant of room 307 was another George D. Bryson![14]

Or consider this case: In 1914 a German mother photographed her son on a film plate, and then left the plate at a processor to be developed.

World War I broke out and she couldn't return to the city to get the picture. Two years later, she bought a film plate in another city 200 miles away to take a picture of her new daughter. When the plate was developed, it was a double exposure—her daughter was superimposed over her son![15]

Such events are astonishing, and can lead people to believe that something mysterious, mystical, or even divine is happening. In fact, stories like these led the psychologist Carl Jung to propose his concept of synchronicity. He maintained that such coincidences are the work of some unknown force trying to impose order on the events of the world. Once again, we have a case where someone, in this instance a very influential psychologist, is asserting that some mysterious force is the underlying cause. But let's apply Occam's razor. Is there a simpler explanation?

When thinking about coincidences such as these we shouldn't think in terms of the likelihood of these specific events happening. If we focus on the odds of my two professors meeting in London during their respective vacations, we'll likely conclude it's too low to be just a chance occurrence. But we shouldn't think about the meeting in that way. Yes, the odds of meeting that person, at that time, on the streets of London five thousand miles away from home, are extremely low. However, the odds that we meet someone we know, at some distant location, at some time in our life, are much greater. In fact, when you look at the millions and millions of people who travel every year, it's very likely that some of them will have chance meetings with someone they know. (Within one month, I saw, by coincidence, the same professor from our school at the Orlando, Florida, airport and again in a toy store in New York City.)

When thinking about the George D. Bryson coincidence, we shouldn't focus on the likelihood that the prior occupant of the room was another George D. Bryson. Instead, we should ask ourselves how likely it is that two successive occupants in some room in some hotel in some city at some point will have the same name.[16] When thinking about my roulette winnings, don't focus on that one case. Think about the millions of people who place millions of bets on the roulette table. Given the sheer numbers, it's likely that some will win a few times in a row, even with their "lucky" numbers.

It seems incredible that such coincidences occur, and so we want to attribute them to otherworldly explanations. But given the billions and billions of events that occur every day, there are bound to be many such coincidences. In fact, it would actually be incomprehensible if coincidences didn't occur. For example, if we flipped five quarters, there's only a 3 percent chance of getting all heads. However, if we flipped these coins one hundred times, there's a 96 percent chance that one of those trials would give us all heads. As you can see, when we consider the vast number of events occurring, it's very likely that coincidences will occur. As Penn Jillette says, "Million to one odds happen eight times a day in New York."[17]

However, many people still want to attribute mysterious causes to coincidences. A woman came up to Michael Shermer and said, "How do you explain coincidences like when I go to the phone to call my friend and she calls me? Isn't that an example of psychic communication?" Shermer replied, "No . . . it is an example of statistical coincidence. Let me ask you this: How many times did you go to the phone to call your friend and she did not call?" The woman later said she figured it out, she only remembers when it happens and forgets all the times it doesn't. Shermer said "You got it. It's just selective perception." She replied, "No, this just proves that psychic power works sometimes but not others." As James Randi said, believers in the paranormal are like "unsinkable rubber ducks."[18]

SUPERSTITION

Wade Boggs was one of the most proficient hitters in the history of baseball. He won the batting title five times and had a lifetime batting average of .363. He is also highly superstitious. Early on in his career he formed the belief that he could hit better after eating chicken. For that reason, he ate chicken almost every day for twenty years when he played baseball. He is not alone in his superstitious behavior. Wayne Gretzky, the great hockey star, always tucked in the right side of his jersey behind his hip pads. Jim Kelly, the Buffalo Bills quarterback, forced himself to vomit before every game. Bjorn Borg did not shave after he began to play in a major tennis tournament. Bill Parcells would buy coffee from two different coffee shops before every game when he coached the New York Giants.[19]

Superstitious behavior is not confined to the sports arena. Like Wade Boggs, Michael Crichton, author of *Jurassic Park*, has the same thing for lunch every day when he's working on a new novel. One study found that between 20 to 33 percent of students rely on superstition and magic to bring good luck when taking exams. They wear special clothing, use certain pens, listen to lucky songs, knock on the exam room door, circle the building, or practice a number of other rituals.[20] Some people believe that walking under a ladder or breaking a mirror will bring bad luck, and many fear the number thirteen. In fact, there's even a company in France that provides emergency dinner guests so that thirteen people never have to sit at the table together.[21] And gamblers are notorious for exhibiting superstitious behavior.

A superstition is a belief that one thing affects something else, even though there is no logical relation between the two things. Superstitious behavior is often an outgrowth of coincidence. What happens? By coincidence, one event follows another, and a person then draws a causal association between the two events. For example, if a basketball player bounced a ball three times before attempting a crucial free throw, and then made the basket, he may associate the successful basket with the number of times the ball was bounced. In effect, the bouncing pattern was reinforced by the successful basket, resulting in a shooting ritual, a personal superstition.[22] Wade Boggs most likely had one or two great batting days after he ate chicken, which launched his superstition. Superstitions caused by coincidences can be seen every day in casinos around the world. I've talked to many a gambler who are convinced that they have to put coins in a slot machine by hand, instead of using credits accumulated on the machine (which is much easier), in order to win. Why? They once had a big hit right after inserting coins by hand, and the coincidence created the superstition.

Linking superstitious beliefs and behaviors to coincidental events occurs because of a process that psychologists call operant conditioning. Psychologist B. F. Skinner, the foremost proponent of operant conditioning and author of the famous article "Superstition in the Pigeon," convincingly demonstrated that coincidence develops superstitious behavior. Skinner put pigeons into separate cages and had a prize (food) dropped periodically (remarkably similar to slot machine payouts!). After just a few minutes, each bird exhibited a different bizarre behavior. Some bobbed their heads up and down, others walked in circles, while still others thrust their heads into different places in the cage. It turned out that the birds repeated the behaviors they performed just prior to receiving the food. Since they were doing different things just before food arrived, they developed different rituals. In essence, the pigeons' behavior was the result of a coincidence based on what they were doing when the food appeared. So it is with many human superstitions.[23]

While operant conditioning explains how many superstitions form, an underlying question remains: Why do they form? We live in a world of uncertainty. Many of life's events are unpredictable, and superstitions provide a way for many people to cope with the uncertainty. Superstitious behavior often makes us feel we have control over the situation; that, in some way, our behavior can affect the outcome. Consequently, superstitious behavior is likely to arise in situations that are more uncertain, random, and uncontrollable.

As we've seen, baseball and other sports figures are notorious for developing superstitions. Why? Uncertainty plays a big part in most sports. The best professional basketball players typically make only about half of their shots from the field. Quarterbacks in the NFL complete an average of about 58 percent of their passes. When such uncertainty exists, superstitions are bound to arise. This occurs even within a sport. If a baseball player gets a hit 30 percent of the time he is known as a premier batter, while hitting 26 percent makes him only average. In contrast, a fielder usually catches a ball that he's expected to catch, or throws a batter out, about 97 percent of the time. As a result, baseball superstitions tend to center most around hitting and pitching—many players feel less need for such superstitions when playing the field.[24]

Our superstitious beliefs are often reinforced by a biased interpretation of future events. As noted earlier, many people think that things come in threes. To support that belief, they point to many instances where three bad or three good things happened over a period of time. However, evidence for such a superstition is problematic. Why? We remember the times that three things seemed to happen fairly close to one another, and forget all the times when three things didn't happen together. Once again, we remember the hits and forget the misses. Also, as we noted, there's never a time horizon stated. Do the three things have to happen within a week, a month, or a year? Sooner or later, three similar things are likely to occur. We can interpret just about any data as supporting the things-come-in-three superstition—if we wait long enough. As Stuart Vyse stated, "The fallibility of human reason is the greatest single source of superstitious belief."[25]

Chapter 5: Seeing Things That Aren't There

Things are not always what they seem.
—Phaedrus

We like to think that we perceive the world as it actually exists, but the fact is our senses can be deceived. We can actually see and hear things that aren't really there. While this may seem far-fetched, research in psychology and neurobiology indicate that to understand perception, we have to abandon the notion that the image we see is an exact copy of reality. Perception is not just replicating an image in our brain; instead, perception requires an act of judgment by our brain.[1]

Most of us are familiar with the picture of the cube presented in figure 5. We see the cube as pointing either up or down depending on how our brain interprets the picture, even though the image remains constant on our retina. External reality hasn't changed, but our interpretation of that reality has. Our perception is also affected by the context in which it occurs. A 5' 10" sports announcer looks quite small when he interviews a basketball player, but quite tall when he interviews a jockey.[2] Thus, our vision is a constructive process—the simple act of seeing is open to interpretation and judgment.

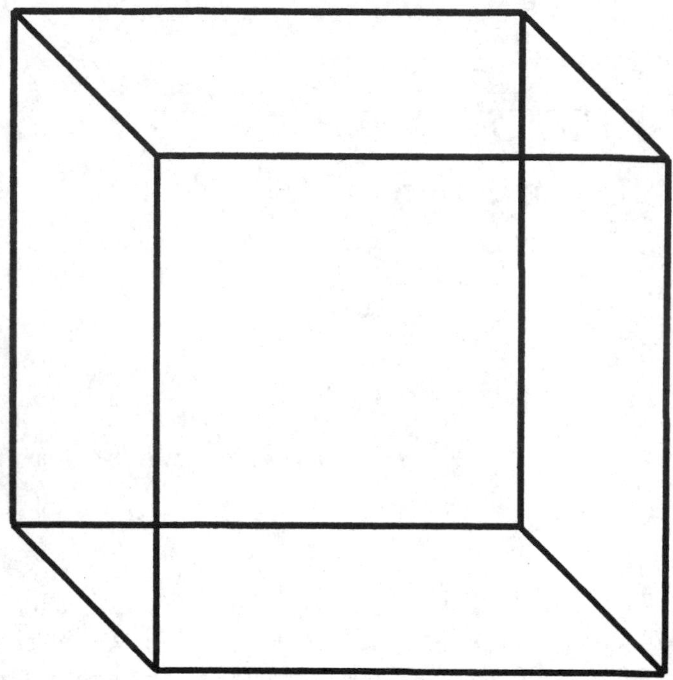

Figure 5. Cube points up or down depending upon a person's perception.

Of course, our perceptions are often quite accurate (or at the very least, they're good enough). It would be difficult to lead normal and productive lives if they weren't. But when we do misperceive, we can form some pretty weird and erroneous beliefs. Research has found that two factors significantly influence how we perceive the world—we see what we *expect* to see and what we *want* to see. That is, we often see things because our prior experiences have led us to expect them, or our desires have led us to want to see them.

SEEING WHAT WE EXPECT

The eye sees only what the mind is prepared to comprehend.

—Henri-Louis Bergson

Read the following:

PARIS
IN THE
THE SPRING

If you're like many people, you read the phrase as "Paris in the Spring."[3] But look closely—the word *the* is stated twice. We don't expect to find two in a row, so we see only one. As another example, when people were quickly shown a playing card that illustrated a black three of hearts, many of them were sure it was a normal three of hearts or a normal three of spades. Why? We don't expect to see a black heart, so we interpret it to be consistent with our expectations.[4] As these simple examples illustrate, we can misperceive our world when reality doesn't match our expectations.

Our expectations can actually make us see things that never happened. For example, when a researcher told people that the light in a room would blink at random intervals, many said the light blinked, even though it never did.[5] Other research demonstrates that people can experience electric shocks or smell certain odors when they don't actually exist.[6] These misperceptions also occur outside the lab. When a panda bear escaped from a European zoo, people called from all over to say they saw the bear. However, the bear traveled only a few yards from the zoo before it was tragically hit by a train. All of the reported sightings were products of overactive imaginations—people expected to see the bear, and so they did.[7] Expectations can lead to hallucinations!

What if you thought that a full moon caused people to act strangely? You would expect to see weird behavior on nights with a full moon, and would likely be on the lookout for such behavior. Many studies have systematically shown that there is no such thing as a "lunar effect"—full moons do not cause abnormal behavior. However, when nurses were asked to note any unusual behavior in their patients during a full moon, those who believed in the lunar effect said they saw more unusual behavior than those who didn't believe.[8] If we expect to see something, we'll interpret our world to see it.

Our expectations also affect how we judge others. Consider the following description of a person called Jim:

> Jim is intelligent, skillful, industrious, warm, determined, practical, and cautious. Circle the other traits you think Jim is most likely to have (circle one trait in each pair):
>
> Generous———Ungenerous
> Unhappy———Happy
> Irritable———Good-natured
> Humorous———Humorless

When people respond to this task, about 75 percent to 95 percent think Jim is generous, happy, good-natured, and humorous. However, when the word *warm* is changed to *cold* in Jim's description, only 5 percent to 35 percent think that Jim will have these traits.[9] Other researchers have found that if army supervisors think subordinates are intelligent, they also see them as having better character and leadership ability. If people are thought to be attractive, we typically think they are happier, have a good personality, and produce better quality work.[10]

Why? If we think a person has a good quality on one dimension, we expect that she will have good qualities on other dimensions. In essence, we attribute characteristics to a person that are consistent with what we already believe about the person. This phenomenon, known as the halo effect, can affect many of the decisions we make concerning others. For example, Jerzy Kosinski was a well-respected author of many acclaimed books. At one point in his career, he wrote a novel called *Steps*, which won the National Book Award for fiction. Someone retyped the book and sent it with no title and a false name to fourteen publishers and thirteen literary agents, including Random House, who actually published Kosinski's book. Not one of the publishers or agents recognized that the book had already been published—and all twenty-seven rejected it! Without Kosinski's name to create a halo effect, the book was considered to be a fairly mediocre piece of fiction.[11]

Does something as seemingly irrelevant as the color of one's uniform affect our expectations, and hence our perceptions and judgments of others? We tend to associate the color black with evil. Black Thursday ushered in the Depression. When the Chicago White Sox deliberately lost the 1919 World Series, they were known as the Chicago Black Sox. Psychologists Mark Frank and Thomas Gilovich found that people think black uniforms look more evil, mean, and aggressive, as compared to nonblack uniforms.[12] But will this negative perception actually affect our judgments about the people wearing black? Frank and Gilovich analyzed the penalty yards and minutes given to professional football and hockey teams between 1970 and 1986. Amazingly, they found that all the teams in the NFL and NHL who wore black uniforms were penalized more than the average of the other teams. In fact, switching to black can actually increase the penalties given to a team. The Pittsburgh Penguins switched to black uniforms during the 1979 to 1980 season. During the first forty-four games, when they were wearing blue, the team averaged eight penalty minutes per game. For the final thirty-five games, when they wore black, the team averaged twelve minutes per game!

Frank and Gilovich also had football referees and fans view different plays that contained borderline calls. In one play, two members of the defensive team grabbed a ball carrier, drove him back several yards, and threw him to the ground with considerable force. The participants were asked to indicate on a nine-point scale how they would penalize the defensive team for the play. One end of the scale was labeled "cheap shot designed to hurt the opposing player," while the other end was labeled "legal and somewhat non-aggressive." Some of the referees and fans saw a video with the players wearing black, while others saw players wearing white. Again, the teams with black uniforms received harsher treatment (average score of 7.2) than the teams with white uniforms (average of only 5.3).[13]

Our expectations have consequences not only for our perceptions and judgments, but also for our reactions. For example, an intriguing study investigated the impact of expectations on patients' abilities to recover from abdominal surgery. One group of patients was told what to expect from the surgery, such as how long it would last, the type of pain they would experience, and when they would regain consciousness, while another group was told nothing. Those patients who were told what to expect complained less about the pain, required less medication, and recovered more quickly. In fact, they were discharged from the hospital an average of three days earlier![14] Researchers in another study told students that they were drinking coffee with caffeine, when, in fact, it was actually decaf. The students said they were more alert and tense, and even had significant changes in blood pressure.[15] While it's not used much now, doctors used to prescribe placebos for some patients.[16] As we saw, when a patient expects a pill to work, he sometimes gets better even though the pill has no actual therapeutic effect. It's all about what we expect.

SEEING WHAT WE WANT

While expectations can influence perceptions, our desires are perhaps an even more powerful influence on perception. Why? We have a strong motivation to see things that we want to see in order to maintain consistency in our beliefs. The more we perceive the world as supporting our beliefs, the more we think those beliefs must be true.

A particularly rough football game was played between Dartmouth and Princeton. One of Princeton's star players suffered a broken nose, while a Dartmouth player was carried off with a broken leg. Researchers asked both Dartmouth and Princeton students who started the rough play.[17] When the Princeton students responded, 86 percent said that Dartmouth had started it, while only 11 percent blamed both sides. When the Dartmouth students were asked, only 36 percent said Dartmouth started it, while 53 percent said both sides. The researchers then had other students watch a film of the game and write down any infractions they saw. While Dartmouth students saw about the same number of penalties on each side (averages of 4.3 and 4.4), Princeton students saw 9.8 infractions for Dartmouth and only 4.2 for Princeton. All the students saw the same game, yet they saw very different things.

In a similar vein, researchers have asked voters whether the media coverage for a past presidential election was biased, and, if so, in what direction. One third thought it was biased, and of those, 90 percent thought it was biased against their candidate.[18] Perceiving a negative, as opposed to a positive, bias toward our preferred candidate is so common that it's actually been termed the "hostile media effect." Other researchers showed both a rigged "successful" demonstration of ESP, and an unsuccessful demonstration, to skeptics and believers. While the skeptics tended to recall both demonstrations accurately, those who believed in ESP tended to recall the unsuccessful demonstration as successful.[19] Our desires influence our perceptions.

Since religion is a powerful motivating force in many people's lives, the impact of desires on perception can be especially strong when people are zealously religious. People have traveled from Canada to Houston because they thought the image of the Virgin of Guadalupe could be seen in an ice cream stain on the sidewalk. In June 1997 the virgin was seen in another stain (thought to be either urine or water) on a Mexico City subway platform. So many worshipers made the pilgrimage that the stain was eventually moved above ground to a permanent shrine in order to accommodate the crowds. In 1978 a New Mexico housewife thought that she saw the face of Jesus Christ in a burned tortilla. Thousands came to see her tortilla. Other "miraculous" visions have been seen on everything from the rust stains of a grain silo to the backs of highway signs.[20]

You may think that such visions are isolated instances, but that's not the case. I'm sure you can find such occurrences where you live. One of our local newspapers recently ran a story that described a number of such instances in my area.[21] In one case, a man claimed the Virgin Mary came in through his window and told him to go to Colt Park in Hartford, Connecticut. He went, saw her again, and spread the news. Hundreds have since come to see what they're calling the Virgin of Hartford in the foliage of a thirty-foot locust tree. On a single day about two hundred people were pointing at the tree and exclaiming, "You see her, you see her!" In another instance, in July 1998, over one thousand people went to a house in the nearby town of Greenfield to see statues of the Virgin Mary and Jesus, which appeared to be bleeding. And, parishioners in a Catholic Church in another local town, Ware, started seeing visions of the Virgin Mary after they thought their church was going to be closed.

Are these really spiritual signs? Is it reasonable to conclude that an all-powerful, supernatural being would be communicating with us through tortillas or ice cream and urine stains? Is there a simpler explanation? It is well known that we look for patterns in things, and this pattern seeking can lead to biased perception, especially when the data we see are ambiguous. For example, when the Viking spacecraft photographed Mars in 1976, some people immediately saw a form that looked like a face, and thought that an alien civilization must have sculpted it. But should we believe in the alien civilization, or believe that our own constructive human perception leads us to see things that we want or expect to see. Even our culture can have an impact on our perception. When observing the moon, Americans see a man in the moon, Samoans see a woman weaving, East Indians see a rabbit, and the Chinese see a monkey pounding rice.[22] The forms on Mars and the moon are vague, and therefore open to interpretation, especially if we have a preconceived notion of what to see.

Have you seen the picture of the World Trade Center disaster in figure 6? Some people see the face of the devil in the smoke—they say it makes sense because the attack was such a horrendous deed. But if we look hard

Figure 6. Devil face in the smoke of the World Trade Center disaster (reprinted by permission, © 2001 Mark D. Phillips/markdphillips.com. All Rights Reserved).

enough, we'll see many different images in ambiguous stimuli. In fact, it's a common human perceptual phenomenon, called pareidolia. Just lie on the grass on a beautiful summer day and look up at the sky. All kinds of images will take form in the clouds overhead.

Our desires also affect how we judge ourselves and others. One of the most documented findings in psychology is that we want to think flattering thoughts about ourselves. A great majority of us think we are more intelligent, more fair-minded, and less prejudiced than the average person (and a better driver, too).[23] A survey of one million high school seniors found that 70 percent thought they were above average in leadership ability, while only 2 percent thought they were below average. All students thought they were above average in their ability to get along with others; in fact, 25 percent believed they were in the top 1 percent. The same goes for teachers. A study of college professors found that 94 percent thought they were better at their jobs than the average professor. Furthermore, most of us think that more favorable things will happen to us than to others. We think we're more likely to own a home and earn a large salary, and less likely to get divorced or become afflicted with cancer, as compared to others.[24] Of course, these beliefs can't all be true, but our desires lead us to those biased beliefs.

Consider the following study. Psychologist Peter Glick examined two groups of students—one that believed that horoscopes accurately describe a person's personality and another that did not. Each group read one of two versions of a horoscope. In one version, the horoscope was generally positive, saying that the person was dependable, sympathetic, and sociable. In the other group, the horoscope gave negative traits, indicating that the person was overly sensitive and undependable. When asked how accurate the horoscopes were, the believers said they were very accurate, whether flattering or not. On the other hand, those who didn't believe thought the flattering version was accurate, while the unflattering version was not. Also, the people who initially didn't believe in astrology indicated a significantly greater belief after they received the flattering version of the horoscopes.[25] We see what we want to see. If we have a firm belief in astrology, we'll see the predictions as accurate. If we initially don't believe, we'll be more inclined to believe if the horoscope tells us something we want to hear.

HALLUCINATIONS

Do you remember the movie *A Beautiful Mind* that won the Academy Award in 2002? It was based upon the life of John Nash, a brilliant mathematician who won the Nobel Prize for economics. Amazingly, Nash was also schizophrenic. He would have constant visions, seeing aliens and people that didn't actually exist. When asked why he believed in them, Nash said that his hallucinations came to him in the same way that his best mathematical ideas did. They were very real to him, as they are to other individuals with schizophrenia.

We tend to think that only people with mental disorders such as schizophrenia hallucinate. So when someone we consider normal says he saw a ghost or alien creature, we think that maybe there's something to it. However, research shows that otherwise normal individuals can hallucinate at various times in their lives. Ever since the inception of the International Census of Waking Hallucinations in 1894, surveys have indicated that about 10 percent to 25 percent of normal people have experienced at least one vivid hallucination in their lives. That is, they hear a voice or see a form that isn't actually there. Studies show that if sleep is interrupted for a few days during REM sleep (when we dream), we'll start to hallucinate during the day. Hallucinations can also be elicited by emotional stress, fasting, fever, sensory deprivation, and drugs.[26]

Years ago, neurophysiologist Wilder Penfield demonstrated that when various parts of the brain are electrically stimulated, vivid hallucinations can result. Another neuroscientist, Michael Persinger, has reported that people have out-of-body experiences, a feeling that someone is in the room, and even deep religious feelings when a helmet containing electromagnets is placed on their heads.[27] Patients experiencing epileptic seizures in the temporal lobes of the brain can have very intense spiritual experiences. As one patient indicated, he experiences bright lights, a rapture that makes everything else pale, and a feeling of oneness with God. In actuality, there are circuits in the brain that are involved with religious and other supernatural experiences, which may be activated by outside stimulation or seizures.[28]

A psychological syndrome called sleep paralysis makes people immobile, anxious, and prone to seeing hallucinations like ghosts, demons, and aliens. It's interesting to note that most alien abductee experiences occur when falling asleep, waking up, or on long car drives. We know that we can experience hypnogogic hallucinations, which occur while falling asleep, and hypnopompic hallucinations, which happen while waking up. In these states, individuals experience floating out of their bodies; feeling paralyzed; and seeing ghosts, aliens, and loved ones who have died. There's also a strong sense of being awake during these hallucinations. Remember my ghostly encounter? It's more common than you think. One study found that out of 182 university students, about 63 percent experienced auditory or visual hypnagogic imagery and 21 percent experienced hypnopompic imagery.[29]

Research has also shown that a small group of individuals (about 4 percent of the population) fantasize a large part of the time. These people often see, hear, smell, and touch things that aren't there, and they also have a decreased awareness of time. In fact, a biographical analysis of 154 people who said they had been abducted by aliens revealed that 132 of them appeared normal and healthy, but had fantasy-prone personality characteristics.[30] In addition, many people are extremely suggestible—5 percent to 10 percent of us can be easily hypnotized—and enhanced suggestibility can influence our perceptions and beliefs. You would think that these misperceptions should make us question the validity of personal accounts of extraordinary events. But our penchant for a good story usually wins out.

Thus, our perception is not a one-to-one mapping of external reality. Instead, it's a constructive process that's determined not only by what our senses detect, but also by what we expect and want to see. In addition, we can, at times, experience vivid hallucinations, and can even have collective hallucinations, where two or more people experience the same thing.[31] These collective hallucinations can be so powerful that they can actually lead to mass hysteria.

MASS HYSTERIA

In Mattoon, Illinois, in 1944, a woman said a stranger came into her bedroom late at night and sprayed her with a gas that left her legs temporarily paralyzed. The local newspaper ran stories on the Phantom Gasser of

Mattoon, and over a nine-day period, twenty-five separate incidents, involving twenty-seven women and two men, were reported to the police. They said the intruder came into their homes and sprayed a sweet smelling gas that left them nauseated, dizzy, and temporarily paralyzed in their legs. After a couple of weeks of investigation, however, no physical evidence or chemical clues were uncovered. Police and newspapers began attributing the experiences to wild imaginations and mass hysteria, and then the reported intrusions stopped.[32]

Over a two-week period in 1956, twenty-one people in Taiwan said they were cut by a stranger while out in public (termed the Phantom Slasher of Taiwan). Police eventually concluded that any cuts that occurred came from everyday contact in public places that would normally go unnoticed if it weren't for the media coverage. Between March and April 1983, 947 Palestinian residents of the Israeli-occupied West Bank reported fainting, headache, abdominal pain, and dizziness from supposedly being gassed. Medical tests showed there was no gas, and the reports subsequently disappeared. Just recently, as noted earlier, a monkey-man delusion occurred in India. During the first three weeks of May 2001, people around New Delhi reported seeing a half human–half monkey creature with razor-sharp fingernails, superhuman strength, and incredible leaping ability. On May 16 alone, police had forty reported sightings, often from different areas of the city. Two people actually died when they tried to run away from the creature.[33]

In various parts of Asia, a particularly disconcerting type of mass hysteria sometimes emerges—penis-shrinking panics. Men in some regions become panic stricken by the belief that their penises are shriveling up or retracting into their bodies. As a preventative measure, the men often place clamps or strings on their penises, or have family members hold their private parts in relays until they can get treatment. In October and November 1967, hospitals in Singapore were inundated—Singapore Hospital treated about seventy-five cases in a single day. The panic occurred when rumors were spread that eating pork vaccinated for swine fever triggered penis shrinking. About five thousand people thought that their genitalia were shrinking in the Guangdong province of China between the summer of 1984 and 1985. Another panic occurred in India from July to September 1982. Thousands of men thought that their penises or testicles were shriveling up, and women thought that their breasts were shrinking.[34]

It sounds funny, so we tend to laugh at the naivete of the Chinese and Indians who believe these things. But we have our own delusions as well. Since the 1730s people in central and southern New Jersey have been seeing a three-to-four foot-tall creature with a head like a horse and bat-like wings. In January 1909 over one hundred people in more than two dozen communities reported a sighting. Townspeople stayed behind locked doors, schools and factories were shut down, and posses were formed to find the creature. In fact, the New Jersey Devils hockey team is named after the elusive creature. During the Salem witch trial hysteria of the 1600s, people were put to death. Other forms of hysteria still occur today. In the 1980s, thousands of Satanic cults were thought to be operating in the United States. The cults were supposedly sacrificing and mutilating animals, sexually abusing children, and performing other Satanic rituals. However, the evidence for such widespread abuse was nonexistent. And what about the multiple sightings of UFOs and aliens that pop up from time to time?

In effect, mass hysterias and delusions have occurred throughout the years, where false or exaggerated beliefs are rapidly spread throughout a segment of society.[35] Why do they happen? One reason is that our perceptions can be faulty, and when those misperceptions are combined with our inherent suggestibility, weird beliefs can prevail, even when there is no hard evidence.

NEUROBIOLOGICAL PROBLEMS AND PERCEPTUAL ISSUES

Neurobiological research is uncovering many reasons for our misperceptions of the world. It turns out that perception is dependent upon a number of interacting brain functions, and that problems can arise in any one of them. For example, research suggests that there are approximately thirty distinct visual areas in the brain, and that these areas specialize in perceiving different attributes, such as depth, motion, color, and so on.[36] If a person experiences damage to the middle temporal area of the brain, she can suffer from "motion blindness." Such individuals can identify objects, people, and even read books. But if a car is passing by on the street, they see a series of static strobelike snapshots, instead of continuous motion. Pouring coffee for them is an ordeal because it's difficult to estimate how fast the coffee is rising in a cup.

Neuroscientist V. S. Ramachandran and science writer Sandra Blakeslee report on a number of bizarre perceptions that occur because of damage in certain parts of the brain.[37] Individuals experiencing these hallucinations are not mentally ill; going to a psychiatrist would be a waste of time. They are rational and lucid, but their perceptions are flawed. For example, people with damage to their visual pathways can suffer from Charles Bonnet syndrome. They are often partially or completely blind, yet they experience vivid hallucinations that seem more real than reality. Author James Thurber was shot in the eye with a toy arrow when he was six years old. Blind by age thirty-five, he started hallucinating brilliant images, which could have been the basis for his outrageous stories and cartoons. One woman saw cartoon characters in a large blind spot that developed in her field of vision, while another saw miniature policemen leading a little person to a tiny police van. Others with Charles Bonnet syndrome have seen ghostly figures, dragons, shining angels, little circus animals, and elves.

Consider the amazing case of Larry, a Charles Bonnet patient. Larry was twenty-seven when he had a car accident that fractured the frontal bones above his eyes. When he came out of a coma he said, "The world was filled with hallucinations, both visual and auditory. I couldn't distinguish what was real from what was fake. Doctors and nurses standing next to my bed were surrounded by football players and Hawaiian dancers. Voices came at me from everywhere and I couldn't tell who was talking." He slowly improved, except for one amazing problem. He could see perfectly normal in the top half of his vision, but he had vivid hallucinations in the bottom half, where he was blind. When Dr. Ramachandran interviewed him, Larry said, "As I look at you, there is a monkey sitting in your lap." He said that the images fade after a few seconds, but when they're there, they are vibrant and extraordinarily vivid. In fact, they look too good to be true. As he said, "Sometimes when I'm looking for my shoes in the morning, the whole floor suddenly is covered with shoes," making it hard to find the real ones.[38]

The noted neuroscientist and author Oliver Sacks reported on a patient with neurological problems who, during his exam, took his shoe off. When Sacks asked him to put it back on, the man put his hand on his foot and said, "This is my shoe, no?" Sacks said, "No, it is not. That is your foot. There is your shoe." To which he replied, "Ah! I thought that was my foot." When he was leaving, he looked around for his hat, took hold of his wife's head, and tried to lift it off to put it on his head, which gave rise to Sacks' famous title for his book *The Man Who Mistook His Wife for a Hat*.[39]

Our temporal lobes enable us to recognize faces and objects. When portions are damaged, patients can't recognize their own parents. In other cases, patients suffering from Capgras' delusion come to regard their close relatives as imposters. They recognize the face, but feel the person is posing as their parent, brother, or sister. This may result from damage to the link between the temporal lobe and the limbic system within the brain. The temporal lobe recognizes the image (e.g., mother) and then passes it on to the amygdala which determines the face's emotional significance (e.g., mother associated with love). If the pathway to the amygdala is damaged, the person may recognize the face, but not experience any emotion, leading to the belief that the person is an imposter.[40]

What we see can also be influenced by what we experienced in the past. For example, a man who gained his sight after being blind for most of his life sometimes saw new things only after he could touch them. That is, if he was exposed to a novel item that he had no experience with in the past, he wouldn't "see" it until he felt it, which was how he perceived things most of his life.[41] Research indicates that cats raised in environments where they see only vertical lines typically don't perceive horizontal objects, while cats raised in horizontal environments don't perceive vertical objects. If a cat experienced only vertical lines when very young, and was later put in a normal environment, it would walk off the end of a table because it wouldn't see the table's horizontal edge.[42]

Problems in perceiving the world arise not just from visual perception. Consider the case of phantom limbs. Patients who lose an arm or leg sometimes feel that the appendage is still there. In fact, the phantom limb can cause excruciating pain, which has even led some to contemplate suicide. One physician had a pulsating cramp in his leg caused by Buerger's disease that was so painful he had the leg amputated. Amazingly, and unfortunately for him, the pain continued in his phantom limb! Some patients feel that their amputated hand is extremely painful because they think it's curled in a tight fist, with their fingers digging into the palm of their lost hand. Dr. Ramachandran created a box with a mirror so that if a patient put his good hand in one side, it would appear that the amputated hand was also there. He would tell his patients to put their hands into the box with their fingers clenched into a fist, and then try to unclench both hands. For many patients, the visual feedback from the mirror made them feel that their phantom fist opened up, so their pain was relieved.[43]

As these cases demonstrate, our perceptions of the world depend upon the complex interconnected neural structures in our brain. At birth, our brains contain over one hundred billion neurons. Each neuron has a primary axon, which sends out information to many other neurons, and tens of thousands of branches, called dendrites, which receive information from other neurons. Neurons make contact with one another at points called synapses, and every neuron has from one to ten thousand synapses. As a consequence, a piece of brain the size of a grain of sand has about one hundred thousand neurons, two million axons, and one billion synapses, all talking to one another. If problems arise somewhere in these neural connections, our perceptions of external reality can be vastly different from reality itself.

IMPLICATIONS

As we have seen, our senses can be fooled. We often see what we want or expect to see, and we can, at times, experience vivid hallucinations. Interestingly, the problems that arise in our perceptions can come from mechanisms that are often very useful to us in coping with the world. For example, seeing what we expect to see frequently serves a very useful purpose. For the most part, things occur as we expect. Cars generally stop at red lights and go on green, and so we've come to expect that they will continue to do so. If we didn't make this assumption, we would have to pay attention to every car as we go through an intersection. You can easily see how we would be overwhelmed with information if we had to attend to everything. Our expectations simplify our lives, and since what we expect to see or occur often happens, those expectations can be quite useful. However, if things don't happen as we expected them to, we can misperceive the world.[44]

Given our misperceptions, we can't always trust that our senses are giving us an accurate read of reality, which is a main reason why we can't rely on anecdotal evidence when evaluating the truth of a claim. Just because someone said they had an experience with a ghost or an alien, that doesn't provide reliable evidence for their existence. Ghost and alien sightings could be the result of fasting, emotional stress, drugs, hypnagogic or hypnopompic hallucinations, or even problems in the ocular pathways. Remember, Occam's razor says we should accept the explanation with the fewest assumptions. We don't need to assume that ghosts or aliens are visiting the earth to explain people's personal experiences; human misperceptions can easily account for such reports. And yet, given our storyteller history, we continue to place considerable importance upon personal testimonials and stories.

As psychologist Robert Abelson has said, our beliefs are like possessions.[45] We buy our possessions because they have some use to us. So it is with our beliefs. We often hold beliefs not because of the evidence for those beliefs, but because they make us feel good. How can we overcome perceptual biases that lead to faulty beliefs? It's difficult, but a good place to start is by asking three questions: (1) Do you want this belief to be true? (2) Do you expect this event to occur? and (3) Do you think you would perceive things differently without these wants and expectations?[46] If the answer is yes to these questions, you should be very careful in how you interpret your perceptions of the world.

CHAPTER 6: SEEING ASSOCIATIONS THAT AREN'T THERE

You can't depend on your eyes when your imagination is out of focus.

—Mark Twain

We have evolved to be pattern-seeking animals. As we noted earlier, we come from ancestors who were constantly on the lookout for the causes of things. Of course, searching for relationships in the world is often beneficial because it can lead to new knowledge. Our built-in tendency to seek out causes is so great, however, that we start to see associations when none exist. We can thus come to believe that two things are related when, in fact, they are not. This especially occurs when we want or expect to see an association. Let's look at two cases where very intelligent people are making major financial and health decisions on the basis of erroneous associations.

CHARTING THE WATERS

Your stockbroker calls and exclaims, "I'm glad I caught you—it's time to jump in and buy stock in Natural Water Inc.!" When you ask why, he says, "I've just analyzed the company's past stock prices, and it's a classic case. I've seen this pattern a thousand times before. When a stock acts like this, it's ready to take off. Do yourself a favor and buy now!" After hearing such news, many of us would dig out our checkbook and throw our hard earned money into Natural Water's stock. But is it the right thing to do?

Stockbrokers who analyze changes in a company's stock price are using a technique known as a technical analysis. Technical analysts (also called chartists) believe they can see patterns in stock price charts that allow them to predict whether a stock will increase or decrease in the future. A chartist doesn't even care what type of business a firm is in—they could be selling computers or Barbie dolls. The trends detected in past stock prices are much more important for the technical analyst. You may have seen stock charts, like the one presented in figure 7. They are printed in financial newsletters, shown on news programs like CNBC, and are part of countless Internet financial sites. In fact, companies that create these charts have recently experienced a boom in sales.[1]

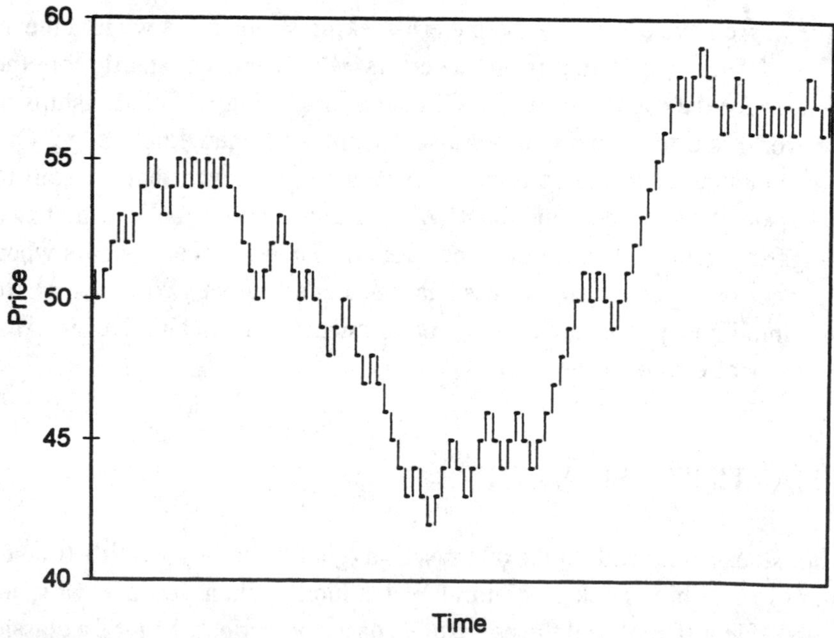

Figure 7. An example of a stock price chart showing the daily price changes for a hypothetical company.

Most investment houses employ technical analysts, who are well paid for their services. These analysts look for patterns like the "head and shoulders" formulation shown in figure 8.

With this chart, the price first rises, then falls a bit. Next, it goes up and down again, but slightly higher this time, forming a head. It then rises and falls somewhat, forming the shape of a shoulder on the right side. Chartists believe that if the price drops below the "neckline" it's a sure sign to sell. How do they know? They've seen the pattern many times before, and it usually results in a big price drop.

Chartists also use filter systems. For example, if they see a low point in a stock price, followed by a 5 percent (or some other percent) upswing, they think it's an upward trend. If the price peaks and then drops by 5 percent, it's a downward trend. A typical chartist rule goes something like, buy a stock that moves up by 5 percent from a low, and hold it until the price goes down 5 percent from a subsequent high.[2] In fact, this technique

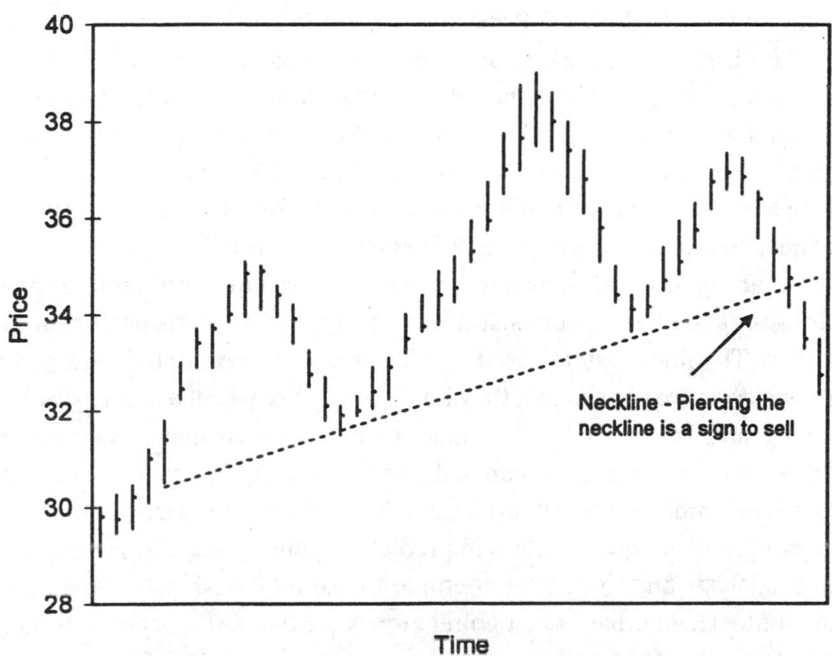

Figure 8. An example of a "head and shoulders" stock price chart. If the stock price drops below the "neckline," chartists believe the price will continue to fall.

is the foundation of stop-loss orders that many brokers recommend, where the client is advised to sell if the stock drops by some percent below the purchase price.

So, does charting work? Very intelligent people see patterns in past prices that they believe are associated with future price increases or decreases. However, those associations don't exist. Look again at figure 7. It seems like there are trends in the stock's price movements, doesn't it? The price starts at $50 a share, rises a bit, levels off, and then experiences a sharp drop to around $42. The stock price then has a period of rapid and consistent growth to around $59, drops a bit, and then appears to level off. With such trends, it seems like the stock's price changes are somewhat predictable. But the fact is, this chart was generated by a random process! Starting at $50, I used a random number generator, which was essentially like flipping a coin, to determine if this hypothetical stock was going to rise by a dollar or fall by a dollar each day. Chartists see all kinds of patterns in such random processes. In fact, Professor Burton Malkiel of Princeton University had his students create similar charts by flipping a coin. One chart showed an upward breakout from an inverted head-and-shoulders formulation, which a chartist would interpret as very bullish. Malkiel showed the chart to one of his analyst friends who almost jumped out of his skin, exclaiming, "What is this company? We've got to buy immediately. This pattern's a classic. There's no question the stock will be up 15 points next week."[3]

Charting has been shown to be useless. A wealth of research, from as far back as the 1960s, demonstrates that technical analysis can't beat the market. The filter systems used by chartists have been tested, and, when trading costs are considered, they don't consistently beat a strategy of just buying and holding on to a stock. In fact, two financial economists, Arnold Moore and Eugene Fama, determined that only about 3 percent of the variation in daily stock prices can be explained by past stock prices, so past prices are quite useless in predicting future prices.[4] And yet, technical analysts on Wall Street continue to see relationships between past and future stock prices when no relationship exists. And people continue to invest millions of dollars on the basis of the analysts' unfounded stock recommendations. In fact, chartists have recently been hired in increasing numbers. Why? Technical analysts recommend a lot of trades. As Malkiel notes, "Trading generates commissions, and commissions are the lifeblood of the brokerage business. The technicians do not help produce yachts for the customers, but they do help generate the trading that provides yachts for the brokers."[5]

IT'S A HORSE—NO, IT'S A BAT

Take a look at figure 9. Do you see a dinosaur, a bird, a laughing face, a person flying?

The picture is a computer-generated image made to resemble an inkblot. Many clinical psychologists and psychiatrists use the Rorschach inkblot test, which consists of ten similar kinds of images, to diagnose whether a patient has certain disorders or tendencies, such as paranoia or suicidal tendencies. How do they do it? Patients state what they see in the images, and the psychologist interprets their responses as indicating certain deep-seated, unconscious thoughts that suggest some type of illness or social tendency.[6]

Figure 9. A computer-generated example of an inkblot. Clinicians have patients describe what they see in similar types of images in order to diagnose various psychological disorders or tendencies.

What did you see in the figure? If you saw something like buttocks, female clothing, or a person of indeterminant sex (e.g., looks like a man below the waist but a woman above), a clinical psychologist is likely to interpret your response as indicating you're homosexual (as Jerry Seinfeld would say, "Not that there's anything wrong with that"). In fact, psychologists Loren and Jean Chapman asked thirty-two clinicians about using the Rorschach test to determine male homosexuality (at a time when homosexuality was thought to be a disorder).[7] The clinicians said that homosexuals were more likely to interpret the inkblots as buttocks, genitals, female clothing, human figures of indeterminate sex, and human figures with both male and female features.

So what's the problem? None of these responses are actually associated with homosexuality. Research has shown that just as many heterosexuals give these responses as homosexuals. And yet, the clinicians were convinced that they had discovered an association between these responses and homosexuality. Why the error? It just seems reasonable to assume that homosexuals would see such images—but that assumption is wrong. The clinicians' expectations of what they thought should correlate with homosexuality led them to perceive associations that weren't actually there.

To investigate these expectations further, Chapman and Chapman gave undergraduate students thirty cards.[8] Each card had an inkblot, what one patient said about the inkblot, and different emotional, personality, or sexual characteristics of the patient. The students were asked if homosexuals made any particular response more often than other responses. The naive undergraduates thought that the signs mentioned by the psychologists (i.e., feminine clothing, anus, confusion between the sexes, etc.) were stated more by homosexuals. However, the thirty cases were constructed to be random. There was no association whatsoever between the patients' responses and their sexual orientation as listed on the cards. Yet, the students saw associations, and they were the very same associations that experienced clinicians see. Thus, untrained students and clinical psychologists are falling into the same trap—they see associations because of their false expectations.

In another compelling experiment, the Chapmans gave students thirty cards that contained a patient's response to an inkblot along with his emotional problem or a statement indicating he was homosexual.[9] Two responses (i.e., seeing a monster or a part human/part animal creature) were always given when the patient stated he was a homosexual (i.e., a perfect correlation). Despite the perfect correlation, the students failed to see the association. Only 17 percent thought these two signs occurred more frequently with homosexuality, while 50 percent thought that seeing things like buttocks, genitals, and female clothing occurred more frequently, even though they were listed at random so no association existed. These studies demonstrate that if we think two variables are related, we'll often see a connection, irrespective of the evidence. This is what is known as illusory correlation—we see associations that don't actually exist.[10]

Other responses from the Rorschach test reveal similar problems. If a patient gives a reflection response like "I see a cat looking into a mirror," clinicians typically interpret it to mean the person is narcissistic, even though studies have shown that there's no association between narcissism and reflection responses. The bottom line is, the reliability and validity of the Rorschach test has not been supported by scientific research. Therapists are seeing associations between responses and illnesses or personality traits because they expect to see them, not because they exist.[11] And yet, people are being treated every day for a variety of mental health issues by clinical psychologists and psychiatrists who use the Rorschach inkblots. Furthermore, psychologists use the test to help courts decide which parent should get custody of a child, whether prisoners should be granted parole, or what should be done about convicted murderers.[12] Hundreds of thousands of crucial decisions are made each year based upon the unreliable Rorschach.

Similar problems exist with other widely used projective tests. For example, with the Draw-a-Person test, a clinician interprets the psychological meaning of a face drawn by a patient. Chapman and Chapman asked clinicians what types of characteristics certain patients might draw, and found that 91 percent of them thought a paranoid patient would draw atypical eyes. However, controlled studies show that there is no difference between the eyes drawn by paranoid patients and by normal subjects. The perceived correlation by clinicians is purely illusionary.[13] And yet, clinicians continue to use the test, even though they know the results of such studies. As one clinician commented, "I know that paranoids don't seem to draw big eyes in the research labs, but they sure do in my office."[14] We can only imagine the number of inaccurate diagnoses made because of clinicians' misguided beliefs in their ability to accurately perceive associations.

Seeing associations that aren't there also occurs in business and government. Graphologists maintain that they can tell many different things about an individual's personality by analyzing handwriting samples. They don't analyze the content of the writing, they analyze how a person crosses her Ts or loops her Os. Empirical research has demonstrated that graphology is completely useless.[15] For example, one study had an "expert" graphologist evaluate a number of handwriting samples, with some of the samples presented more than once. The graphologist gave very different analyses to the same handwriting samples. It's scary to think that about 85 percent of the largest corporations in Europe, and about three thousand corporations in the United States, have, in the past, employed graphology in their personnel selection.[16] You may have been denied a job because of a graphologist's unfounded judgment.

CONSIDER THE NEGATIVES

We all know that sugar can make children hyperactive. Just give a child a few candy bars and he'll start running, jumping, yelling, and generally bouncing off the walls. We've all seen it happen. In fact, researchers observed a number of children, paying close attention to whether they were hyperactive or not. They also noted if the children recently ate candy. Their findings are described in table 4. That is, 250 children were hyperactive after eating candy, while 50 were not. For those children who weren't hyperactive, 50 ate candy, while 10 didn't. Given this information, is hyperactivity associated with eating candy? What information is needed to determine if hyperactivity and sugar consumption are related?

Table 4

Frequencies of Sugar Consumption and Hyperactivity in Children

		Sugar Consumption	
		Yes	No
Hyperactivity	Yes	250	50
	No	50	10

Many of us would say there's a positive association because the yes-yes cell is the largest. We focus on the 250 children that both ate candy and were hyperactive, and conclude there's a relationship because the number is considerably larger than the others. However, all the cells in the table are needed to determine if the two are related. We have to compare the ratio of hyperactivity to no hyperactivity when children eat sugar (250:50) and when they don't (50:10). There's a 5 to 1 ratio in both cases, so the children were 5 times more likely to be hyperactive whether they ate sugar or not. As a result, there's no association between hyperactivity and sugar consumption.

So why do we make the error? We don't attend to the negative cases in the table—the times when sugar consumption or hyperactivity is absent. Ignoring negative information is very common in our decision making, but when we do, we're likely to form erroneous beliefs. While this data was made up to demonstrate a point, research has shown that there is, in fact, no association between sugar consumption and hyperactivity. As another example, consider that many people believe that if a couple with fertility problems adopts a baby, they are more likely to conceive than a problem couple that doesn't adopt. The thinking is that their stress is alleviated, which makes it easier to conceive later on. However, clinical studies show it's not true. Why do we believe it? Our attention is drawn to the couples that conceive after adopting, and not to all those couples who adopt and don't conceive, or who conceive without adopting.[17] To see if a relationship exists, we have to consider all the information—the positives *and the negatives*.

Medical professionals are not immune to this decision error. One study had nurses review 100 cases where hypothetical patient records indicated that a symptom and a disease was either present, or not present, in a patient.[18] Like the data in table 4, there was no association between the symptom and the disease, but 86 percent of the nurses thought a relationship existed.

Erroneous connections are made for all types of beliefs. Politicians like us to believe that welfare has to be eliminated because it breeds fraud. As support, they point to the number of fraud cases involving people on welfare. But do people on welfare commit more fraud than people not on welfare? We would need to know before we accept their argument.[19] In a similar vein, many people believe that God answers prayers because they remember the times they prayed and the event prayed for occurred. But how many times did someone pray and the event didn't occur? We typically ignore those cases. And so, when deciding if two things are related, we should think about table 4 and realize that we need to focus on more information than we normally do.

BUT IS IT THE CAUSE?

Let's assume for the moment that there is, in fact, an association between two variables. What's the best way to measure the degree of association? Statisticians have developed a measure of association called a correlation coefficient, and it ranges from -1 to +1. The closer the coefficient is to +1, the more two variables are related (i.e., if one variable goes up the other variable goes up). If the number approaches -1, the variables are inversely related (as one goes up the other goes down), while a zero means there's no association.[20] Once again, statistics based on empirical data provide our best means to determine if two variables are related—but a few things must be kept in mind when interpreting a correlation.

Correlation Is Not Causation

Many people think that if two variables are correlated, then one variable causes the other. However, correlation does not imply causation. Just because a correlation exists between the amount spent on advertising and the sales generated by a given company, that doesn't mean the ads caused the sales. It could be that improved product quality generated more sales, and the advertising campaign happened to coincide with the improved product. In addition, causation does not necessarily imply a strong correlation. Intercourse causes pregnancy, but not all the time. However, our inherent tendency to look for causes leads us to draw causal inferences from correlations—a temptation we have to strongly resist.[21]

Directionality

In the 1990s researchers noticed a small correlation between student self-esteem—meaning their confidence and self-respect—and school achievement. Many people immediately assumed that one caused the other, and that the causal direction was obvious. Low self-esteem was thought to result in a plethora of problems, including poor school achievement, drug abuse, and teenage pregnancy. This belief led many educational programs to focus their attention on improving student self-esteem. However, if there is a causal association between self-esteem and school achievement, the causal link is just as likely to be in the opposite direction—superior school performance may generate high self-esteem.[22] And so, even if a correlation exists because one variable causes the other, we don't really know if A causes B, or if B causes A.

A Third Variable

Correlations are sometimes spurious. That is, two variables may be related to one another not because there's a direct causal link, but because both variables are related to another, third variable. Studies indicate, for example, that student performance is associated with attending private or public schools. As a result, some people have concluded that private schools are better than public schools. We often hear from public officials and other special-interest groups that we should privatize the educational process or, at the very least, subsidize private schools because they're doing a better job of educating our youth. This argument has led politicians to advocate school vouchers and faith-based initiatives that give more money to private schools. However, support for the superiority of private schools comes from studies that simply correlate student performance and type of school attended. It could be that student performance depends on a number of variables that may be correlated with the type of school attended, such as the education and occupation of the students' parents, their socioeconomic status, the quantity of books in their home, etc.[23]

How do we know if a student's achievement is due to the type of school or to some other variable? With more advanced statistical procedures we can recalculate the correlation of two variables after we account for the influence of other variables.[24] It turns out that when variables like a student's general mental ability and home background are removed, studies find virtually no association between student performance and the type of school attended.[25] And so, the use of more advanced statistics allow us to make better-informed decisions on important social policy issues. Keep in mind, however, these more advanced procedures still can't tell us if there's a direct causal link between two variables—they can only improve our understanding of the associations that exist.

Selection Bias

Your local community is deciding whether to increase the funding for its school system. As expected, the debate on whether additional spending will result in better student performance heats up. Some people point to evidence indicating that teacher salary and class size are related to educational quality.[26] Other people, however, with a different agenda point to studies that say there's little or no relationship between educational expenditures and students' performance on the scholastic aptitude test (SAT), a general achievement measure. So what should we believe? Does more money lead to better student performance or not? To make a more informed decision, we have to determine if there's a selection bias in the data analyzed. That is, we need to determine if the correlations are based on all the relevant data that should be considered, or if they are calculated on only a small sample of the data, specifically selected to bolster one's argument.[27]

Those who are against spending argue that when studies analyze data across the fifty states, there is little or no relation between spending and performance. In fact, they point out that if a study finds an association, it's often in the opposite direction, suggesting that higher spending actually leads to lower performance. What evidence do they have for this conclusion? A number of states with high teacher salaries actually have low average SAT scores, while other states with low salaries have high SATs. For example, students in Mississippi have higher SAT scores than students in California (by over one hundred points, on average). Given that Mississippi pays its teachers the lowest salaries in the nation, it seems pretty compelling that spending more will not increase student performance. In fact, some may argue that we should even cut teacher salaries!

But are schools really better in Mississippi than in California? Other measures show that California schools are superior, so why do we have lower SAT scores in California?[28] The answer is that the SAT is not taken by every high school student. Some state university systems do not require the SAT, they use the American College Testing (ACT) program. Thus, only students who plan on attending college out-of-state take the SATs, and those students are likely to have higher academic achievement than the average student in the state. In addition, states with better educational systems typically have more students who want to go to college, so a greater proportion of students take the SAT, resulting in more students with average abilities sitting for the exam. In fact, a close examination reveals that only about 4 percent of high school students in Mississippi take the SAT, while 47 percent of students in California take the test.[29] And so, there is selection bias in the data analyzed. The 4 percent from Mississippi represent the cream of the crop, and comparing those students to a much larger proportion of students from California is like comparing apples and oranges.

The bottom line is, if we don't critically analyze the data used to calculate a correlation, we can be misled into believing something that's not actually the case. This is especially true if we have a preconceived personal or political bias. For example, one conservative commentator fell into this trap when he argued against expenditures on education, citing the research indicating that greater spending does not lead to higher SAT scores. However, the states that he pointed to as having high scores—Iowa, North Dakota, South Dakota, Utah, and Minnesota—had SAT participation rates of only 5 percent, 6 percent, 7 percent, 4 percent, and 10 percent, respectively. These numbers are quite low given that about 40 percent of all high school seniors take the SAT in the United States. He used New Jersey as an example of low SAT scores and high educational expenditures, but 76 percent of high school seniors take the SAT in New Jersey.[30]

So what is the relation between spending and academic achievement? It turns out that when the proportion of students taking the test is considered in the analysis, states that spend more on education actually have higher scores. It's estimated that spending an additional $1,000 per pupil would yield a fifteen point increase in the average SAT score for a state.[31]

SUMMING UP

We make erroneous associations all the time, and those associations can be quite costly, both financially and in terms of our health. Sometimes we see nonexistent associations because we want or expect to see the association. As we saw earlier, our desires and expectations are extremely powerful forces in our perception and evaluation of the world. It turns out, however, that we don't even need a desire or expectation—we can erroneously conclude that two things are related because we just don't analyze the information we see as rigorously as we should. That is, we usually just look for instances when two things happen, and if we find a number of these cases, we quickly conclude they are related. As we saw in table 4, however, we also need to consider the negatives—pay attention to those times when a thing didn't happen. If we don't, we'll forever see associations that don't exist.

Even if we find that two things are empirically associated with one another, we still have to critically evaluate how the statistics demonstrating their association are calculated. Politicians and special interest groups are constantly attempting to convince us that their position on an issue is right, and they often use statistics, like correlations, to support their point of view. We can easily be fooled into believing something that's not true if we don't understand how those statistics are calculated. As Mark Twain said, "There are three kinds of lies—lies, damn lies and statistics." Statistics typically provide us with the best information we can get to make informed decisions, but we have to know how the statistics were calculated and what they really mean. The moral of the story—look closely at the data before you choose to believe.

CHAPTER 7: PREDICTING THE UNPREDICTABLE

Prediction is very difficult, especially if it's about the future.

—Chinese Proverb, Neils Bohr, Yogi Berra

We humans have a great desire to predict things. We want to know if we'll marry the person we just met, if we'll get that new job, if it's going to rain this weekend, or if the stock we just bought will skyrocket. Our desire to know the future permeates many aspects of our personal and professional lives. As we've seen, however, wanting something often biases our beliefs and decisions. It turns out that our strong desire to predict future events has led us to believe that we can predict things that are essentially unpredictable. And we spend considerable time and money trying to predict them.

PSYCHICS AND ASTROLOGY

The World Trade Center tragedy on September 11, 2001, was a defining moment in our history. We were shocked, emotionally drained, and outraged. In our search for information about the disaster, many people turned to the Internet. CNN reported that the top three Web topics on September 20 were, in order, Osama bin Laden, Nostradamus, and Afghanistan. Nostradamus was number two!

Our history shows that we have always had a desire to predict future events. Written records from five thousand years ago indicate that the ancient world was attempting to foretell the future by using everything from animal entrails to celestial patterns.[1] Alexander the Great had his psychics read the insides of slaughtered animals to ascertain future events. This desire still finances a number of activities, from reading tarot cards, palms, tea leaves, and crystal balls, to listening to mediums who supposedly receive messages from the dead or some unseen power. Many people believe that psychics and astrologers who've been dead for centuries, like the sixteenth-century French astrologer Nostradamus, can predict today's and future events, while others listen to a host of more current foretellers. Major companies have even employed psychics in their personnel hiring decisions, and some police departments have used them in attempting to solve crimes.[2]

So is there any value to psychic predictions? People point to some pretty amazing success stories. For example, Jeanne Dixon supposedly foretold the assassinations of John Kennedy and Martin Luther King, while many people believe that Nostradamus predicted both world wars, the atom bomb, Hitler, and the 9/11 tragedy. When evaluating these predictions, a couple of things must be kept in mind. First, we have to ask ourselves, are the predictions unambiguous, and second, are the predictions more accurate than what we would expect from chance.

Consider the following prophecy of Nostradamus that many people believe predicted the 9/11 disaster:

> Earthshaking fire from the centre of the earth,
> Will cause tremors around a new city,
> Two great rocks will war for a long time,
> Then arethusa will redden a new river.[3]

It certainly seems applicable to the Twin Towers collapse in New York City, referring to "two great rocks" and "a new city." In fact, researchers found that 68 percent of people surveyed thought that the verses might have predicted 9/11.[4] But is that because they were looking for such evidence? To find out, the researchers gave the same prophecy to another group of people and asked if it might have predicted the London blitz, where Germany bombed London for fifty-seven straight nights during World War II. It turned out that 61 percent thought the prophecy referred to the London blitz, where "earthshaking fires" and "tremors" were experienced throughout the city.[5] The bottom line is that the prophecy is ambiguous enough to allow multiple interpretations. To further prove the point, the researchers *randomly* selected lines from different prophecies. Amazingly, 58 percent of the people surveyed thought that this scrambled version accurately predicted World War II!

Even Nostradamus experts can't agree on the meanings of his predictions. For example, two noted experts have interpreted the same verses in very different ways. One expert thought that a certain prophecy predicted the role of Emperor Haile Selassie in World War II, while the other said it referred to Henry IV and the siege of Malta in 1565.[6] In effect, the verses are so ambiguous and open to interpretation that anyone can read whatever they want into them, and so, they are veridically worthless.

In addition to considering their ambiguity, we also have to question whether psychic predictions are more accurate than what we would expect from mere guessing. Thousands of forecasters make millions of predictions every year. With such a large number, some of the predictions will be right some of the time. As we have seen, coincidences happen quite often because of the sheer number of events that occur. In some instances, a coincidence will take place when a psychic foretells an event and the event actually occurs. Many people interpret that happenstance as proof of psychic ability. Why? When we test the hypothesis—psychics can predict the future—we naturally attend to evidence that confirms the hypothesis. Thus, we focus on the few times that psychics may have been somewhat right, and disregard the vast number of times they were wrong.

Psychologists Scott Madey and Tom Gilovich interestingly demonstrated this biased reaction to data. They gave subjects a diary of a student who supposedly had prophetic dreams. The diary contained a number of the student's dreams, along with events that occurred later on in her life. Half of the dreams appeared to come true, while half did not. When subjects were later asked to remember as many of the dreams as they could, they remembered many more that came true. When it comes to prophecies and fortune telling, we remember the hits and forget the misses.[7]

As we've seen, however, we have to pay attention to all the evidence when deciding if psychic predictions are associated with future events. Consider how many times psychic predictions were way off the mark. Even if we forget about the ambiguity in the Nostradamus quatrains, he supposedly predicted that in 1999, "A great king of terror will descend from the skies," and the War of Wars will be unleashed. Did it happen? Of course, we may not have noticed since he also said we would have been at war with the antichrist since 1973.[8] Jeanne Dixon predicted in her 1969 book *My Life and Prophecies* that Castro would be removed by 1970, Spiro Agnew's career would prosper, America would have severe food shortages after 1979, and a comet would strike the earth causing earthquakes and tidal waves in the mid 1980s.[9] Another popular psychic predicted in the year 2000 that Bill Bradley would win the presidential election and David Letterman would call it quits in 2001. Bush won the election and Letterman signed a $32-million-a-year contract in 2002 to continue his nightly TV show.[10]

We also have to ask ourselves, if psychic ability was real, why are so many major events not foretold? The Committee for the Scientific Claims of the Paranormal (CSICOP) noted that the biggest embarrassment for psychics in 1997 was their failure to predict the death of Princess Diana. No psychic predicted the Oklahoma City bombing, the World Trade Center tragedy, or the two Iraqi wars. And, if psychics can predict the future, why aren't they making millions in the stock market? They say they have no need for great wealth—but why don't they do something good for society and donate the money to needy charities? On close examination, psychic ability turns out to give us nothing more than interesting conversation.

Some people also believe that astrology can predict the future. As noted, even Nancy Reagan used an astrologer to determine the best time for her husband's presidential speeches and meetings with heads of state.[11] Astrologers claim to have many clients in large Wall Street investment firms, and some technical stock analysts willingly say that they use astrology to predict the market. You, as stockholders, may unknowingly be paying for that advice![12]

Do you think there must be something to astrology because it's based on ancient wisdom? If so, just remember that the ancients also used to foretell the future by reading the entrails of animals. The Babylonians invented astrology and hepatoscopy. While astrology uses the alignment of the stars and planets, hepatoscopy makes predictions by evaluating an animal's liver. Does it make any sense to believe that animal livers can give us an indication of the future? Probably about as much as believing that planets a million miles away affect our personality and future.

There are over ten thousand professional astrologers in the United States today. So does astrology work? Numerous studies demonstrate that it does not. For example, one study gave thirty prominent astrologers the natal charts of 116 subjects. They were also given three different personality profiles for each subject—one was the subject's profile and two were selected at random. All the astrologers had to do was match the subject's natal chart to his or her correct personality profile, a job that should have been quite easy for these professionals. It turned out that they chose the correct profile only 34 percent of the time, exactly what we would get from simply guessing. In essence, the astrologers' predictions were no better than chance accuracy.[13]

So why do people believe in astrology, palm reading, and other psychic prognosticators? In addition to wanting to believe, a major reason concerns a well-documented phenomenon known as the Forer effect.[14] Mentioned earlier, the Forer effect refers to the fact that we often see some of our own personality traits in very general personality descriptions. Essentially, we see an ambiguous, general description and think that it refers specifically to us. My favorite example of the Forer effect occurred when a scientist put an ad in a Paris newspaper offering free horoscopes. He sent the same horoscope to all one hundred and fifty people who replied, and amazingly, 94 percent said they recognized themselves in the description. I wonder how they reacted when they found out the horoscope was drawn up for a French serial killer![15]

PREDICTING THE STOCK MARKET

> *October. This is one of the peculiarly dangerous months to speculate stocks in. The others are July, January, September, April, November, May, March, June, December, August and February.*
>
> —Mark Twain

While some people believe that fringy prognosticators like psychics and astrologers can predict future events, most of us think that such predictions are worthless. It turns out, however, that there are things that many of us think we can predict quite accurately, which, in fact, we can't. Remember my friend Chris? Like many people, he thought that if he spent the time to learn about the stock market he could make a killing by buying and selling stock. Many people believe they can beat the market, and are willing to spend considerable money for advice from the "experts." So, can we predict the market? We saw earlier that technical analysts can't accurately predict future stock prices, but can anyone else do it? Let's take a look.

One of the largest professional groups that attempt to forecast the future are investment advisers. There are about two hundred thousand investment advisers, and nearly half are stockbrokers. Most all of them are involved in the $71 billion industry that attempts to predict the future movements of investments.[16] Stock analysts are on TV, writing newsletters, and calling their clients to clue them in on the next hot stock pick. Do people listen to them? Just consider how you would react to the following information.

You get a letter in the mail saying, "Accurate stock predictions! Professional stock analysts have recently developed a groundbreaking technique, based on years of research, that's proven successful at predicting stock price fluctuations. These stock predictions will be published in a new financial newsletter that comes out every month." The letter doesn't ask you to subscribe, but it gives you the newsletter's latest pick and asks that you check it out. It says that Macrotech's stock will go up next month. You don't think much of it, but at the end of the month, you notice that Macrotech did rise. Of course, your first reaction is "lucky guess!" The next month you get another letter predicting that Macrotech will go down in the following month. When you check the price that month you find that the stock did fall. A third letter predicts that Macrotech will increase next month, and, amazingly, it does go up. Now you're getting intrigued. You then receive a fourth letter predicting that Macrotech will rise again in the following month. A check of the price reveals that it increased once more. Unbelievable! At that point you get a letter asking if you're interested in subscribing to the newsletter for a mere $400 a year. It sounds like a good deal, so you jump on it.

Now just imagine how those letters could have been generated. Someone sitting in their kitchen could have sent out two thousand letters to different people in the phone book. Half of the letters said that Macrotech would go up and half said it would go down. After Macrotech went up that month, the writer sent letters to only those 1,000 individuals who were initially told that Macrotech would rise. Once again, half the letters said that Macrotech would go up and half said down. When Macrotech went down, letters were sent to the 500 people who were told it was going down, half saying it would rise and half saying it would fall during the following month. The next letter was sent to only the 250 people who received the last correct prediction, with half saying Macrotech will rise and half saying it will fall. Now, you happen to be one of the 125 individuals who received four correct letters in a row. With that track record you figure the newsletter is worth the $400—so you write a check. If the other 124 people feel the same way, the writer sitting in her kitchen has just made $50,000 by sending out a number of cheap form letters![17]

Seems like a big scam, doesn't it? But think about the stock analysts who market themselves as being superior because they perform above average four years in a row. You often see advertisements touting the ability of a stock analyst to beat his peers in the financial newsletters and on TV. However, out of one thousand stock analysts, about sixty-two will perform above average four years in a row by chance alone. As Martin Fridson explains, this beat-your-peers fallacy "is repeated every day in the financial markets. Investment advisers regularly win new clients on the strength of performance records that are not demonstrably better than chance results. Market forecasters routinely persuade investors of their excellence by stringing together just a few correct predictions. If these representations of superior scale can be discredited so easily, why do people persist in relying on them? Investors simply do not understand the basic principles of probability."[18]

Stock analysts imply that if we follow their suggestions we can "beat the market." What does that mean? The market is comprised of thousands upon thousands of stocks, actively traded on exchanges like the New York Stock Exchange. While we're not going to invest in every stock, we can invest in an index fund, which is a fund that reflects the returns we would earn from a broad category of stocks. For example, one index fund mirrors the returns earned by the five hundred stocks included in the Standard & Poor's 500 listing. Index funds are not actively managed—an investment expert is not using her expertise to select the stocks she thinks are valuable, as is the case with the vast majority of mutual funds. Presumably, if stock analysts use their expert knowledge they should be able to do better (i.e., earn a higher return) than an index fund. If not, their advice isn't worth much. So the question is, Can the experts beat the market? Let's look at the evidence.

Fund Managers

One type of evidence comes from the performance of fund managers. These individuals spend their entire professional lives analyzing the market, and buying and selling individual stocks for the funds they manage. In 2005 there were over eight thousand such funds marketed.[19] Do their managed portfolios earn a higher return than an index fund? It turns out that the majority of funds do not beat the average market return in any given year. Considerable research demonstrates this fact, going all the way back to the 1960s. Michael Jensen, a University of Rochester professor, demonstrated that mutual funds from 1945 to 1964 were "not able to predict security prices well enough to outperform a buy the market and hold policy."[20] And that fact holds true today. If you just bought an index fund, which mirrors the returns offered by the overall market, you would have beaten 50 percent to 80 percent of the fund managers in the 1970s, 1980s, and 1990s.[21]

Now you may say, some funds do beat the market. Maybe those fund managers have superior knowledge that they can capitalize on. But the data argues otherwise. While some mutual funds have performed better than an index fund over short time periods, they typically can't achieve that superior performance over the long term. The top twenty performing mutual funds in the 1980s were understandably better than the S&P 500 index in that decade (18.0% vs. 14.1% return). However, those same funds did worse than the S&P index in the 1990s (13.7% vs. 14.9%). A more dramatic example of a fund's inability to stay on top can be seen in the last few years. Riding the Internet bubble, the top twenty funds in 1998–1999 achieved a 76.72 percent return, a staggering three times higher than the S&P 500 index of 24.75 percent. However, those same funds came crashing down to a -31.52 percent return in 2000–2001, a loss three times greater than the S&P index of -10.50 percent. The number one ranked fund in 1998–1999 (Van Wagoner: Emerging Growth) dropped in rank to 1,106, the second best fund (Rydex: OTC Fund; Investor Shares) dropped to 1,103, while the third best fell to 1,098. As can be seen, there is no consistency in superior performance. In fact, the average large cap mutual fund earned about 2 percent *less* per year than the S&P 500 index fund over a twenty-year period ending December 31, 2001![22]

Remember our discussion on chance and coincidence? Before we start to attribute some cause for an event, we need to demonstrate that the event was not the result of chance. So can mutual fund performance be explained by chance? What if we selected a sample of one thousand mutual funds and analyzed the percent that would be in the top half in performance over a number of years by chance alone. If we had one thousand people flip a coin, about five hundred heads would come up. If these five hundred advanced to the second round and flipped again, about two hundred fifty would be heads. About one hundred twenty-five will be heads in the third round, sixty-three in the fourth, and thirty-one in the fifth. So by chance alone, 50 percent of the funds would be in the top half in year one, 25 percent would be in the top half two years in a row, while 12.5 percent, 6.25 percent, and 3.1 percent would be in the top half for three, four, and five years in a row, respectively. And so, by chance alone, 3 percent of funds should perform in the top half five years in a row. Is mutual fund performance significantly different from these results?

William Sherden analyzed the performance of all mutual funds with assets over $500 million between 1991 and 1995. For each of the five years he determined the number of funds that performed in the top half for two to five years in a row.[23] As can be seen in figure 10, 50 percent of funds were in the top half in the first year, 27 percent were in the top half two years in a row, 17 percent performed above average for three years, 4 percent for four years, and 3 percent for five years. These numbers are just about what chance would predict. As Burton Malkiel has stated, "The

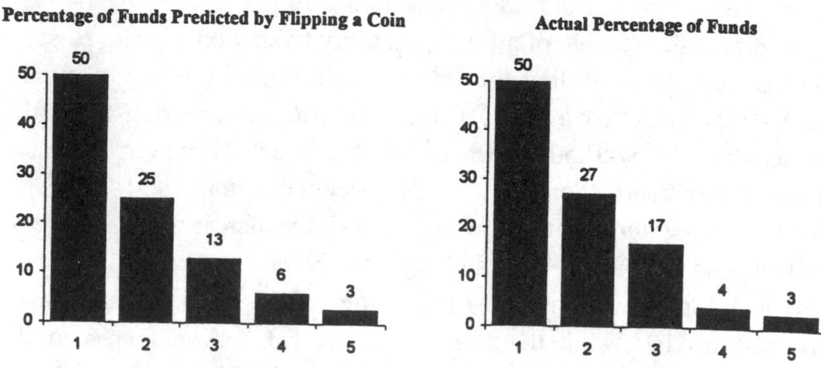

Figure 10. Comparison of mutual fund investment performance with flipping a coin. The graphs show the percentage of major mutual funds that performed better than average over five consecutive years, as compared to the percentage predicted by flipping a coin. (From W. Sherden, *The Fortune Sellers: The Big Business of Buying and Selling Predictions*, Copyright © 1998 by W. Sherden. This material is used by permission of John Wiley & Sons, Inc.)

few examples of consistently superior performance occurred no more frequently than can be expected by chance."[24]

The performance of so-called superior funds is no better. Analyses of the Forbes honor role funds over the period 1973 to 1998 indicate that they underperformed the S&P 500 stock index.[25] The inability of experts to predict the market even led the *Wall Street Journal* to start a dartboard contest in the early 1990s, where the stock picks of four experts were compared to stocks selected by throwing four darts at a stock listing. By the late 1990s, the experts seemed to be ahead by a slight margin. However, if you measure the performance of the experts from a relevant date after their selections were announced in the *Wall Street Journal* (which is more appropriate since their predictions may affect stock prices), the darts were actually slightly ahead.[26]

The above discussion concerns the performance of mutual fund managers, but don't think they're the worst of the lot. It turns out that other investment managers do no better. A number of studies have examined the performance of investment managers from insurance companies, pension funds, foundations, college endowments, state and local trust funds, trust funds administered by banks, and individual accounts handled by investment advisers. Their investment performance is no better. Of course, there are exceptions, but as Burton Malkiel notes, there is no scientific evidence to indicate that the performance of professionally managed portfolios, as a group, is any better than a randomly selected group of stocks.[27]

The Gurus

What about those few individuals who have attained considerable fame for predicting major movements in the stock market? One stock market guru amazingly predicted the 1987 stock market crash. William Sherden analyzed thirteen market predictions that she made between 1987 and 1996 (i.e., predicting that the market would either go up or down), and found that she was right only five out of the thirteen times, worse than what you would get from just flipping a coin. According to Sherden, she never made another long-shot forecast that turned out to be correct, and the fund she managed outperformed the stock market in only one of the six years it was in existence. While it's value increased by 38 percent, the S&P 500 index increased by 62 percent over the same period.[28]

A number of gurus publish financial newsletters that purport to predict the market. While one of these gurus had some early success in the 1970s, he later advised his clients to sell everything when the Dow was in the 800s. The market proceeded to rise to about 1200. According to Sherden, the guru's performance over eight years, ending January 1994, was 38 percent below the market average. Yet another guru predicted the 1980s bull market. However, shocked by the 1987 crash, he stated that the bull market was over and that the Dow would fall to 400 by the early 1990s. Instead, the Dow climbed to 4,000 by 1994. His performance over the ten-year period ending December 1996 was 64 percent below the market average.[29] The bottom line is, people pay up to $500 per year for financial newsletters that help them pick stocks, yet an index fund beats the newsletter picks 80 percent of the time.[30]

Frequent Trades Equal Poorer Performance

Given our belief that we can beat the market, many of us actively manage our own portfolios. We buy and sell stock frequently, attempting to capitalize on some hot issue. However, the data indicate that this is a bad strategy. Consider the following two statements.

(A) Between 1984 and 1995, the average stock mutual fund earned an annual return of 12.3 percent, while the average bond fund earned 9.7 percent per year.
(B) Between 1984 and 1995, the average investor in a stock mutual fund earned 6.3 percent, while the average investor in a bond fund earned 8 percent per year.

Both of these statements are true![31] How can that be? It turns out that instead of investing and holding a fund for an extended period of time, most investors move in and out of funds on a regular basis.[32] Oftentimes, investors move their money into a fund that has experienced good recent performance. However, statistics tell us that we have regression to the mean. That is, if a fund is currently outperforming the market, its performance is likely to drop in the future to bring it back to average. And so, if we buy into a fund right after it has posted recent gains, we're likely to be in for a fall. In effect, going after strong past performance often means we take money out of funds that are likely to rebound, and put it into funds that are ready to drop.[33]

In fact, one study compellingly demonstrated that frequent stock trading results in poor performance. The stock investment performance of individual investors from over sixty thousand households was analyzed between February 1991 and December 1996. The average household earned an average return of 16.4 percent. More importantly, the top 20 percent of investors who traded the most earned an average return of 11.4 percent.[34] These individuals actively traded their stocks because they thought they could beat the market, when in fact, that trading actually resulted in poorer performance.

Why Can't We Predict the Market?

Many researchers argue that the reason we can't predict future stock prices is because the market is efficient. The efficient market hypothesis states that all publicly available information is quickly impounded into a firm's stock price, so we can't beat the market by finding over- or undervalued stocks.[35] While there's considerable support for this hypothesis, there are also anomalies that make some people question whether markets are totally efficient. However, even if the efficient market hypothesis doesn't hold in all cases, that doesn't mean we can predict future stock prices. As Malkiel states, "although I believe in the possibility of superior professional investment performance, I must emphasize that the evidence we have thus far does not support the view that such competence exists."[36]

One reason for the unpredictability of the stock market is that, even when prices are rising, they don't increase in a gradual, steady manner. Instead, a few days a year have big gains, while the rest of the year is relatively flat. As Gary Belsky and Tom Gilovich state, "the stock market is much like that common description of war: long periods of boredom interrupted by episodes of pure terror." Studies show that if you missed the forty best-performing days out of the 7,802 trading days from 1963 to 1993, your average annual return would have dropped from just under 12 percent to slightly above 7 percent.[37] The problem is, we have no reliable way to predict which days are going to be the top performers.

What causes these big shifts in the market? William Sherden offers a plausible explanation when he states, "The stock market is clearly driven by irrational herd mentality and mass psychology. Speculative binges cause stocks to surge to price levels way beyond their economic value in terms of future earnings potential. Panics cause the equally irrational effect in the opposite direction. The stock market is a psychological soup of fear, greed, hope, superstition, and a host of other emotions and motives."[38]

Just look at Black Monday, October 16, 1987, the day the stock market crashed. The crash came and went without any good cause. Compared to the preceding Friday, stocks were worth 30 percent less, and no real new information accounted for the drop. This irrationality suggests that the efficient market hypothesis doesn't give us the whole story about the market. A more complete explanation is that the market is a complex system that has both rational and irrational forces at work. As Sherden states, "While rational forces drive the market toward its fair value, irrational forces of speculation and panic cause the market to diverge from rational value. These irrational forces give rise to explosive nonlinearities that make the market unpredictable."[39] And yet, we are spending billions of dollars to predict it.

So what can we take away from all this? In some sense, the stock market is like flipping a coin. If we flip a coin 1,000 times we can be pretty sure we'll get about half heads and half tails, but we can't tell what will happen on each individual flip. Similarly, if we invest in the stock market, we can be pretty sure that it will go up over the long-term, but it's very difficult to consistently predict which specific stock will outperform the market.[40] As a result, it makes more sense to invest in an index fund, and to hold onto that fund for the long haul, because we can then reap the rewards of the general upward movement in the market. But what about all those stock experts with their hot tips? You have to ask the old adage, "If these people can predict the market, why aren't they all incredibly rich?" The fact is, if stock analysts could predict future prices, it would make infinitely more sense to keep that valuable information to themselves, because they could make a killing in the market if they did. But they don't. They sell it to you.

But We Still Want to Believe

So we have considerable evidence to indicate that it's not worth our time to analyze and pick individual stocks. Of course, if you're doing it for sport—if you enjoy the game—go right ahead. I go to a casino knowing that the odds are stacked against me in the long run, but I enjoy the act of gambling. However, if you think that you can pick stocks to beat the market, you're fooling yourself. And yet, very intelligent people continue to think they can.

I was talking recently with a fellow colleague of mine—one of the most scholarly professors in our school. He told me that he could pick superior stocks by using fundamental analysis, a technique that attempts to determine the intrinsic (true) value of a stock based on a firm's underlying economic variables. The technique assumes that when the market price is below the intrinsic value, the stock is undervalued and the price will rise when the market properly adjusts.[41] It seems to make sense, and so many people believe that fundamental analysis can work. In fact, my friend told me he had supporting evidence, and referred to the research of

Benjamin Graham, the father of fundamental analysis. As Professor Burton Malkicl notes, however, "The academic community has rendered its judgment. Fundamental analysis is no better than technical analysis in enabling investors to capture above average returns."[42] In fact, Graham himself reluctantly concluded that fundamental analysis could no longer produce superior returns, stating, "I am no longer an advocate of elaborate techniques of security analysis in order to find superior value opportunities. This was a rewarding activity, say, 40 years ago, when Graham and Dodd was first published; but the situation has changed. . . . [Today] I doubt whether such extensive efforts will generate sufficiently superior selections to justify their cost. . . . I'm on the side of the 'efficient market' school of thought."[43]

I saw my friend a few days later, gave him the quote, and said, "Wasn't this the person you were referring to for support?" His reaction was telling—he ripped up the quote and exclaimed, "That doesn't mean a thing!" Even though the person he was using as support said the technique is no longer effective, my friend refused to believe it. Instead, he reiterated, once again, that fundamental analysis has given him many successful stock picks. When I pressed him on this issue, he said, "Sometimes I'm right, and sometimes I'm wrong." I said, "What if you're wrong 60 percent of the time and your portfolio drops?" He replied, "Then it's my fault and I'll learn from it." I said, "What if it doesn't work year after year?" He responded, "Then I have to learn how to do it better." In effect, he wasn't willing to question his belief in fundamental analysis—even in the face of considerable empirical evidence to the contrary. Why is that? He was relying on his personal experience instead of scientific investigation, and, as we've seen, relying on anecdotal information is one of the main causes of erroneous beliefs.

Fundamental analysts often attribute their gains to using fundamental analysis, and their losses to alternative explanations, such as a downturn in the overall economy. But with this rationale, fundamental analysis is unfalsifiable, and something that's unfalsifiable is worthless. What should you do if you decide to pick individual stocks for investment? Keep track of your wins and losses; in effect, pay attention to both the hits and the misses. As time goes by, you'll likely realize that you're not earning any more than if you just invested your money in an index fund. Without such an approach, you'll be doomed to make extremely costly mistakes, as another colleague of mine recently discovered. He had his money in an index fund until he was convinced by a mutual friend to pick individual stocks—which went on to lose 40 percent of their value when the overall market was rising!

ECONOMIC FORECASTING

While some people pay astrologers to foretell the future, and others pay stock analysts for stock tips, we, as a society, spend billions of dollars on economic forecasts. A number of government agencies and hundreds of private organizations sell economic forecasts. How good are they? A review of twelve studies on forecasting accuracy, covering the periods 1970 to 1995, concluded that economists can't even predict the major turning points in our economy.[44] One study analyzed the error rates in forecasting the gross national product (GNP) growth and inflation eight quarters into the future for six major economic forecasters: the Federal Reserve, the Council of Economic Advisers, the Congressional Budget Office, General Electric, the Bureau of Economic Analysis, and the National Bureau of Economic Research. Forty-six of the forty-eight forecasts did not predict our economy's turning points.[45]

Another study revealed that the forecasting track record of the Federal Reserve was, again, worse than chance. Over the period 1980 to 1995, the Fed called the major turning points in real GNP growth only three out of six times (the same as chance), and was unsuccessful in predicting the two turning points in inflation. Thus, the Fed was accurate only 38 percent of the time (three out of eight). The turning point predictions of the Council of Economic Advisors (CEA) and the Congressional Budget Office (CBO) between 1976 and 1995 faired no better, with overall accuracy rates of only 36 percent and 50 percent, respectively.

These data indicate that the major economic forecasting organizations can't predict whether there'll be a major turning point in our economy. As William Sherden notes, "Economic forecasters have routinely failed to foresee turning points in the economy: the coming of severe recessions, the start of recoveries, and periods of rapid increases or decreases in inflation. . . . In fact, they have failed to predict the past four most severe recessions, and most of them predicted growth instead for these periods."[46]

Most economists were forecasting a severe downturn after the stock market crashed in October 1987, and yet the economy expanded vigorously during the last quarter of 1987. The bottom line is, most economic forecasts are no better than just predicting that next year will be about the same as this year. In fact, they can actually be worse, because if change is predicted, there's a good chance the direction will be wrong.[47]

In addition, the expertise of economists or the sophistication of economic models does not improve forecast accuracy. Predictions based upon large models having over one thousand equations are no better than predictions from simple models with only a few equations. No matter how sophisticated the models are, they still can't reliably predict the future. A particularly telling test was revealed in 1995, when the magazine the *Economist* published the results of a contest held in 1985. They asked people with different backgrounds to accurately predict the British economy ten years into the future. Who won? A group of sanitation workers tied for first place with a panel of four chairman of multinational firms.[48] Once again, the amount of knowledge we have in a certain area will not help us predict what will happen if the events are inherently unpredictable. As Michael Evans, founder of Chase Economics, states, "The problem with macro [economic] forecasting is that no one can do it."[49]

Also, no specific economic ideology does a better job than the others in predicting the economy's future. Forecasts are typically influenced by the particular beliefs and assumptions that an economist holds, and those assumptions can lead to vastly different predictions about our economic future. In fact, economics seems to be the only discipline where two people can receive a Nobel Prize for saying the exact opposite thing. This has led to a belief in the "First Law of Economics: For every economist, there's an equal and opposite economist."[50] When different economists predict very different things, it's difficult to place much credence in those predictions. Why are there such diverse views from economists? One reason may be that economics typically does not use the scientific method, where hypotheses are tested by observing what goes on in the economy. Instead, economists often develop elaborate theories that may be logically consistent, but are often based upon unrealistic concepts. For example, a basic assumption of economics is that people are consistently rational in their behaviors. However, we are psychological and social beings who often display inconsistencies and errors in decision making.

Money is not our only motivator—we are also affected by conformity, power, love, revenge, charity, laziness, etc. Have you ever heard an economist's joke? Here's one: Two economists are walking down the street. One says, "Hey, there's a dollar bill on the sidewalk." The other says, "That can't be so—if there was, someone would have picked it up."[51]

Given their poor track record, some say that forecasters are actually worse than useless because they can cause long-term damage to the economy.[52] Why? People can make bad financial decisions by relying on erroneous forecasts. Interestingly, more and more people have recently questioned the value of those forecasts. In fact, a few corporations have disbanded their economics departments. However, many economists still attempt to predict the future, and the cost of that useless information to our society runs into the billions. So why do we do it? Our desire to predict the future is extremely powerful, whether we're trying to predict matters in our own personal life or the economy as a whole.

IT'S GOING TO BE SUNNY—UNLESS IT RAINS

Weather forecast for tonight: dark.
—George Carlin

You're planning a ski trip at the end of the week, so you turn to the Weather Channel on Monday to get the five-day forecast. "It's going to snow on Friday," it reports. Psyched, you can't wait for the weekend. On Tuesday, you check the weather again to see if Friday's storm will be huge, but now they say it's going to be sunny. What happened to the storm? Disappointed, you check the forecast a little later and this time it predicts rain for Friday. We hear long-range forecasts all the time, and they're reported with considerable certainty. And yet, those forecasts are constantly changing. What's going on? It turns out that we can't predict the weather that far ahead. In fact, weather prediction is reasonably accurate only about twenty-four to forty-eight hours in advance.[53]

And yet, we spend billions of dollars to make long-range forecasts. The World Meteorological Organization estimated that the global budget for weather forecasting was around $4 billion in 1995. About half of that is spent in the United States by the National Oceanic and Atmospheric

Administration, which is the parent organization of the National Weather Service, the Climate Analysis Center, the Severe Storms Forecasting Center, and the National Hurricane Center. The National Weather Service issues daily forecasts as well as three-to-five- and six-to-ten-day forecasts. The Climate Analysis Center gives us monthly and seasonal outlooks, predicting weather patterns for the next thirty days, ninety days, and even eighteen months into the future. We do this knowing that the weather is a chaotic system, and is therefore impossible to predict that far ahead.[54]

Research indicates that the National Weather Service can produce reasonably accurate forecasts of temperature, cloudiness, and rain twelve to forty-eight hours ahead of time. Heavy snows are more difficult to predict. For example, New England experienced the great blizzard of 1978 on February 6. The day before the blizzard, the *Boston Globe* made no mention of a big storm, and predicted that the winds would only be ten to fifteen miles per hour in an easterly direction. As William Sherden notes, "For the period more than 48 hours in the future, weather forecasting enters the twilight zone, where accuracy and reliability decline to a point of very limited usefulness. In fact, the prediction of the specific time and places of precipitation beyond two days becomes indistinguishable from random guessing."[55]

It's no surprise, therefore, that the long-range forecasts of the Climate Analysis Center aren't any better than chance. If you wanted to predict whether a certain part of the country would have normal, above-, or below-average temperature over the next three months, which is what the Climate Analysis Center does, you would do just as well by throwing darts at a map to predict those three options.[56]

Some people believe that the *Old Farmer's Almanac* is quite accurate in its weather forecasts. In fact, the editors of the almanac claim that their forecasts are 80 percent to 85 percent accurate. Sounds impressive, doesn't it? But consider the evidence. William Sherden analyzed the monthly average temperatures for the previous thirty years in Omaha, Nebraska, and found that the almanac was accurate 49 percent of the time in predicting whether they would be above or below seasonal norms. Given that there's a 50/50 chance of being right in this prediction, we might as well just flip a coin. The almanac's accuracy in predicting temperature was 73 percent, which is close to the 80 percent that it claims.

Sounds pretty good—but to determine the real value of the almanac forecast we have to compare its accuracy to some benchmark, like that attained from a naive forecast. What if, for example, we just used the seasonal average temperature to naively predict the current temperature. Amazingly, we would get an accuracy rate of 90 percent. So relying on the almanac gives us less accurate predictions than if we just used past seasonal averages, which require no forecasting skill at all.[57]

What can we take away from this evaluation of weather forecasting? In recent years, meteorologists have made great strides in storm detection and short-range forecasting over a one- to two-day time horizon. In fact, Sherden notes that meteorology is the only forecasting profession that shows signs of improvement. However, long-range forecasting is just voodoo. So you have to wonder, why are we spending billions of dollars to make long-run forecasts? It seems more like wishful thinking than anything else.

TECHNOLOGICAL AND SOCIAL TRENDS

Technology gurus constantly make predictions about the new gadgets that will change our lives. Are they accurate? Professor Stephen Schnaars of Baruch College analyzed the forecasts published between 1959 and 1989 in sources like the *New York Times*, the *Wall Street Journal*, and *Business Week*, and found that they were wrong about 80 percent of the time. The predictions of major think tanks fair no better. In fact, *Futures* magazine once analyzed 1,556 technological forecasts and found that the experts were no better than nonexperts in their prediction accuracy. [58]

So-called technological experts over the past forty years have predicted that, by now, most people would be using video telephones, ultrasonic dishwashers and showers, moving sidewalks, and jet-powered cars. Some experts even predicted that the average person would be working only about ten hours a year—by the year 2000. Moreover, innovations that have had a major impact on our lives, such as cellular telephones, atomic energy, compact discs, and the computer, were not predicted. In fact, the dictionary definition of a computer was "a person who computes" as recently as 1950. In 1956 RCA predicted that by the year 2000, there would be only 220,000 computers in existence.[59] The evolution of technology is so complex and uncertain that it is just about impossible to predict what the next breakthrough innovation will be. As Sherden states, "The main difference between technology forecasting and science fiction is that the former is sold under the pretense of being factual."[60]

One reason it's tough to predict which consumer product will take off is because it's not always the best product. For example, Sony's Betamax came out at about the same time as VHS. Most experts thought that Betamax was a superior product, but VHS gained a market share advantage in the video rental stores, which pushed Betamax into oblivion. In the early days of personal computers, many experts thought the Macintosh operating system produced by Apple Computer was superior to Microsoft's DOS operating system that was used in IBM computers. However, Apple refused to license the Macintosh software until 1995, so when other companies started mass producing low-cost computers, they installed the DOS system.[61] Just compare the market share of the two companies today.

What about all those futurists who predict major trends in our society? As you might surmise, they're typically wrong. For example, if you believed Paul Ehrlich's book *The Population Bomb*, published in 1968, you would have thought that war, pestilence, and famine would engulf us by the 1990s, killing around 500 million people. In 1970 Alvin Toffler wrote *Future Shock*, in which he predicted we would experience a psychological melt down by the 1990s because of too much change in our lives. In fact, we appear to be adapting quite well. Once again, it seems like the only difference between these types of books and works of fiction is that they are sold as nonfiction.[62]

WHY WE CAN'T PREDICT—BUT STILL TRY TO

As we've seen, we attempt to predict many things that are essentially unpredictable. Why aren't they predictable? Two major reasons come to mind: chaos and complexity. The weather is inherently unpredictable beyond a couple of days because it is a chaotic system. Chaos theory applies to a limited number of physical systems, like the weather and fluid turbulence. With chaos, turbulent behavior is determined by nonlinear laws that magnify small errors in the initial conditions of the system, making it extremely unpredictable beyond a short period of time. You may have heard of the butterfly effect, where something as small as a butterfly flapping its wings in a far-off place may have consequences for the weather you're experiencing here and now.

The economy and other social systems are unpredictable because they are complex systems. In complex systems, order emerges from the complex interactions among components of a system, influenced by one or more guiding principles. For example, our ecosystem developed because of the complex interactions of many different life-forms guided by the principle of natural selection. Complex systems are unpredictable because it's practically impossible to know the outcome caused by countless interacting variables. These systems have periods of order interrupted by unexpected turmoil, and they can evolve, exhibiting new, unexpected behaviors. And so, chaos relates to many aspects of the physical world, while complexity relates to our biological and social world. In either case, accurate predictions are just about impossible to make.[63]

So why do we believe predictions that have no basis in reality? As with many of the topics discussed so far, we believe we can predict the future because we *want* to believe it. We abhor uncertainty. We like to feel in control, and the thought that we can predict the future gives us a better sense of control. Also, we are easily influenced by people who are in authoritative positions. We attribute expert status to economists, meteorologists, and stock analysts because they've had years of training in their respective disciplines. But as we've seen, some things are essentially unpredictable, no matter how much training a person has.

As William Sherden says, "The theories of chaos and complexity are revealing the future as fundamentally unpredictable. This applies to our economy, the stock market, commodity prices, the weather, animal populations (humans included), and many other phenomena."[64] In effect, some things are just not knowable. We would be well advised to follow the lead of Winston Churchill, who gave up trying to predict what was to come, complaining that the future was just one damned thing after another. The sooner we realize that many things in our environment are essentially unpredictable, the sooner we'll be able to make more informed decisions on what to believe and how to use our resources.

Chapter 8: Seeking to Confirm

I can't give up smoking—coughing is the only exercise I get.

—My friend Harry

In 1941 Admiral Kimmel, commander in chief of the Pacific fleet, was repeatedly warned about the possibility of war with Japan. On November 24, he was informed that a surprise attack could occur in any direction. However, Kimmel didn't think the United States was in any great danger, and since Hawaii was not specifically mentioned in the report, he took no precautions to protect Pearl Harbor. On December 3, he was told that American cryptographers decoded a Japanese message ordering their embassies around the world to destroy "most of their secret codes." Kimmel focused on the word "most" and thought that if Japan was going to war with the United States they would have ordered "all" their codes destroyed. One hour before the attack on Pearl Harbor, a Japanese sub was sunk near the entry to the harbor. Instead of taking immediate action, Kimmel waited for confirmation that it was, in fact, a Japanese sub. As a result, sixty warships were anchored in the harbor, and planes were lined up wing to wing, when the attack came. The Pacific fleet was destroyed and Kimmel was court-martialed.[1] Our desire to cling to an existing belief in the face of contradictory evidence can have disastrous effects.

We have a natural tendency to confirm. That is, we selectively attend to information that supports our existing beliefs and expectations. Studies have shown, for example, that when we view a presidential debate, we pay more attention to information that's consistent with our political point of view. When believers in ESP are shown experimental results contrary to their belief, they remember less of that data than if the results had supported ESP.[2] As I write this, President George W. Bush is under attack for starting a war with Iraq based on questionable intelligence. Although United Nations inspectors could find no evidence of weapons of mass destruction prior to war, and some intelligence and policy advisors thought that Iraq was not an imminent threat to the United States, Bush (and Vice President Cheney) wanted to eliminate Saddam Hussein. Consequently, many experts now believe that Bush and Cheney "cherry-picked" the evidence, focusing on anything that supported a war, and discounting evidence that did not. After the invasion, we found that most all of their supporting evidence was wrong.[3] Using a confirming strategy can lead to dire consequences.

Confirming strategies maintain consistency in our beliefs. How does that happen? New information that's consistent with our existing beliefs is quickly accepted at face value. On the other hand, information that contradicts our beliefs is often ignored or critically scrutinized and discounted.[4] For example, a team of psychologists had people read summaries of two studies relating to the effectiveness of capital punishment in preventing crime. The results of one study supported capital punishment while the other did not. It turned out that if the study's results were consistent with a person's beliefs, he thought that the study was well conducted. On the other hand, if the results were not consistent, he found numerous flaws in the study to discount its relevance. If we don't ignore contradictory evidence, we often find reasons why we shouldn't consider it.[5]

At times, the reasons we give to rationalize conflicting evidence can be quite laughable. Do you remember the psychic mentioned earlier who thought he could remotely view distant objects without his eyes? To provide support for his ability, he said that the CIA spent millions on remote viewing, proving that there must be something to it. However, when asked why the CIA would shut down a successful program, he said that the cold war is over, and so it's not needed. This, of course, makes no sense because it implies that we have no need for intelligence gathering around the world. If that's the case, why is the CIA still in operation? When the psychic was asked why he wasn't rich if he had the ability to predict the stock market, he said that once a person knows he can do it, he is at such peace with his life that he doesn't feel the need for money. Again, one wonders why he wouldn't use his powers to generate considerable wealth for charity. Wouldn't that be a wonderful use of his gift? When I hear such comments I'm reminded of the quote at the start of this chapter. While said as a joke, it's indicative of the amazing lengths that people will go to rationalize what they want to believe.

As Michael Shermer has indicated, most of the time we form our beliefs not because of empirical evidence or logical reasoning. Rather, we have belief preferences for a host of psychological and emotional reasons, including parental or sibling influences, peer pressure, education, and life experience. We then search for evidence to support those predilections. In fact, this process is a main reason why smart people believe weird things. As Shermer notes, "Smart people believe weird things because they are skilled at defending beliefs they arrived at for non-smart reasons."[6]

Gamblers are notorious for rationalizing away their losses so as to maintain a belief in their gambling strategy. If you listen closely, they actually rewrite their history of successes and failures, accepting their successes at face value, and fabricating reasons for their losses. My friend uses a basic strategy in blackjack to determine when he should take a card. Like many gamblers, he usually attributes the outcome of the game to his strategy when he wins. However, when he walks away a loser, he finds a number of reasons for the loss, none of which has to do with his play. The dealer may have changed, someone new sat at the table and ruined the flow of cards, there were too many players, or a person at the table's end took a bad hit. It's extremely common for gamblers to evaluate their outcomes in such a biased manner. Winning is interpreted as a reflection of one's gambling skill, while losing is explained away, and thereby discounted, by some outside forces beyond the player's control.

Sometimes gamblers even evaluate their losses as "near wins." If a gambler bets on a winning football team, she is likely to believe the win is due to her superior insight and skill, even though it may have been caused by a fourth-quarter fumble by the opposing team, which allowed her team to score. If she bet on the losing team, however, she probably wouldn't question her skill or insight. Rather, she would think the loss was caused by a fluke fumble, and that if it didn't happen, she would have won. In effect, she interprets the outcome not as a loss, but as a near win.

Don't think that gamblers are the only ones fooling themselves. Many of us believe that our successes are due to what we did, and our failures are due to external events. Athletes attribute their wins to themselves and their losses to bad officiating. Students who perform well think a test is a valid assessment of their ability, while those who perform poorly think the test is unfair. Teachers believe that their students' successes are due to their teaching skills, while their students' failures are due to the students' lack of ability or motivation. If a manuscript is rejected for publication, researchers think it's due to the arbitrary selection of a particularly critical reviewer, as opposed to the quality of what they wrote.[7]

And so, we evaluate evidence in a biased fashion. We pay particular attention to evidence that supports our point of view, and either ignore or discount the importance of evidence that contradicts our beliefs. In fact, the desire to maintain our beliefs often makes us avoid situations that would unearth contradictory evidence in the first place. We typically associate with like-minded people and read books and magazines with orientations similar to our own. Seldom do we read a conservative magazine if we're liberal, or a liberal magazine if we're conservative, to get a better understanding of an opposing viewpoint. I once told a good friend, who is a staunch conservative, that he should read Al Franken's new book *Lies, and the Lying Liars who Tell Them.* I said, "The book is hilarious, I think you'll enjoy it even if you don't agree with its liberal bent." He flatly refused. I said, "You don't have to reward Franken by putting money in his pocket—read my copy." Again, a resounding no! Such a desire to attend to evidence supporting our beliefs acts as a filter mechanism that can actually be self-fulfilling. By avoiding contradictory data, it seems like there's more data supporting our preconceptions, which, of course, reinforces our belief that we were right all along.

CONFIRMING OUR HYPOTHESES

It is the theory which decides what we can find.
—Albert Einstein

Our tendency to confirm is so ingrained in our cognitive makeup that we confirm even if we don't have a prior belief or expectation—all we have to do is test a hypothesis. Whether we realize it or not, we act as intuitive scientists, continually developing and testing hypotheses when we make our professional and personal judgments. For example, a doctor forms hypotheses about the potential causes of a patient's disease, and then tests them by gathering information from the patient and other medical procedures. An investor tests whether a firm's future net income will increase (or decrease) when making investment decisions. We even hypothesis test in our everyday lives when we decide whether we like a person or not. In essence, we constantly test hypotheses when forming our judgments; and if we use confirming strategies, those judgments can be biased.

Imagine that you're talking with your friend John about a mutual friend, Barry. John tells you, "I always thought that Barry was outgoing—he's a real extrovert." You haven't thought about it before, but you recall that Barry was at a party last week, he sometimes tells jokes, and he likes to go to a bar to wind down. Before long, you come to believe that Barry must be an extrovert. What's wrong with this thinking? When deciding whether Barry is an extrovert, we naturally start to think of the times he exhibited extroverted behavior. In effect, we think of things that confirm the hypothesis we're testing. If we focus on the times Barry was extroverted, we're likely to conclude that he is, in fact, an extrovert. The problem is, people are complex, and can exhibit both extroverted and introverted behavior at different times and under different circumstances. And so, if your friend started off by saying he thought Barry was an introvert, you would have likely thought of a number of instances in which he exhibited introverted behavior. You might remember that he reads a lot and likes to spend time at the library. After focusing on these instances, you would likely conclude that Barry was more introverted. Thus, the way the hypothesis is framed can have a major impact on our final judgment.

Our bias to confirm can also affect how we search for information.

For example, what if you didn't know Barry, but you had to decide if he's an *extrovert* by asking him two of the following four questions.

(1) In what situations are you most talkative?
(2) What factors make it hard for you to open up to people?
(3) What would you do to liven things up at a party?
(4) What things do you dislike about loud parties?

Which two questions would you ask? Most people select questions 1 and 3. However, when asked to decide if Barry is an *introvert*, people have a tendency to select questions 2 and 4. Why? Questions 1 and 3 relate to more extroverted behavior, while 2 and 4 concern introversion.[8] Even the questions we ask to make our judgments (test our hypotheses) can bias us in favor of finding that hypothesis to be true. If we ask Barry, "In what situations are you most talkative?" to see if he's an extrovert, we'll begin to focus on those instances in which Barry talks a lot, and ignore those situations in which he doesn't. Given that people exhibit extroverted behavior in some cases, and introverted behavior in others, we can usually find a number of extroverted behaviors, even for a person who is more of an introvert.[9]

Research has found that we consistently employ confirming strategies in social interactions. In fact, psychologist Mark Snyder notes that our tendency to confirm is so entrenched in our cognitive makeup that it doesn't seem to matter whether a hypothesis comes from a source of high or low credibility, how likely it is that the hypothesis is true, or whether substantial incentives (e.g., monetary rewards) are given for accurate hypothesis testing.[10] Our ingrained tendency to focus on confirming data usually wins out.

It's one thing to use confirming strategies to judge whether someone is an extrovert or introvert—the consequences of a wrong judgment will not be that important. But what about judgments that may have significant implications for a person's life? Would confirming strategies still occur? Several years ago, the TV show *60 Minutes* asked three different polygraphers (let's call them A, B, and C) to conduct a lie detector test on three employees (let's call them X, Y, and Z) to determine who was stealing from a firm. A was told that X was suspected, B was told that Y was suspected, while C was told that Z was suspected, although no reason was given for the suspicion. You can probably guess the results. Polygrapher A found X to be guilty, B found Y to be guilty, and C found Z to be guilty. Research has shown that lie detector tests are quite unreliable—they're open to a lot of subjective interpretation. If a polygrapher has a preconceived notion of who's guilty, he can interpret the data to confirm to his preconceived belief, spelling real trouble for suspected individuals.[11]

Could confirming strategies actually affect the type of sentences handed down in court? One study investigated the sentences that would be given if jurors considered the harshest, versus most lenient, verdict first.[12] In most criminal cases, a jury is told to first decide if the defendant is guilty of the greatest offense that he or she is charged with. If reasonable doubt exists on that charge, they then proceed down the list to progressively lesser charges. For example, a jury often considers whether a defendant is guilty of first-degree murder, and if they can't agree on that verdict, they evaluate second-degree murder. This approach may bias the verdict delivered. People often cling to the first hypothesis considered, and then search for confirming evidence to support that hypothesis. If juries consider the harshest (most lenient) verdict first, they may focus on data supporting that charge, and render a harsher (more lenient) verdict.

Two experiments investigated this issue. In the first, participants, acting as jurors, decided whether a defendant was guilty of first- or second-degree murder, voluntary or involuntary manslaughter, or was not guilty. The case materials were adapted from an actual murder trial, where there were no eyewitnesses and most of the evidence was circumstantial. Half of the participants were asked to consider the harshest verdict first (murder in the first degree) and then proceed to progressively more lenient verdicts, while the other half started with the most lenient verdict (not guilty). Amazingly, 87.5 percent of the jurors chose not guilty if they started with a lenient verdict, while only 25 percent chose not guilty when starting with a harsh verdict!

A second experiment examined more jurors and added some new twists (e.g., whether the jurors were rushed or not rushed to enter a verdict). The verdicts were scored on a scale, with one indicating not guilty and five indicating guilty of first-degree murder. When jurors were not rushed, the average verdict in the harsh to lenient condition was 3.26, while it was only 2.20 in the lenient to harsh condition. That could mean the difference between being found guilty of voluntary manslaughter versus involuntary manslaughter, convictions that carry very different sentences. Thus, defendants can receive harsher verdicts when a harsher crime is considered first, and more lenient verdicts when a lenient outcome is first evaluated. These results suggest that it may be better for a judge just to provide definitions of the charges, and not dictate the order in which they should be considered. In fact, one could argue that since we have a presumption of innocence that considering the most lenient verdict first would be more in line with our judicial philosophy.

YES! YES! YES!

Our search for confirming data is one of the main ways we stick to our current beliefs. It's also indicative of a fundamental cognitive strategy that we employ. We use a positive-test strategy when forming our judgments. That is, our cognitive system is set up to focus on positive, as opposed to negative, instances. This doesn't mean that we're optimistic—always looking on the bright side of life. Rather, it means we like to think in terms of yesses instead of noes when we consider a certain issue. When testing whether a person is an extrovert, we attend to more data that suggests that the person is an extrovert—the data says yes, the person is an extrovert.

To see a positive test strategy in action, consider the following series of three numbers:

2 4 6

What if I told you these numbers obey a certain rule, and that you have to determine what the rule is. To decipher the rule, you can choose other sequences of three numbers, and you'll be told yes, they obey the rule, or no, they don't. Think about what the rule might be, and write down a sequence of three numbers to test your hypothesis.[13]

When we form a hypothesis about the rule, such as "even numbers increasing by two," we often pick numbers like 12, 14, 16—numbers that conform to the rule. If we're told, Yes, they obey the rule, we then pick something like 50, 52, 54, and are again told yes. After selecting a couple more triplets that conform to our rule, we become convinced it's "even numbers increasing by two," and are flabbergasted when told it's wrong. Undaunted, we think again and decide to test a different rule, such as "any three numbers increasing by two." After mentioning 3, 5, 7, and 21, 23, 25, we state that rule—and are told it's wrong. What's going on? What could the rule be? It's "any three numbers in increasing order."

Why do we have a hard time discovering the rule? We try to prove our hypothesis correct by searching for examples that confirm the hypothesis, not for examples that disconfirm it. That is, we look for examples that yield a yes response. The problem with this strategy is that we could give a thousand examples which conform to the hypothesis and still not get a definitive answer on the correct rule. Why? If we think the rule is "even numbers increasing by two," and we give many series of numbers consistent with the rule, those numbers may also be consistent with other rules as well, such as "even numbers increasing" or "any three numbers increasing." So continually looking for confirming data doesn't get us any closer to the truth. On the other hand, if we choose some numbers that are inconsistent with our hypothesis "even numbers increasing by two," such as 7, 9, 11, and are told that they conform to the rule, we immediately discover that our hypothesis concerning even numbers is incorrect. In effect, if we use a case that disconfirms the rule that we're testing, we can quickly learn more information than if we continue to search for confirming cases.

As philosopher Karl Popper indicated, a general hypothesis can never be completely confirmed because we may uncover an exception the next time around. It was once thought that all swans were white, until we found black swans in Australia. To determine if a hypothesis is likely to be true, we should try to prove it false. Why? It's impossible to prove a hypothesis is correct with certainty, but we can disprove it with one observation.[14] And so, disconfirming evidence can be very useful in our decision making.

Consider the following problem:

> Suppose the letters and numbers below are on separate cards. The cards have a number on one side and a letter on the other, and someone tells you: "If a card has a vowel on one side, then it has

an even number on the other side." Which of the cards would you need to turn over in order to decide whether the person is lying?

E K 4 7

If you're like most people, you would say E and 4, or possibly just E. When 128 people answered the problem, E and 4 was the most common response (59), followed by E (42).[15] Why? Once again, we choose cards that give us confirming evidence. However, the correct answer is E and 7. Think about the problem this way. If a card has a vowel, then it has an even number (if X then Y). The only way to falsify an if-then statement is to find a case of X and not-Y (i.e., a vowel and an odd number). The only cards that can disconfirm the rule are vowels or odd numbers (E and 7). Even numbers or consonants are not relevant (an even number is not relevant because the rule doesn't say even numbers can't have a consonant on the other side). Once again, searching for disconfirming, as opposed to confirming, evidence would answer the problem. And yet, four out of five experienced mathematical psychologists—people who should know better—couldn't solve this problem correctly.[16] Such is our ingrained desire to confirm.

Interestingly, self-fulfilling prophesies are related to confirming strategies. Self-fulfilling prophecies occur when we act a certain way because we believe something to be true, and our act makes it come true. As such, our belief leads to acts that will likely result in confirming evidence. For example, researchers told grade school teachers that certain students would bloom academically in the coming year. Eight months later, those students' IQs improved more than that of the other students. However, the "high achievers" were selected at random. Teachers apparently gave the bloomers more attention and praise, which resulted in a greater improvement. Thus, not only do we see what we expect to see, we can actually *cause* what we expect to see.[17]

SO WHAT'S THE DEAL?

As with the other decision strategies discussed here, a confirming strategy can yield correct answers in many cases. We obviously use it extensively, often making many accurate decisions. However, we can also make grossly inaccurate judgments if we rely on confirming data too much. Why is that? There is often considerable evidence that both supports and contradicts the hypothesis tested. If we focus primarily on the supporting data, we're more likely to accept that hypothesis, even though the contradictory information may be more compelling. In essence, when we use a confirming strategy, we rely on incomplete information, a main source of bad decision making.[18]

So why do we use confirming strategies if they can have such negative consequences? It's cognitively easier to deal with data that confirm. We have more trouble dealing with negative statements. In fact, our preference for positive responses starts early in life. When children are given twenty questions to determine an unknown number between 1 and 10,000, they seek a yes answer. For example, when they ask if the number is between 5,000 and 10,000? and they hear yes, they're happy and they cheer. If they hear no they groan, even though that answer is just as informative (if it's not between 5,000 and 10,000, then it's between 1 and 5,000). Why is that? A no response requires an extra cognitive step.[19] In effect, we appear to have built-in circuitry that prefers yes answers. As we've seen, however, placing too much importance on positive instances can result in believing things that just aren't true.

How can we overcome our penchant for confirming evidence? While the jury is still out, some research suggests the following. Telling decision makers to disconfirm their hypothesis does not always work. One study found that even when people were told to disconfirm, they still sought confirming evidence about 70 percent of the time.[20] A possible solution would be to frame a question in a way that encourages disconfirming evidence. For example, a top investment analyst specifically solicits disconfirming evidence before making a decision. If he thinks a certain industry is becoming less price competitive, he will ask executives a question that implies the opposite, such as, Is it true that price competition is getting tougher?[21] As we saw before, one of the best things we can do to improve our decision making is to consider alternative hypotheses. By considering additional competing hypotheses, we'll likely focus our attention on data that confirm those hypotheses (and possibly disconfirm our initial hypothesis), giving us a more balanced evaluation of the evidence.

Chapter 9: How We Simplify

Simplify, Simplify, Simplify
—Henry David Thoreau

Our decisions can be quite complex. In fact, if we wanted to maximize the accuracy of our judgments, we would have to gather an enormous amount of information. Just consider the decision to get a new job. To maximize the enjoyment, fulfillment, and financial rewards from a new position, we would need to gather data on the type of work involved in a variety of different careers, the educational requirements for those careers, the salaries offered, and on and on. After we picked a career, we would have to investigate all the companies in the field that we could work for. As you can gather, if we did a thorough search to maximize our decision accuracy, we'd spend more time deciding where to work than actually working. We can't live our lives like that. Thus, we use heuristics when we make our decisions.

Heuristics are general rules of thumb that we use to simplify complicated judgments. These simplifying strategies can be quite beneficial: they reduce the time and effort required to make a decision, and they often result in reasonably good decisions. While heuristics give approximate, rather than exact, solutions to our problems, approximate solutions are often good enough. The problem is, heuristics can also lead to systematic biases that result in grossly inaccurate judgments. So let's look at a few of the heuristics we commonly employ, and the biases that arise from their use.[1]

OF COURSE IT'S THE SAME—IT LOOKS THE SAME, DOESN'T IT?

Imagine that you just met Steve, and after talking with him for a time, you develop a thumbnail sketch of his personality. He seems very helpful, but somewhat shy and withdrawn. It also appears that he likes things orderly and has a passion for detail. What do you think is Steve's occupation? Given a choice between a farmer, a salesperson, an airline pilot, a librarian, or a physician, most people say librarian.[2] Why? Steve's characteristics are similar to our stereotypical view of librarians. We often make judgments based on similarity. If A is similar to B, we think A belongs to B. In effect, we think that like goes with like. This strategy is known as the "representativeness" heuristic, because we're making our judgment based on the degree to which A is representative of B.

This heuristic works quite well for many decisions—things that go together are often similar. However, it also causes us to overlook other relevant data, and thus can lead to decision errors. For example, when considering our judgment of Steve's occupation, we overlook the fact that, in any given town, there are many more stores than there are libraries. There are therefore many more salespeople than librarians. Even though you may think that salespeople usually aren't shy and withdrawn, given their much greater number, there are likely to be many that are. In fact, there are likely to be more shy salespeople than there are librarians, so a better answer would be salesman. But we don't pay attention to that background statistic. Instead, we base our judgment on an ambiguous personality description because we think it's representative of a librarian.

Believing that like goes with like also leads us mistakenly to think that one thing causes another. Why? We think that effects should resemble their causes. This has resulted in some pretty strange medical practices over the years. At one time, ground-up bats were prescribed for vision problems in China because it was mistakenly assumed that bats had good vision. In Europe, fox lungs were used for asthmatics because it was thought that foxes had great stamina. Certain alternative medical practices prescribe raw brains for mental disorders.[3] Much of psychoanalysis follows a similar approach to thinking. For example, psychoanalysts maintain that a fixation at the oral stage (the breast) when one is young will lead to a preoccupation in adult life with the mouth, resulting in smoking, kissing, and talking too much.[4] The idea that like causes like is also a fundamental feature of astrology, where people born under a specific sign are believed to have certain personality characteristics. If you're born under the Taurus (bull), you're thought to be strong willed, under Virgo (virgin), you're shy. There is no physical evidence for these beliefs, but the causes and effects have similar characteristics.

And so, basing judgments on similarity can result in a number of bizarre beliefs. Why? When we use the representativeness heuristic we typically ignore other potentially relevant information that should influence our decision. Here are some important decision errors that we fall prey to because of this simplifying strategy.

Neglecting Base Rates

Do you remember the virus test mentioned earlier? Your doctor gave you a screening test for a certain type of virus, and the results came back positive, indicating that you have the virus. How concerned should you be? What if your doctor said:

- The test is 100 percent accurate in indicating a person has the virus when they actually have it.
- The test indicates a person has the virus when they don't actually have it 5 percent of the time.
- The virus is present in one out of five hundred people.

So what's the probability that you actually have the virus? Many people say it's around 95 percent. Recall that the right answer is only around 4 percent! How can that be? Let's use a little logic and number crunching. If one out of five hundred people have the virus, the other 499 don't. However, if the test indicates that a person has the virus when she doesn't in 5 percent of the cases, the test will say that about twenty-five of the virus-free individuals are infected (0.05 times 499). This 5 percent is called a false positive rate, because the test positively identifies a person as having the virus when, in fact, she doesn't. As a result, the test indicates that twenty-six people (twenty-five wrong and one right) out of five hundred have the virus when only one actually has it. One in twenty-six is about 4 percent. So even though the test says you have the virus, there's only about a 4 percent chance you do.[5]

Don't feel foolish if you thought the answer was close to 95 percent. When a similar problem was given to sixty doctors, medical students, and house officers at four Harvard Medical School teaching hospitals, the answer given most frequently was 95 percent. About half of the medical practitioners said 95 percent, while only eleven gave the right answer.[6] Even medical professionals fall prey to judgment errors that relate to their work. As it turns out, intelligent people are usually not trained to think about issues like these in the right way.

There's usually some error associated with most predictive tests. While the virus test indicated a person has the virus when she actually has it 100 percent of the time (the true positive rate), it also indicated a person has the virus when she doesn't 5 percent of the time (the false positive rate). It would be one thing if a test was perfect in prediction, but the overall accuracy is almost never 100 percent. Thus, we first have to consider the base rate—the background statistic—which indicates how often the event occurs. We normally don't think about this background stat, but it's crucial information. In our example, one in five hundred have the virus, which is a base rate of only 0.2 percent. Next, that base rate should be adjusted given the result and "diagnosticity" of the test. To evaluate a test's diagnosticity, we have to compare the true positive and false positive rates. In the virus example, the true positive was 100 percent while the false positive was 5 percent, so we should adjust the base rate by a factor of twenty (100 percent ÷ 5 percent). This number indicates how much information we get from a test—the higher the number, the more the test results should influence our judgment.[7]

The diagnosticity of a test is extremely important when we make decisions based on test information. For example, many people rely on lie detector tests. Police and lawyers use them in criminal investigations, and the FBI uses them to screen employees.[8] However, the diagnostic value of a lie detector test has been estimated to be as low as two to one.[9] As we saw in the medical example, a twenty to one diagnosticity yielded only a 4 percent probability of having a virus, given that the base rate of infection was very low. A lie detector test is much less reliable, indicating that we get little useful information from polygraphs. And yet, lawyers, police, and federal agencies place great emphasis on their results (thankfully, they're not admissible in a court of law). In fact, since the base rate of being a criminal is usually quite low, some argue that the only time you should take a lie detector test is when you're guilty. Why? When the base rate is low, and there's a significant false positive rate, there can be many more cases where the test says guilty for an innocent person than for a guilty person. In effect, there's a chance you may beat the test if you're guilty, while there's a significant chance of being found guilty when you're innocent.

Corporate leaders are also not immune to base rate neglect. For example, auditors use bankruptcy prediction models when they decide the type of audit opinion to report. One study told auditors that a bankruptcy model had a 90 percent true positive and a 5 percent false positive rate, and that about 2 percent of all firms fail. Given this information, there would be a 27 percent probability that a firm will go bankrupt if the model predicts bankruptcy. However, the average probability estimated by audit partners was 66 percent, and their most common response was 80 percent. While these experts seem to perform a bit better than novices, they still do not appreciate the full significance of base rates when making probability decisions.[10]

If base rates are so significant, why do we ignore them? Representativeness is one reason. The test tells us that we have characteristics similar to people with the virus, or that a firm is similar to other firms that have failed, and so we focus on that information. But ignoring base rates could also be due to other reasons as well. Because we are storytellers, not statisticians, we think that background statistics aren't very important. But they are! So what should we do? For crucial decisions, we may want to formally calculate the probabilities. Even if we don't go through formal calculations, however, just knowing that we should pay attention to the background statistics should help us arrive at more informed judgments.

Disregarding Regression to the Mean

At the 2000 British Open, Tiger Woods started the last day with a six-stroke lead—but David Duvall was closing fast. He sank four birdies in five holes, and was within three strokes of Tiger when the announcers exclaimed, "Duvall is on fire—it looks like he's going to catch Woods." But was it realistic to think that Duvall could keep up his blistering pace? If he kept playing at that level, he would have ended the day with a score of 59, unheard of in the world of professional golf. So it's extremely unlikely Duvall could have done it—but the announcers didn't consider that fact. In effect, they didn't take into account a statistical concept known as regression to the mean.

Extreme values of any measurement are typically followed by less extreme values. While very tall parents are likely to have tall children, those children are usually not as tall as their parents; instead, they're closer to the average height of people in general (i.e., they "regress" to the mean of the population).[11] Similarly, if Duvall is making more birdies than normal now, it's likely he will regress to his average and not make them later on in the game.[12] But we often don't consider that fact; rather, we think that he's on a hot streak (or he's got a "hot club").

So what happened at the British Open? Woods won by eight strokes. Interestingly, Woods started the day ahead by six strokes after playing three rounds, which means he was better than the other players by an average of two strokes a day. After the fourth round, he added another two strokes and won by eight. While the numbers don't always work out this simply (e.g., players can have a bad day, as Greg Norman found out when he blew a large lead at the final round of the Masters in 1996), it's very unrealistic to assume that a player's performance on a short sequence of holes (e.g., Duvall's four birdies in five holes) will continue throughout the match. It makes much more sense to assume that his performance will regress back to his average performance.

Our failure to understand regression to the mean can be detrimental to learning. For example, flight instructors in one study noticed that when they praised a pilot for an exceptionally smooth landing, the pilot usually had a poorer landing on the next flight. On the other hand, criticism after a rough landing was usually followed by an improvement on the next try.

The instructors concluded that verbal rewards are detrimental to learning, while verbal punishments are beneficial. But are punishments really better than rewards for learning? It's more likely that we would get such a sequence of events because of regression to the mean.[13]

An often-used management practice, management by exception, is also subject to this bias. With this procedure, managers intervene when very high or low employee performance occurs. Management may therefore attribute any subsequent change in performance to their intervention, when the change may simply be due to employees regressing back to their average performance. Or consider the *Sports Illustrated* jinx. A sports figure often makes the cover of *Sports Illustrated* when he has an outstanding year. In the following year, his performance typically drops off, leading many to believe that making the cover is a curse. But it's just regression to the mean—any outstanding year will likely be followed by one that is not so stellar.

Disregarding Sample Size

What if your town has two hospitals, and about forty-five babies are born each day in the larger hospital, while fifteen are born in the smaller one. As you know, around 50 percent of all babies are boys, but the exact percentage varies from day to day; sometimes it may be higher, and sometimes lower. Over the last year, each hospital recorded the days on which more than 60 percent of the babies born were boys. Which hospital do you think recorded more such days—the larger hospital, the smaller hospital, or would they be about the same (i.e., within 5 percent of each other)?[14]

When asked this question, the majority of people think that both hospitals would have about the same number of days. However, we should expect more 60 percent days in the smaller hospital. Why? There's a greater variability of outcomes in small samples, so there's more chance that seemingly unrepresentative events will occur. But we don't recognize the importance of sample size when making our judgments. Instead, we erroneously believe that small samples are as representative as large samples.

If you flip an unbiased coin six times, which of the following sequences do you think is more likely to occur?

(A) H T H T T H

(B) H H H T T T

Is it A, B, or do they have the same probability? Most people say A, when, in fact, A and B are equally likely. Why is that? Since each coin flip is independent of the next, each has a 1/2 probability of being a head or a tail. To get the probability of each specific sequence, we have to multiply 1/2 by itself six times (the number of times we flip). The result is 1/64, or 1.5 percent, for either sequence. However, we tend to believe that even short sequences of a random process will be representative of that process. Thus, we think that every part of the sequence must appear random, and since random processes switch between heads and tails, option A seems more likely.[15]

As you can see, we have a mistaken belief that small samples will mimic the population more closely than they actually do. We consequently think that small samples are as reliable as large samples when making our judgments. This can lead to all sorts of decision errors. One study showed, for example, that students often select their courses by relying on the recommendations of a couple of students, rather than on the formal written evaluations of dozens of students. Why? Students focus on a few personal accounts, and ignore the unreliability of that small sample size.[16] But small samples are less likely to be representative of the population—a couple of students in class may have very different views than the class as a whole. Realizing that small samples are not as representative as large samples will go a long way in helping us form better beliefs and decisions.

Conjunction Fallacy

You just met Linda, who is thirty-one years old, single, outspoken, and very bright. As a student, she majored in philosophy, was deeply concerned with issues of discrimination and social justice, and participated in antinuclear demonstrations. Which do you think is more likely? (A) Linda is a bank teller, or (B) Linda is a bank teller and is active in the feminist movement.[17] Or consider this decision: What's more likely? (A) an all-out nuclear war between the United States and Russia, or (B) an all-out nuclear war between the United States and Russia in which neither country intends to use nuclear weapons, but both sides are drawn into the conflict by the actions of a country such as Iraq, Libya, Israel, or Pakistan.[18]

If you're like most people, you said B in both cases. In fact, nearly nine out of ten people believe it's more likely that Linda is a feminist bank teller than only a bank teller. Also, more people believe that a war triggered by a third country is more likely. However, these decisions violate a fundamental rule of probability. That is, the conjunction, or co-occurrence, of two events (e.g., bank teller and feminist) cannot be more likely than either event alone. There have to be more bank tellers than bank tellers who are feminists, because some tellers aren't feminists.[19] But we think the description of Linda is representative of a feminist, and so we rely on that similarity information when making our decision. We have to keep in mind, however, that as the amount of detail in a scenario increases, its probability can only decrease. If not, we'll fall for the conjunction fallacy, which can result in costly and misguided decisions. As psychologist Scott Plous indicates, the Pentagon has spent considerable time and money developing war plans based upon highly detailed, but extremely improbable, scenarios.[20]

Stereotyping

Many, if not most, people judge others by using stereotypes. A stereotype is a type of simplifying strategy, because when we use stereotypes we don't spend much time thinking about a person to decide how she will act. We just pigeonhole the person as a certain type, and immediately attribute a variety of characteristics to her.[21] Stereotypes are then perpetuated because our confirming bias causes us to notice things that support the stereotype. So, if we buy in to the view that blonds are dumb, or that the Irish love to drink, we are more likely to notice those people who conform to our preconception and ignore those who don't. Our stereotypes are also reinforced because we typically label different groups, and by using labels we see them as being more different than ourselves. One study found, for example, that if we simply label short lines as A and longer lines as B, people think there is a bigger difference in the length of the lines than if no labels are given at all.[22] Imagine what labels do to our subjective judgments of others.

While stereotypes are simple to use, they can lead to many decision errors. People are very complex creatures. Remember the bell curve? There's a distribution around most things. Within a certain group of people, there will be very intelligent individuals and some that are not very bright, some that like to drink and some that don't. In effect, there is often a much bigger difference in the traits and characteristics between two individuals within a group than there is between groups. Remember, the smaller the sample size, the greater the variability. Pick any one individual from a group, and you can get someone with characteristics that are very different from your preconceived notions of the group. As a result, we need to pay particular attention to our use of stereotypes—they can lead to a number of erroneous judgments concerning the attributes of others.

IT'S WHAT COMES TO MIND

Which do you think is a more likely cause of death in the United States: being killed by falling airplane parts or being eaten by a shark? Most people say shark, but you're actually thirty times more likely to die from falling airplane parts![23] Or consider the following pairs of potential causes of death: (1) poisoning or tuberculosis, (2) leukemia or emphysema, (3) homicide or suicide, (4) all accidents or stroke. Which cause do you think is more likely in each pair? The second cause is more common, but most people choose the first.[24] In fact, we think we're twice as likely to die from an accident as from a stroke, when we're actually forty times more likely to die from a stroke.[25]

Our errors in judging these frequencies are due to a heuristic called availability. When using this heuristic, the estimated frequency or probability of an event is judged by the ease with which similar events can be brought to mind. For example, is it more likely that a word starts with the letter *k*, or that a word has *k* as its third letter? Most of us think that *k* appears more often as the first letter, even though there are twice as many words where *k* is the third letter. Why do we make the error? It's easier to search for words that begin with *k*, while it's tougher to bring to mind words with *k* in the third position.[26] The availability heuristic often serves us well, because common events are usually easier to remember or imagine than uncommon events. However, sensational or vivid events are also easily remembered, and so availability can cause us to overestimate those events.

Suppose you're taking a seven hundred fifty-mile plane trip and your friend drives you twenty miles to the airport. When he drops you off at the terminal, he says, "Have a safe trip." Rarely do you tell him to have a safe trip back home, but, ironically, your friend is three times more likely to die in a car crash on his return trip than you are on your plane trip.[27] While driving a car is more dangerous than flying, phobias about driving are rare, while flying phobias are ubiquitous. Images of plane crashes more easily come to mind given the attention that the media gives to them. In 1986 the number of Americans traveling to Europe dropped sharply because of a few publicized plane hijackings. However, Americans living in cities were in greater danger by staying home. Just consider the effects that the hijackings on 9/11 had on the travel industry in the United States. People stayed closer to home, driving instead of flying, which actually increased their risk of death.

When parents were asked what worried them most about their children, high on the list was abduction, an event that has only a one in seven hundred thousand chance of occurring! Parents were much less worried about their children dying in a car crash, which is well over one hundred times more likely than abduction.[28] Why? Abduction cases are given considerable attention by the media, while car crashes are not. In the mid 1980s, rumors were spread that seventy thousand children had been abducted around the country. It turned out that the figure referred to runaways and children taken by parents involved in custody battles. In fact, the FBI recorded only seven abduction cases by strangers nationwide at that time.[29] But sensational stories get airtime, distorting our evaluation of the risk.

Availability and the Media

As we saw earlier, the beliefs we set are often linked to media coverage. A major reason for this influence is availability. Consider, for example, what happened when George Bush (senior) became president and declared in his first televised address that "the gravest domestic threat facing our nation today is drugs." In the next few weeks the number of drug stories on network newscasts tripled. A survey conducted by the *New York Times* and CBS two months into the media barrage indicated that 64 percent of people thought that drugs were the country's greatest problem. The number was only 20 percent five months earlier.[30]

Research demonstrates that public opinion is linked to media coverage. In one study, the number of stories that included the words *drug crisis* was analyzed, along with changes in public opinion, over a ten-year period. Drugs were sometimes ranked as the country's most important problem by only one in twenty Americans, while at other times nearly two out of three thought it was our most pressing issue. It turned out that the variations in public opinion could be explained by changes in the media coverage.[31] Why is that? When the media plays up drug stories, they more readily come to mind—they're more available to us. And so, our beliefs can easily be manipulated by politicians, or any other special interest group, the media decides to cover—with long-reaching effects.

In an effort to show how pervasive crack cocaine had become in our cities, Bush held up a plastic bag marked evidence during his television address and said, "This is crack cocaine seized a few days ago by drug enforcement agents in a park across the street from the White House." The country was aghast to learn that drugs were being sold right next to the White House. However, the *Washington Post* later learned that Bush asked DEA agents to find crack in Lafayette Park. When they couldn't find a dealer there, they recruited a young crack dealer from another part of town to make a delivery across from the White House. Unfamiliar with the area, the dealer even needed directions to find the park.[32] The push was on to make the public view crack and other drugs as a serious national problem, when, in fact, drug use in the United States had actually declined over the previous decade. The media highlighted crack as "the most addictive drug known to man," even though the Surgeon General reported that less than 33 percent of the people who try crack become addicted, while 80 percent of people who smoke cigarettes for a certain length of time get addicted.[33]

What was the result of such political and media sensationalism? By the end of the 1980s, Congress mandated much harsher prison sentences for the possession of crack cocaine than for the possession of cocaine powder. Since a greater proportion of African Americans used crack (whites used more cocaine powder), by the mid 1990s, three out of four people in prison for drug-related crimes were African American, even though many more whites used cocaine.[34] Consider, also, the media coverage of the anthrax scare after 9/11. Millions of dollars were spent to combat anthrax, which affected only a small number of people. At the same time, a large number of deaths were caused by other infections.[35] And so, while the availability heuristic can provide fairly accurate probability estimates, it can also lead to judgment biases that affect many aspects of our lives. The moral of the story—whenever possible, pay attention to the statistics—not the story!

ANCHORS AWAY

It is well known that many cases of management fraud go undetected. How prevalent do you think executive-level management fraud is in public companies? Do you think the incidence of significant fraud is more than ten in one thousand firms (i.e., 1 percent)? First, answer yes or no. After you answer, estimate the number of firms per one thousand that you think have significant executive level management fraud.[36]

What if I first asked whether you thought there were more than two-hundred fraud cases in one thousand firms? Would that change your overall estimate of the number of firms with fraud? Most people would say, "Of course not—it won't have any effect. I'm just indicating whether my estimate is above or below that number." But, in fact, changing that arbitrary number does affect judgments. For example, when auditors responded to these two conditions, the average number of frauds was sixteen in the first condition (i.e., ten out of one thousand), and forty-three in the second condition (i.e., two hundred out of one thousand). While ten and two hundred should be irrelevant, professionals' judgments of significant executive-level fraud almost tripled when the higher number was given. Why? They were using a heuristic called anchoring and adjustment. When using this heuristic, we select an initial estimate or anchor, and then adjust that anchor as new information is received. Problems arise when we use an irrelevant anchor, or when we make an insufficient adjustment from the anchor.

Now you may say, maybe the researcher was giving the auditors hints about the level of fraud with the initial question, so their estimates should be affected. But that's not the case. Anchoring and adjustment is such a powerful phenomenon that it affects our judgments even when we know that the anchor is totally meaningless. For example, psychologists Amos Tversky and Daniel Kahneman asked people to estimate the percentage of African nations in the United Nations.[37] Before answering, a wheel with numbers one through one hundred was spun and the participants were asked whether their answer was higher or lower than the number on the wheel. Subjects were influenced by that number even though they knew it was determined totally by chance. For example, the median estimates were twenty-five and forty-five for those groups who spun the numbers ten and sixty-five, respectively.

As another example, consider the following case. Without actually performing any calculations, give a quick (five second) estimate of the following product:

$$8 \times 7 \times 6 \times 5 \times 4 \times 3 \times 2 \times 1 = ?$$

What number did you get? When people responded to this problem, their average answer was 2,250. However, another group of individuals was asked to respond to:

$$1 \times 2 \times 3 \times 4 \times 5 \times 6 \times 7 \times 8 = ?$$

Their average was 512, even though the numbers are the same. Why? We anchor on the initial numbers, and since those numbers are higher in the first case, our response is much higher.[38]

Anchoring simplifies our decisions. It allows us to focus on a small amount of information at one time, as opposed to simultaneously considering all the information relevant to a decision. We first pay attention to some initial data, and then adjust our initial impression for any new information we receive. While this approach may be appropriate for many decisions, it can lead to errors when we anchor on initial data that is totally irrelevant to the decision at hand. And even if the initial data is relevant, we often pay too much attention to that data, and thereby fail to make sufficient adjustments when new information becomes available.

Anchoring can affect judgments in many aspects of our personal and professional lives. The prices that we negotiate in our financial decisions are extremely susceptible to anchoring effects. For example, one study found that when retailers and manufacturers negotiated the price of auto parts, an irrelevant initial anchor of $12 resulted in a price of $20.60, while an irrelevant anchor of $32 yielded a price of $33.60.[39]

How much are you going to pay for your new house? One study investigated the appraisal values that real estate agents attach to houses on the market.[40] The agents were given tours of a house and a ten-page packet of information that included all the information normally used to value a house. They were also given different initial listing prices (which should be irrelevant), and were asked to judge what they thought the house was worth. The initial listing prices ranged from $119,900 to $149,900, which caused the agents' appraisal values to increase from $114,204 to $128,754. In effect, you could pay $14,550 more for a house just because of an irrelevant initial anchor used by a real estate agent.

Anchoring can also affect your stock decisions. Remember my colleague who thought he could use fundamental analysis to beat the market? He once told me that if a company was selling at $25, and then drops to $3 a share, it's a good investment. This is an anchoring problem. The price we pay for a stock often becomes our anchor when evaluating that stock in the future. In fact, we don't even have to buy the stock, we just have to know what it was selling for at a certain point in time. Just consider how people reacted to the stock price changes of Enron or WorldCom. Enron's stock was selling at close to $90 a share in the year 2000. The price dropped to around $55 early in 2001, and when compared to its high, the stock looked cheap. Many people rushed in to buy at that price, and they looked pretty smart when the price rebounded to over $60. But we all know what happened. By 2002, Enron's stock was selling for twelve cents a share![41] Using anchoring in our decision processes can be quite costly.

Anchoring can have even more severe consequences. Remember the study that investigated the verdicts handed down by juries when told to consider the harshest or most lenient verdict first? Considering the harshest verdict first (standard practice in murder trials) resulted in harsher verdicts handed down than if juries considered lenient verdicts first.[42] Our simplifying strategies can lead to a number of disastrous judgments.

SIMPLIFYING ISN'T ALL BAD

As you can see, we simplify our decisions, and simplifying can get us into trouble. But the picture isn't all gloomy. We obviously make many correct decisions and hold many correct beliefs. If we didn't, we wouldn't have survived very long. In fact, simplifying strategies serve us very well in many instances. When we use availability, we don't conduct an exhaustive search of all the relevant information, we just retrieve data from our memory that's the easiest to remember. This usually works well because we often retrieve common things, and common things are more likely to occur. We think the probability of getting a cold is greater than getting cancer because we see more people with colds, which leads to a correct judgment. However, we also easily retrieve sensational items that are not common, and so we judge their likelihood to be greater than they actually are. As a result, we overestimate the danger from anthrax, drugs, crime, and a host of other risks because the media emphasize these threats, making them foremost in our minds.

Judging by representativeness also can work well, because similar things often go together. However, if we focus only on similarity, we ignore other relevant information that should affect our decision, such as base rates and the reliability of the data. And so, these simplifying strategies can lead us astray. This can happen in the personal decisions we make every day of our lives, as well as in our professional decisions that have severe consequences for large numbers of people. One encouraging point: research suggests that when professionals perform job-related tasks, the biases evident in their judgments are usually not as great as when novices perform abstract tasks.[43] Expert knowledge in decision-making tasks appears to reduce, but not eliminate, biased judgments. The bottom line is, we need to be aware that we use simplifying strategies when making our decisions, and that they can lead to problems, if we're not careful. Recognizing that fact is the first step to correcting a number of our decision errors.

CHAPTER 10: FRAMING AND OTHER DECISION SNAGS

Some people think of the glass as half full. Some people think of the glass as half empty. I think of the glass as too big.

—George Carlin

Imagine that the United States is preparing for an outbreak of an unusual Asian disease that's expected to kill six hundred people. Two different medical programs to combat the disease have been proposed, and their consequences are as follows:

- If program A is adopted, two hundred people will be saved.
- If program B is adopted, there is a 1/3 probability that six hundred people will be saved, and a 2/3 probability that nobody will be saved.

Which of these two programs would you favor?[1] If you're like most people, you would choose program A. Now consider the following case. Imagine, once again, that an outbreak of an Asian disease is expected to kill six hundred people. Two other programs (C and D) are available to combat the disease.

- If program C is adopted, four hundred people will die.
- If program D is adopted, there is 1/3 probability that nobody will die, and a 2/3 probability that six hundred people will die.

Which of these two programs would you favor? Most people choose program D. In fact, psychologists Amos Tversky and Daniel Kahneman found that when these decisions were given to two different groups of people, 72 percent who saw the first context preferred program A, while 78 percent who saw the second context preferred program D. You may not have picked A and D since they were presented side-by-side and you could directly compare them, but if you saw only one condition, there's a strong likelihood you'd pick A in the first case and D in the second. What's wrong with that? Program A is identical to program C, while program B is identical to program D. If two hundred lives will be saved (program A), then four hundred people will die (program C), so to be consistent, if you picked A, you should have picked C.

These two decision scenarios offer the same choices, but we react very differently. Why? The "frame" of the problem has changed. In the first case, we focus on saving lives and are in a gain frame, while in the second scenario we focus on losing lives and are in a loss frame. In essence, our decisions can change if we frame the problem as a gain or a loss. Viewing the proverbial glass as half full or half empty really does affect our judgments!

This framing effect has been found in a variety of personal and professional decision contexts. For example, seventy-one experienced managers responded to a similar decision in a business context. In this case, the managers would either lose $400,000 or save $200,000 if they chose the first alternative. Only 25 percent of the managers chose that alternative when it was framed as losing $400,000, but 63 percent chose it when framed as saving $200,000.[2]

Framing can even affect life and death decisions. One study asked 1,153 patients, doctors, and graduate students if they would choose radiation therapy or surgery for lung cancer. Some saw the decision framed in terms of living, while others in terms of dying. For example, about half were told that, with surgery, there was a 68 percent chance of living for more than one year. The other half was told that, with surgery, there was a 32 percent chance of dying by year's end. Surgery was selected 75 percent of the time in the survival frame and 58 percent in the mortality frame.[3] Even for decisions as important as surgery, many people would make a different choice depending upon the language of the frame. You can imagine the power that some people have to manipulate public opinion just because they know how to ask a question to get their desired response.

So the framing of a decision can affect our choices—but why? It turns out that we have a natural tendency to be risk avoidant for gains and risk taking for losses. To see what I mean, choose between the following two options.

Option A: A sure gain of $1,000
Option B: A 50% chance of gaining $2,000, and a 50% chance of gaining nothing

Most people are risk avoidant for this decision. They want the guaranteed gain of $1,000, as opposed to a gamble where they could gain $2,000, but may also gain nothing. Now consider the following decision:

Option A: A sure loss of $1,000
Option B: A 50% chance of losing $2,000, and a 50% chance of losing nothing

Most people choose B in this case because they don't want to experience a certain loss of $1,000. We're willing to take a chance of losing a greater amount if there's also a chance of losing nothing. In essence, we're generally risk averse for gains (we go for the sure thing) and risk taking for losses (we're willing to take a gamble). That's okay—it's just a natural human tendency. But these risk preferences can cause us problems. As we saw in the "lives saved / lives lost" decision, our judgments for identical alternatives can change just because the options are framed as gains or losses. So we have to be aware that our decision frame can affect our choice. What can we do about it? Whenever possible, frame the decision in different ways and see if your judgment changes. If it stays the same, we can be confident in our choice—but if it changes, we need to think a bit more about our preferences.

We Hate to Lose!

Imagine that you just lost $1,000. How would you feel? Now imagine that you just won $1,000. Most of us would love to win $1,000, but would have a stronger reaction to losing $1,000. A loss of $1,000 is felt more than a gain of $1,000. This is a phenomenon that psychologists call loss aversion—losses loom larger than gains for most of us. In essence, we hate to lose! Our loss aversion is one reason we're willing to take more risks in loss contexts—we just don't want to accept a sure loss.

This desire to avoid losses leads to a number of faulty decisions. For example, investors tend to sell winning investments quickly and hold on to losing investments. Studies show that we're more likely to sell stocks that rise in price rather than those that fall. This is often a bad decision. In fact, one study found that the stocks investors sold outperformed the stocks held by about 3.4 percent over the subsequent twelve months.[4] Why do we do it? We want to lock in a sure gain, and we don't want to accept a sure loss. As a result, we sell stocks that go up in price to realize the gain, and hold stocks that drop, hoping they'll recover. Unfortunately, some of those stocks continue to drop and we lose more money than if we had just cut our losses. In our attempt to avoid the pain of a loss, we hold on to losers much too long, causing us greater pain down the road.

Loss aversion also explains an interesting phenomenon known as the endowment effect. Consider the following decision.

> What if you won a pair of tickets to a sporting event that you want to go to. Someone you don't know finds out that you have the tickets and wants to buy them. What's the minimum price you would be willing to sell the tickets for?

Now assume that you don't have tickets to the sporting event, but you want to go. How much would you be willing to pay someone for the tickets?[5]

We typically demand about twice as much to sell a ticket we already have, compared to the price we would pay to buy the ticket. Why? We don't want to lose what we have. We therefore overvalue what belongs to us and undervalue what belongs to others.[6] As a demonstration, Professor Richard Thaler gave a group of students a coffee mug embossed with their school's logo. When the students were later asked how much they would be willing to sell the mug for, their average price was $5.25. But other students without a mug would only pay an average of $2.75 to buy one.[7] Ownership actually increases the value of what we have.

Our propensity to overvalue the things we have is exploited every day by the business community. Marketers understand that when we buy a product and take it home, the endowment effect will take over and we won't want to return it. And so, we see furniture retailers enticing us to take home a new dining room set today—without starting our payments for one full year. In other cases, we can get a free Internet connection, or a reduced rate on cable TV or phone service, for a number of months. Getting a product on a trial basis or for a reduced initial price lures us in, and once we have it, we're reluctant to give it up.[8]

At some gas stations, fuel is less expensive if purchased with cash instead of credit. Credit card companies encourage the stations to call the difference a cash discount as opposed to a credit card surcharge.[9] Why? Surcharges are seen as out-of-pocket losses, while cash discounts are viewed as gains. Although the fee structure is the same for both, we react more to a surcharge "loss," so we're less likely to use a credit card if a surcharge is involved. Loss aversion may also complicate our negotiations with others, because each party considers its concessions to be losses, and those losses loom larger than the gains received from the other negotiating party. Loss aversion may even explain an incumbent politician's advantage in elections, since the potential loss from an unfavorable change may be viewed to be greater than the potential gain from a favorable change in leadership.[10] Our desire to avoid losses can have far-reaching effects.

MENTAL ACCOUNTS

What if you bought a ticket for $75 to see your favorite sports team play, and when you go to the ballpark, you realize that you lost the ticket. Are you going to spend another $75 to see the game? Now suppose that you go to the ballpark expecting to buy a $75 ticket at the window. When you check your wallet, you realize that you have more than enough money to buy the ticket, but that you just lost $75. Would you buy the ticket?

When people are given decisions like these, most answer no to the first question and yes to the second. One study found, for instance, that only 46 percent of us would buy the ticket in the first case, while 88 percent would buy it in the second.[11] Why is that? In the first case, we put both cash outlays of $75 in the same "mental account" because both amounts relate to buying the ticket. We start to think that the game is costing us $150, which is more than we're willing to spend. In the second case, the two amounts are put in different mental accounts because we don't associate the lost money with the ticket price, and so we buy the ticket. But we're in the same position at the end of the day if we buy the ticket—we get to see the game and we're out to the tune of $150. Yet our decisions differ.[12]

With mental accounting, we pigeonhole our money into different categories or accounts, and then treat that money differently depending upon the account in which it's kept. In fact, we can waste our money because of mental accounts.[13] Traditional economics says that all money should be fungible—it shouldn't matter if it comes from our salary, from a gift, or from gambling winnings. The money in each case should have the same value to us, so we should spend it the same. But that's not how we act. We often spend money which we receive as a gift or from gambling much more freely than money we had to work for. This even applies to our tax refunds. We frequently think of our tax refund as a windfall, and so we're more likely to spend it frivolously. However, a refund is really a deferred payment of our salary, a type of forced savings. If we save money from our paycheck, we typically give considerable thought to how we're going to spend it, but we don't do that with a tax refund. Why? We put the refund into a separate mental account.[14]

I often travel to Australia to present and discuss research projects at various universities. Any stipend that I receive is quickly, and extravagantly, spent. I buy more expensive meals and spend much more on wine and beer. I'll often buy a $75 bottle of wine to have with dinner down under, while back in the United States I spend only around $25. Why? I don't consider my stipend to be part of my normal salary, and so it goes in a different mental account. While I have a great time, I'm making very different financial decisions than I would if I were at home—all because of my mental accounts.

The size of our mental accounts can also affect our financial decisions. How would you act in the following two situations?[15]

> You're at a store to buy some new computer software that costs $100. The salesperson tells you that the same software is on sale at another store that's a ten-minute drive away for $75. Would you go to the other store?
>
> You're at a store to buy a new computer that costs $1,900. The salesperson tells you that the same computer sells for $1,875 at another store that's a ten-minute drive away. Would you go to the other store?

Most of us would go to the other store in the first case, but not the second. The percentage reduction in price should not matter; we should only compare the dollar savings with the time spent to get that savings. However, we use mental accounts and compare the savings to the size of the account. Since we want a good deal, we're more than willing to make the drive to save $25 in the first case, but not the second.[16]

Credit cards are a type of mental account. Somehow, our money gets devalued if we use plastic, which is ironic since credit cards typically cost us more after we factor in the large interest rates. As an example, two professors at MIT conducted a sealed bid auction for tickets to a Boston Celtics game. Half of the participants were told that if they won the bid they would have to pay for the tickets in cash, while the other half were told they would have to pay by credit card. Amazingly, the average credit card bid was about twice as high as the average cash bid![17] Our credit card mental account can cost us big bucks.

Mental accounts can also affect our risk-taking behavior. Finance professor Richard Thaler asked a group of divisional managers if they would invest in a project that had a 50 percent chance to gain $2 million and a 50 percent chance to lose $1 million. The expected value of the project is a profit of $500,000—not a bad investment—but only three out of twenty-five executives would take the gamble.[18] Why? They were using a narrow mental account that included only one investment project, and were not willing to take the chance of losing on the project. But if they expanded their account to include other similar investments, they might be more than willing to take the risk. In fact, when the company

CEO was asked if he would invest in twenty-five such projects, he enthusiastically said yes, because in the long run the company is likely to come out ahead. The moral of the story—if you're too risk averse in your business dealings, you should expand your mental account.[19]

Mental accounts also make us evaluate the results of our financial decisions in a faulty manner. Remember my friend Chris's story? Someone he knew made a killing on just a couple of stock investments. When I asked about his friend's other investments, he downplayed their importance—because they were losers. Many investors put their stock gains in one mental account and their losses in another. They then focus on the gains and explain away the losses (e.g., some outside force beyond their control, like an overall downturn in the economy, may have caused the loss). This is a classic case of focusing on the hits and de-emphasizing the misses. If we want an accurate evaluation of our investment performance, we need to expand our mental account to include both gains and losses.

Do mental accounts lead you to make poor financial decisions? Ask yourself the following two questions: (1) Do I have emergency or other money in a savings account that's not for retirement? (2) Do I owe money on my credit cards that's carried over from month-to-month? If you answered yes to both questions, you're making poor decisions because of mental accounting. Why? You're paying a high interest rate on your debt, and receiving a low rate on your savings. It's better to pay off your credit card, and if you need money for an emergency down the road, put it on the card.[20] When making your personal financial decisions, it's usually smarter to pay off your debt as soon as possible. If you have a $3,300 balance on your credit card and you're charged 18 percent interest, it would take nineteen years to pay off the debt if you make the minimum monthly payment. If you paid just $10 more than the minimum each month, you would pay the debt in only four years and save about $2,800 in interest![21]

So what can we take away from all this? We pigeonhole our money into mental accounts, and that accounting can result in a number of unwise financial decisions. How can we overcome those problems? Treat all your money equally, whether you get it from your salary, savings, gifts, or gambling winnings. One of the best ways to do that is to first put all your money into a savings or investment account before you spend it.

This little bit of advice seemed to help a student in my critical thinking course. He went to a casino and won $800, a considerable sum for an undergraduate student. On his way to blowing his windfall, he stopped and thought about how his mental accounts were affecting his decision. He was in dire need of cash at the time, so he came home with the money, put it in the bank, and used it to live off of for a couple of weeks. It's one thing if you have excess money to blow, but if not, treating all your money equally will reduce reckless spending and result in more informed financial decisions.

20/20 HINDSIGHT

Why do blacks dominate basketball? All sorts of reasons have been proposed, including genetics. Some people believe that blacks are better basketball players because they can jump higher and run faster. Through this logic, it's no wonder blacks are superior at the game; in fact, some people could not imagine it otherwise. But when making such inferences, they're being caught up in the hindsight bias. No matter what the event, people can come up with causal explanations that make the event seem as if it was obvious from the start. It's obvious to many people that blacks dominate professional basketball for genetic reasons. But consider the following facts.

At one time, Jews dominated the game. Basketball was primarily an east-coast, inner-city game from the 1920s to the 1940s, and it was played, for the most part, by the oppressed ethnic group of that time—the Jews. Investigative journalist Jon Entine noted that when Jews dominated basketball, sports writers developed many reasons for their superior play. As he states, "Writers opined that Jews were genetically and culturally built to stand up under the strain and stamina of the hoop game. It was suggested that they had an advantage because short men have better balance and more foot speed. They were also thought to have sharper eyes . . . and it was said they were clever."[22] Paul Gallico, one of the premier sports writers of the 1930s, said the reason basketball appealed to Jews was that "the game places a premium on an alert, scheming mind, flashy trickiness, artful dodging and general smart aleckness."[23] Notwithstanding the insulting stereotype, I'm amazed how we think we know the cause for something after the fact—even if that presumed cause is quite absurd.

Were World War II, the attack on Pearl Harbor, the *Challenger* and *Columbia* space shuttle disasters, and the escalation of the Vietnam War inevitable? With hindsight, people often answer yes. But if these events were so inevitable, why weren't they predicted? There are usually many uncertainties before an event occurs. But when we know the outcome, we forget about those uncertainties and think that the event was likely to happen all along. Psychologist Baruch Fischhoff interestingly demonstrated this tendency with a true historical account of a battle between British forces and the Gurkhas from Nepal.[24] Fischhoff had people read about the battle, told some of them that the British actually won, and told others nothing about the outcome. They then had to assess the likelihood that the British won, the Gurkhas won, or a stalemate occurred, based only upon the battle's description (i.e., assuming they didn't know the outcome). Those who were told the British won thought there was a 57 percent probability of a British victory, while those not told the outcome thought there was only a 34 percent chance that the British won the battle.

Once we know an outcome has occurred, two things happen: (1) The outcome seems inevitable, and (2) We easily see why things happened the way they did. In effect, if we know the outcome of an event, we restructure our memory. We don't remember the uncertainties that were evident before the event occurred; instead, we reconstruct the past given our knowledge of what actually happened.[25] It's the curse of knowledge!

Why is hindsight bias important? For one thing, it affects how we judge others. If our company lost market share and put our job in jeopardy, we may think, "Our CEO should have known that the competition was going to market a new innovation—just look at the evidence." But if we consider all the uncertainties that existed prior to knowing the outcome, we might have made the same decision as the CEO. Hindsight bias also inhibits how we learn from experience, because if we're not surprised by an outcome, we tend not to learn much from that outcome.

So how can we mitigate the problems of hindsight? Just informing people about the bias is typically not enough. As with many other problems discussed here, one of the best ways to reduce the bias is to consider the alternative—consider how an alternative outcome *could* have occurred. In so doing, we pay attention to information that supports an alternative outcome, which should open up the possibility that the actual outcome may not have been obvious from the start.[26]

OVERCONFIDENCE

With all the ways our decisions can go wrong, you would think we'd have a little humility about our ability to make accurate judgments—but we don't. Research has consistently demonstrated that we're overconfident in the judgments we make. And these include the judgments of professionals like doctors, lawyers, security analysts, and engineers. One study showed, for instance, that when doctors diagnosed pneumonia, they were 88 percent confident in their diagnoses, even though their patients had pneumonia only 20 percent of the time. Sixty-eight percent of lawyers believe that they will win their case, when only 50 percent can. When people predicted whether stocks were going to rise or fall from market reports, only 47 percent of their predictions were correct, but their average confidence was 65 percent. Over 85 percent of us think we're better drivers than the average person. In most every aspect of life, we consistently overrate our knowledge and abilities.[27]

Of course, in some cases overconfidence helps us achieve things we normally wouldn't. Few people would start a new business if they thought it wasn't going to succeed, yet over two-thirds of small businesses fail within the first four years of their start-up. However, overconfidence can also cause catastrophic results. Before the space shuttle *Challenger* exploded, NASA estimated the probability of a catastrophe to be one in one hundred thousand launches. That's equivalent to launching the shuttle every day for three centuries! With such confidence, it's no wonder NASA thought they could launch the shuttle under extremely adverse conditions.

Overconfidence also leads to the planning fallacy. Do you normally underestimate the time or expense to complete a project? Most of us do. When students estimated how long it would take to write their theses, their average estimate of 33.9 days fell way short of the 55.5 days it actually took.[28] Government projects are particularly susceptible to the planning fallacy. When the Australian government decided to build the famous Sydney Opera House in 1957, they thought it could be completed by 1963 at a cost of $7 million. In fact, a scaled-down version opened in 1973 at a cost of $102 million. The city of Boston recently constructed a new underground highway system known as the "big dig." The initial estimates indicated the project would be completed in 1998 and cost $2.6 billion. The majority of the work was completed by 2005, with a price tag of over $14 billion![29]

Research consistently reveals little or no relation between our confidence and accuracy. As an example, when clinical psychologists and students repeatedly evaluated patients after receiving increasing amounts of information, confidence in their judgments went up, but accuracy stayed about the same.[30] Particularly disconcerting, psychologist Elizabeth Loftus, who studies the relationship between eyewitness court testimony and accuracy in criminal identification, concluded, "One should not take high confidence as any absolute guarantee of anything."[31] Even when eyewitnesses are extremely confident in their identifications, they are often wrong. Studies have also found no relation between confidence and accuracy when clinicians diagnose brain damage, or when physicians diagnose cancer or pneumonia.[32] In effect, physicians are as confident on the cases they misdiagnose as they are on the cases they diagnose correctly. Just because we think we know something, doesn't always mean we do.

One reason we're overconfident is we remember the hits and forget the misses—we often remember the times we're successful, and forget the times we fail. It's a bit more complicated, however, because sometimes our failures are our most vivid memories. It turns out that even when we remember our failures, we interpret them in a way that still bolsters our belief. Eileen Langer, a Harvard psychologist, calls it the "Heads I win, tails its chance" phenomenon.[33] As we saw with gamblers' behavior, if we're successful, we think the positive outcome was caused by our knowledge and ability. If we're unsuccessful, we think the negative outcome was caused by something we had no control over. As a result, we reinterpret our failures to be consistent with an overall positive belief in our abilities.

So what can we do about overconfidence? Try to think about the reasons why your judgment may be wrong. In a sense, this is similar to considering alternative hypotheses. If we evaluate alternative hypotheses, and the reasons why those alternatives could be correct, we'll implicitly consider evidence contrary to our current belief or judgment, which should keep our overconfidence in check. Considering the alternatives is one of the most effective methods we have to counter many of our problematic judgment biases.

INTUITIVE JUDGMENTS

Since we're often overconfident, we tend to think that our intuitive judgments are quite accurate. When we make intuitive judgments, we collect various pieces of information, evaluate the importance of the information, and then somehow combine the data in a subjective way to arrive at our decision. We like to think that these intuitive judgments are more accurate than just relying on statistical data alone because subjective assessments allow us to use our own personal expertise in the decision process. Of course, these judgments can be pretty good at times. But as you might expect, they can also result in errors and serious consequences. This is especially true when professionals make intuitive judgments that have a significant impact on our lives. Consider, for example, the college admissions decision.

When we apply to college, our fate is in the hands of an admissions committee. While admission members examine hard, statistical data like a student's prior grade point average and SAT scores, they (for some schools) also place considerable importance on interviewing the prospective student. Committee members like to think they can see some intangible quality during an interview that allows them to predict whether the student will be successful in college. They then subjectively assess all the information to arrive at their own intuitive assessment of the applicant.

The problem is, interviews are notoriously unreliable in predicting future success. As psychologist Robyn Dawes points out, it's presumptuous to think that someone can learn more about a student's abilities in a half-hour interview than by examining their grade point average, which describes the student's performance over four years.[34] In fact, personal assessments from interviews can be harmful, because they lack both reliability and validity. Dozens of studies have shown that an interviewer's assessment isn't a good indicator of an applicant's future success—and different interviewers often don't even agree with one another's assessment.[35] Yet, many colleges employ interviews as a main ingredient in their acceptance decisions.

Why do we continue to believe in the value of interviews? We think that our intuitive judgment is better than relying on statistical data. Part of the problem comes, once again, from remembering the hits and forgetting the misses. An admissions committee member is likely to remember the time he accepted a student with poor grades on a hunch, and the student went on to perform very well in school. Such a memory can only bolster one's confidence in his intuitive judgment. Unfortunately, the committee member is likely to forget the times he accepted a student on a hunch, and the student performed poorly. It's no wonder that we think we have special skills that just can't be replicated by relying on only statistical data. In addition, we think it's just not right to base major decisions on statistics alone—we think it's soulless. Many students would vehemently complain if rejected based solely on their past statistics, arguing that they need to be interviewed to uncover their true potential as a student.

The fact is, however, volumes of research indicate that we would make more accurate decisions if we relied on statistical predictions instead of intuitive predictions. With statistical prediction, we don't use our subjective judgment to assess and combine different bits of information. Instead, we combine the information statistically or mathematically. In the college admissions case, for example, we can just add up a student's grade point average, SAT score, and numerical evaluations of recommendation letters, and then use that sum to predict a student's future success in college.[36] The higher the number, the more likely the student will perform well. No overall subjective assessment is needed.

Decades of research have demonstrated that such simple statistical models do a better job than intuitive judgments in many decision contexts. In fact, statistical prediction has been shown to be better than intuitive prediction in over one hundred studies. These include predicting the success of students in college, the suicide attempts of psychiatric patients, the job satisfaction of engineers, the growth of corporations, when a parolee will violate their parole, whether patients are neurotic or psychotic, the amount of psychiatric hospitalization required, and a patient's response to electroshock therapy.[37] And, in most all of these cases, experts are providing the intuitive predictions.

For example, one study investigated the accuracy of the graduate admissions committee at the University of Oregon. The committee used their professional judgment to predict the future success of students, given information like undergraduate grade point average (GPA), Graduate Record Exam (GRE) scores, and assessments of the quality of the undergraduate institution.[38] The judgments of the admissions committee were then correlated with student performance in school after a two- to five-year period (based on faculty ratings at that time). It turned out that they correlated only 0.19, a very poor accuracy rate. In contrast, just adding up student scores on the relevant variables (e.g., GPA, GRE scores, etc.) yielded a correlation of 0.48. We would be more accurate if we just relied on basic statistical data combined in a very simple way, as opposed to relying on the intuitive assessments of the professionals. [39]

What about the decision to grant a criminal parole? Parole boards rely heavily on interviews with criminals. One study found that out of 629 criminals who were granted parole, all but one of the decisions were consistent with the recommendation of the interviewer. But was the interviewer's intuitive judgment any good? The parole board thought that about 25 percent of their decisions were failures within one year of release because the parolee committed another crime or violated parole. A model that used only background statistics, like the type of crime originally committed, the number of past crimes, and the number of prison rules violated, was much more accurate than an interviewer in predicting these failures.[40]

Even the intuitive predictions of medical doctors can be poor when compared to statistical predictions. One study had doctors estimate the life expectancies of 193 patients with Hodgkin's disease. Although the doctors thought they could accurately make the prediction, their judgments were totally unrelated to a patient's survival time, and a statistical model performed considerably better.[41] One area in which statistical prediction is used extensively is in loan applications. About 90 percent of consumer loans and all credit card issuances are based on statistical models, which is probably a good thing, because when experienced bank officers rated the creditworthiness of clients, more of their selections resulted in defaults as compared to those chosen by a statistical model.[42] In effect, considerable research indicates that the intuitive judgments of professionals often don't add much beyond what we would get from just relying on statistics. In fact, for most of the decisions investigated, intuitive judgments are worse. But we are still very confident in our intuitive decision making.

Why are these expert judgments so poor? Some things are difficult to predict because the information we have isn't very good. For example, there may be no reliable test available to determine if a person has a certain psychological or physical disorder (of course, we usually try to make the prediction nonetheless). In other cases, the information we have is useful, but we may misinterpret or misuse that information (e.g., we often overvalue less important information and undervalue more important data). In addition, if we have to make a large number of decisions, as in the admissions committee case, we may not apply our decision strategy consistently. We're not machines—we have our days. Sometimes we're bored, sometimes we're distracted, and sometimes we're tired. As a result, we may make different decisions at different times, and that inconsistency increases our decision errors.[43] Statistical models, on the other hand, don't get tired, bored, or distracted—they always apply the same decision rule, time after time.

And so, many of our decisions would be more accurate if we relied on statistical prediction rather than intuitive judgments. Of course, I'm not advocating that we never rely on professional judgment. We obviously need the advice of doctors, lawyers, and other professionals for many of the decisions we face in life. Doctors have expert knowledge of current medical practices that can save our lives. But we have to recognize the limits in our ability to predict. As we've seen, predicting many different types of future events is very difficult, especially if they involve human behavior. The research indicates that intuitive judgments do not provide great insight into these decisions. While many professionals believe they have expert insight that allows them to make these predictions, the fact is, relying on statistical prediction would result in better decision making. As psychologist Stuart Sutherland has said, "Suspect anyone who claims to have good intuition."[44]

JUDGMENTS ABOUT INDIVIDUALS VERSUS GROUPS

You may have heard the phrase, "Statistics don't apply to the individual." We may know, for example, that 70 percent of people with a certain disease will die within a year, but that doesn't tell us whether a specific person with the disease will die. Or we may hear that 60 percent of people coming from a certain socioeconomic background will commit a crime, but, once again, we don't know if a specific individual with that background will turn to crime. But remember, we have an inherent desire to predict things. As a result, many people, including professionals, believe they can use their intuitive insight to make predictions about an individual's behavior.

Take, for instance, the field of clinical psychology. Some clinical psychologists claim that their training gives them unique insight into how an individual will act, beyond what we can get from general statistics. They're routinely brought into our courtrooms to provide expert testimony on an individual's psychological state—and they make their pronouncements with a great deal of confidence.[45] The problem is, the field of psychology, and the social sciences in general, don't give us that kind of information. Psychology does not allow us to make definitive predictions about a single individual; instead, it indicates the tendencies that exist in a group of individuals.[46] As a result, intuitive judgments about individuals are frequently in error. The best information we have available to make such judgments is, once again, general statistics.

How do we know that clinical prediction is no better than just relying on statistics? There's no evidence to indicate that years of experience as a psychotherapist leads to a better patient outcome. Also, studies have found that licensed clinical psychologists do no better than unlicensed practitioners (e.g., social workers).[47] In fact, psychologist Robyn Dawes argues that "the effectiveness of therapy is unrelated to the training or credentials of the therapist. We should take seriously the findings that the best predictors of future behavior are past behavior and performance on carefully standardized tests, not responses to inkblot tests or impressions gained in interviews, even though no prediction is as good as we might wish it to be."[48]

The bottom line is, we can be reasonably confident only in our aggregate predictions; that is, how a group of people will tend to behave. Any attempt to predict the behavior of a single individual is open to so much error and uncertainty that, either we should not do it at all, or it should be done with strong caveats.[49] As Dawes states, "A mental health expert who expresses a confident opinion about the probable future behavior of a single individual (for example, to engage in violent acts) is by definition incompetent, because the research has demonstrated that neither a mental health expert nor anyone else can make such a prediction with accuracy sufficient to warrant much confidence."[50] Yet such opinions are given every day in our courts of law.

Since psychology finds general tendencies in groups of people and doesn't allow us to accurately predict what an individual from the group will do, the conclusions discussed here relate to our general tendencies. When I say we're risk avoidant for gains and risk taking for losses, we search out confirming evidence, or we see associations that are not there, I mean that there's a tendency for us to act in these ways. But we can't predict with certainty how any one of us will act, no matter how hard we try. The best we can do is make probabilistic assessments based upon general statistics.[51] While statistics don't apply to the individual, they allow us to say things like, "Based on past statistics, there's a 70 percent chance that a person with this disease will die within a year." It's not perfect, but it's the best we can do. Anything else, and we're just fooling ourselves.

Chapter 11: Faulty Memories

I have a photographic memory, but once in a while I forget to take off the lens cap.

—Milton Berle

Do you remember the repressed-memory example discussed earlier? A policeman comes to your door, reads you your rights, and slaps on a pair of handcuffs. As you're carted off to jail, you learn that your twenty-eight-year-old daughter has accused you of molesting her when she was eight. Why does she believe it? She recently started therapy for some emotional issues, and the therapist thought that childhood abuse might be the cause of her current problems. Your daughter had no prior recollection of abuse, but when the therapist put her under hypnosis, she started to remember a number of vivid instances when you sexually molested her. The police were called in, and on the testimony of her twenty-year-old memory, you're sent to prison for thirty years—even though you know you didn't do it! It sounds crazy, but similar events have occurred in the United States. How can this happen? It all has to do with how our memory works.

IT'S THERE, I KNOW IT IS

Many of us think that our memory is a permanent store of past experiences. For example, which of the following two statements best reflects your view of how memory works?[1]

(1) Everything we learn is permanently stored in the mind, although sometimes particular details are not accessible. With hypnosis, or other special techniques, these inaccessible details can eventually be recovered.
(2) Some details that we learn may be permanently lost from memory. Such details would never be able to be recovered by hypnosis, or any other special technique, because these details are simply no longer there.

If you chose the first option, you're not alone. When psychologists asked people from various parts of the United States this question, approximately 75 percent selected the first description. We seem to think that our memories are literal snapshots of our experiences. Of course, we can't remember everything; in fact, we often complain about our memories. But when we say we have poor memories, we typically mean that we can't recall things at the present time. We think the memory is stored somewhere—we just can't bring it to mind right now. And, when we do recall something, and are confident in that recollection, we think the memory is quite accurate. But this is not how our memory operates.

As time passes, new experiences can change the memory we have for past experiences, without our even knowing it. In effect, our memory is a reconstruction of the past. Every time we recall a past event we reconstruct that memory, and with each successive reconstruction, our memory can get further and further from the truth. As Elizabeth Loftus and Katherine Ketcham state, our memory can be changed "by succeeding events, other people's recollections or suggestions, increased understanding, or a new context . . . truth and reality, when seen through the filter of our memory, are not objective facts, but subjective, interpretive realities."[2] As a result, our recall of the past is not fixed in stone. It is constantly changing—some memories are lost, while others are transformed.

To illustrate this point, two British psychologists secretly recorded a discussion that occurred at a Cambridge Psychological Society meeting. Two weeks later, the participants of the discussion were asked to write down everything they could remember. It turned out that they omitted about 90 percent of the specific points discussed, and when something was recalled, nearly half of the items were substantially incorrect. The individuals transformed off-the-cuff remarks into full-blown discussions, and remembered hearing comments that were never actually made.[3]

Even our memories of surprising and emotionally charged events can be in error. Do you remember how you heard about the space shuttle *Challenger* and *Columbia* disasters, or the collapse of the World Trade Center? The details of these flashbulb memories, as they are sometimes called, are often very vivid. We remember the place we heard the news, who told us, how we felt, and so on. Years after the event has occurred, these "facts" are ingrained in our memory. But are they always as accurate as we think they are?

Shortly after the space shuttle *Challenger* explosion in January 1986, researchers asked a number of students how they first heard the news.[4] They asked those same students the identical question two and a half years later. Most of the students said their two-and-a-half-year-old memories were accurate—but not one of their memories was entirely correct, and more than a third were very inaccurate. In addition, the students were so confident in their memories that when they learned of their inaccuracies, they still didn't believe their revised memories were mistaken. In fact, they insisted their current memories were more accurate than what they said right after the *Challenger* exploded! As psychologist Ulric Neisser indicated, original memories are not just there—they are replaced with new, reconstructed realities.[5]

What about the recall of people who have photographic memories? Do you remember the Watergate scandal that occurred during the Nixon presidency? When White House counsel John Dean testified in front of the House committee investigating the scandal, he gave a number of highly detailed accounts of conversations with Nixon that seemed to be verbatim memories of what actually happened. At the time, people thought that Dean was amazing—he obviously had a photographic memory. But did he? Dean remembered the following from a meeting with Nixon and Robert Haldeman on September 15, 1973:

> The President asked me to sit down. Both men appeared to be in very good spirits and my reception was very warm and cordial. The President then told me that Bob—referring to Haldeman—had kept him posted on my handling of the Watergate case. The President told me I had done a good job and he appreciated how difficult a task it had been and the President was pleased that the case had stopped with Liddy. I responded that I could not take credit because others had done much more difficult things than I had done. As the President discussed the present status of the situation, I told him that all I had been able to do was to contain the case and assist in keeping it out of the White House. [6]

Fortunately for us (not for Nixon), the President taped his conversations. When the tapes were played back, it was revealed that Nixon did not ask Dean to sit down, did not say Haldeman kept him posted, or that Dean did a good job, and did not mention Gordon Liddy. In effect, Dean remembered the gist of the conversation—that Nixon knew about the cover up—but a number of the specific details were changed or added. The bottom line is, our memory is not an exact copy of reality. We can forget some details that occurred and change others without even realizing it. Even more troubling, we may create entirely new memories that didn't actually happen, and these erroneous memories can lead to a number of severe consequences.

IF YOU SAY SO—THE POWER OF SUGGESTION

Consider the following true story. A young woman was sexually assaulted in 1987. Her assailant was caught and sentenced to eighteen months in prison, but the woman continued to be plagued by nightmares. To cope with her feelings of grief and rage, she sought the help of a therapist. In the midst of therapy, she began to believe that her parents sexually abused her as a child, and that her dreams were manifestations of those repressed memories. The woman told her sister and sister-in-law to keep their children away from their grandparents. A little worried, the sisters took their children to a therapist who specialized in childhood sexual abuse. While in therapy, one of the children started having nightmares of frightening creatures that she identified as her grandparents. The therapist diagnosed the children with post-traumatic stress disorder, supposedly caused by sexual abuse, and the grandparents were arrested.

During the trial, the children testified that their grandparents made them touch their genitals. One child also said her grandparents put her in a giant cage in the basement, and threatened to stab her mother in the heart if she told. Because of these memories, the grandparents were convicted of multiple counts of rape and indecent assault and battery. No physical evidence existed to corroborate any of the charges. However, the grandparents were sentenced to nine to fifteen years in prison because of memories that didn't exist until someone had a bad dream.[7]

In the 1980s and 1990s, a number of therapists were proclaiming that victims often repress childhood sexual abuse, and that these memories could be recalled by hypnosis and other suggestive techniques. These therapists believed that if a memory could not be recalled, the person must have repressed it to protect herself from an emotionally overwhelming event. They also thought that when an unpleasant memory is buried from a person's consciousness, the emotions attached to the memory can bubble up and cause havoc in her day-to-day life. To deal with these problems, the therapists thought the memories must be recovered.

A variety of methods have been used to recover these so-called lost memories. Therapists put people under hypnosis, asked them to visually imagine the event, and asked a number of suggestive and leading questions. They also had their clients read books on recovered memories, watch videotapes of talk shows on recovered memories, and participate in group counseling with others who supposedly had recovered memories. Clients usually had no memories of sexual abuse at the outset, but developed them after weeks and months of this therapy.[8]

These suggestive techniques have led many people to believe they were sexually abused in childhood. In fact, in 1988 Ellen Bass and Laura Davis published *The Courage to Heal: A Guide for Women Survivors of Child Sexual Abuse*, which sold 750,000 copies and started a recovered memory movement that involved dozens of books, talk show programs, and magazine articles. The problem seemed so pervasive that Bass and Davis estimated that as many as one third of all women were sexually abused as children.[9] Surely some were abused, but do these estimates make sense? Are these recovered memories accurate? Many people think so and, in fact, a number of people are in jail because they were convicted on nothing more than a recovered memory.

But can false memories be created? A considerable amount of research indicates that memories can be created by the suggestions of others, especially when hypnosis and other suggestive techniques are used. For example, Martin Orne, one of the world's leading experts on hypnosis, put subjects in a hypnotic state after they were asleep for the entire previous night. While under hypnosis, he asked the subjects if they heard two loud noises during the night (the noises didn't actually occur). The subjects typically said that they heard the noise, awoke, and went to investigate what happened. If Orne asked when the noise occurred, they gave a specific time. Thus, Orne obtained very specific responses to events that didn't happen just by asking leading questions during hypnosis. And, when the subjects came out of their hypnotic state, they actually believed the events occurred. In essence, Orne's leading questions produced erroneous memories.[10]

In another series of studies, adults were put under hypnosis and told that they lived in an exotic culture, and were a different sex and race, in a previous life. A significant number of them actually developed "past life identities" that reflected the experimenter's suggestions. When other people were told that they were abused as children, they reported more abuse than people who were not given the suggestion.[11] And so, false memories can easily be implanted with the use of hypnosis, leading questions, and other suggestive techniques.

These suggestive techniques are so powerful that the accused may actually start to believe they committed the crime. Consider, for example, another amazing case in which a young woman accused her father of sexually abusing her when she was a child.[12] The woman gave a detailed story to police investigators, claiming that the abuse began in primary school, and that her father would have sex with either her or her sister. Her father had no memory of abusing his children. During his interrogation, however, detectives told him that he buried his memories because he couldn't face the fact of what he did to his own children. They offered him bits and pieces of information from his daughters' statements, hoping to stimulate his memory, and kept repeating three statements: (1) His daughters would not lie about something like this; (2) Sex offenders often repress their own crimes; and (3) If he admitted the allegations, his memories would return.[13] After hours of interrogation, he began to remember events similar to those the detectives described. The visions were sometimes distant, but when he produced an image, the detectives (or attending therapist) would ask a leading question to bring them into focus. In the end, he confessed to sexually molesting his daughters on numerous occasions, and impregnating one of them when she was fifteen, later arranging for an abortion.

Over the next two months, the accusations grew from sexual abuse to satanic ritual abuse, alleging blood drinking, cannibalism, ritual abortions, sadistic torture, and the murder of twenty-five babies. The two girls then accused their mother and two others of belonging to a cult and having sex with the girls on numerous occasions. There was no physical evidence that the girls had been abused, sexually or otherwise. There also was no evidence of infant murders or animal mutilations, and the two daughters' memories often conflicted with one another.[14]

Because the girls' stories were becoming increasingly more bizarre, Richard Ofshe, an expert on cults and mind control from the University of California at Berkeley, was brought in to evaluate the case. Ofshe conducted a field experiment, telling the father, "I was talking to one of your sons and one of your daughters, and they told me about . . . a time when you made them have sex with each other while you watched. Do you remember that?" He did not. Why should he—Ofshe made up the story. However, Ofshe assured him it happened, and that both children remembered it. Ofshe said, "Try to think about the scene, try to see it happening." In time, the father began to recover a "memory" of the event, and later handed Ofshe a three-page handwritten confession, complete with dialogue about the forced incestuous relation between his son and daughter. When Ofshe told him that he fabricated the entire story, the father became agitated and insisted that the images were real—as real as all of the other images he remembered.[15]

The court decreed a sentence of twenty years for six counts of rape. The other charges of satanic ritual abuse were dropped due to lack of evidence, as were the charges against his wife and two friends. At the sentencing hearing, the defendant denied ever sexually abusing his children, crimes he confessed to just one year earlier. Unfortunately, as Loftus and Ketcham state, "Confessions, unlike memories, do not fade with time.

Tape recorded, signed, and sealed, they stay on the books, uncontaminated and intact, forever."[16]

During the Salem witch trials of 1692, nineteen people were hanged, one was pressed to death, and hundreds were jailed. We like to think that things like that can't occur today, but unbelievable things are happening. We have our own brand of witch trials in the form of repressed memory cases. Even without physical evidence of abuse or other criminal behavior, people are sitting in jail cells because of recovered false memories. Fortunately, these witch hunts typically run their course. Science eventually weighs in and lawsuits are filed. For example, the Associated Press reported that a jury ordered therapists and an insurance company to pay $5.08 million to the family of a woman for making her falsely believe she was abused by her relatives.[17] After such events, movements like recovered memory typically die out, but many people are left to pick up the pieces of their destroyed lives.

False Memories for the Rest of Us

Now you may say, "I agree, if you put a person through hypnosis you can create a false memory, but that doesn't happen in our everyday lives." The fact is, we don't have to go through therapy, hypnosis, or serious interrogation to have memories implanted in our brains. False memories can be created by simple suggestions and leading questions. For example, studies have asked adults to remember events that supposedly occurred in their childhood, some of which were true (provided by a family member), and some false (fabricated by the researcher). False events included being lost in a shopping mall or staying overnight at a hospital for a possible ear infection. In these studies, people were typically asked to think about the events for a few days or write detailed descriptions of what happened. When interviewed days later, anywhere from 20 percent to 40 percent of people believed the false event actually occurred. In fact, false memories have even been created for traumatic events like serious animal attacks or accidents in about one third of people tested. And so, it's possible to implant entirely false memories in some individuals simply by asking them to remember the event, write it down, or continue to think about it.[18]

Memory reconstruction does not just apply to events that occurred in early childhood. We also reconstruct our recent experiences. To illustrate this fact, students were shown films of traffic accidents and then asked, "About how fast were the cars going when they 'smashed' each other?" Other students responded to the question with the verb *smashed* changed to either *hit*, *collided*, *bumped*, or *contacted*. Those who saw the word *smashed* estimated the automobile speed to be 40.8 mph, while those who saw *contacted* estimated the speed at 31.8 mph.[19] So the mere suggestion of a more extreme verb led to increased speed estimates. But did that affect memory? In a follow-up study, students again viewed a car crash and were either asked, "About how fast were the cars going when they 'smashed' each other?" or "About how fast were the cars going when they 'hit' each other?" One week later, they were asked whether they saw any broken glass in the accident film (in fact, there was no broken glass). When the question contained the word *smashed*, 32 percent said there was broken glass, while only 14 percent of those who saw the word *hit* remembered the glass. Thus, some students who thought the collision was more severe actually reconstructed their memory to include broken glass.[20]

In another study, subjects saw a film of a car stopped at a stop sign. Some subjects were then asked whether a second car passed the first car when it was stopped at the stop sign, while other subjects responded to the question with the words *stop sign* changed to *yield sign*. When the question mentioned a stop sign, 79 percent of the subjects correctly identified the sign as a stop sign when asked later. However, when the question mentioned a yield sign, only 41 percent accurately identified the sign as a stop sign. A simple change in the wording of subsequent questions can create inaccurate memories.[21]

This reconstruction from suggestive questioning can even occur for real-life events. In 1992 an El Al cargo plane crashed just after takeoff, killing forty-three people. Researchers questioned 193 individuals about the crash, asking them whether they had seen the television film that captured the moment when the plane hit the apartment building. More than half of the people (107) reported seeing the film—but there was no film of the crash![22]

MIXING THINGS UP— THE PROBLEM OF MISATTRIBUTION

I was having lunch with a number of colleagues one day when my friend Dick started to tell an amazing story about something that had happened to his wife. We were all laughing at the absurdity of the situation that his wife found herself in, when another colleague at the table said, "Didn't that just happen on *The Simpsons* last week?" It turned out that Dick mixed up what happened on the TV show *The Simpsons* with his wife's account of what happened to her during the day. While it may seem hard to believe, this is a very common memory error, called misattribution.[23]

We have a tendency to take past experiences and jumble them up. We attribute one person's comments to someone else, or think we did something at one time or place, when, in fact, it was actually at another time or place. This misattribution can contribute to the memory errors that we make when asked suggestive and leading questions. For example, it's possible that people recalled seeing the El Al plane crash on TV because they misattributed a film they saw for another crash to the El Al crash. People may have believed they were lost in a mall because they combined a genuine experience of being lost someplace with their actual memories of the mall in question.[24]

Former President Ronald Reagan had a habit of misattributing fiction to fact. When running for office in the early 1980s, he repeatedly told a story of a World War II bombing raid over Europe. After a B-1 bomber was hit by antiaircraft fire, the gunner cried out that he couldn't eject from his seat. To comfort him, the captain of the plane said, "Never mind, son, we'll ride it down together." Reagan ended the story by noting that the commander was posthumously awarded the Congressional Medal of Honor for his heroism. A journalist curious about the story researched the incident and found no record of the award. However, he did find a scene in a 1944 movie called *A Wing and a Prayer* that sounded very similar to Reagan's account. In the movie, the captain of a Navy bomber rode the plane down with his wounded radioman, saying, "We'll take this ride together." When the White House was questioned about the story Reagan presented as reality, a spokesman replied, "If you tell the same story five times, it's true."[25]

Eyewitness Court Testimony

Misattribution can have severe consequences in many aspects of life. Consider the case of Timothy Hennis, a sergeant in the US Army. Hennis was convicted of murdering three people in July 1986, even though he had an airtight alibi at the time that the murders were committed.[26] Why was he convicted? An eyewitness positively identified Hennis as the man walking down the victims' driveway about 3:30 am on the night of the murders. Another eyewitness remembered seeing Hennis use a bank ATM around the same time that someone with one of the victim's stolen ATM card withdrew money from her bank account.

There was a complete lack of physical evidence to convict Hennis—no fingerprints or hair samples matched him. In the opinion of the experts, the bloody footprints found in the house were made by a size 8½ to 9½ shoe, while Hennis wore a size 12. There were no traces of blood on his clothing, and no physical evidence in his car. In fact, an expert told the jury that there wasn't one piece of evidence that tied Hennis to the crime scene.

After two days of deliberation, the jury found Hennis guilty of murder and the judge sentenced him to death by lethal injection. The testimony of the two eyewitnesses sealed his fate. But did the eyewitnesses really see Hennis? Six months before the trial, one eyewitness admitted that he could have been mistaken in his identification. He even signed an affidavit to that effect. In fact, prior to seeing a photo lineup, he initially described the man as having brown hair, standing six feet tall, and weighing about 167 pounds. Hennis was blond, six-foot-four, and weighed 202 pounds. In addition, the other eyewitness initially told the police and lawyers that she didn't see anyone at the bank that day.

Why were these two people so positive at the trial when they pointed their finger at Hennis and said that he was the one? Were they lying? Not necessarily. After months of television and newspaper coverage reporting that they may have seen the murderer, they could have reconstructed their memories. In fact, the eyewitness at the ATM machine may have seen someone who looked similar to Hennis at another time, and then misattributed that recollection to her ATM memory. And when this reconstructed memory was rehearsed for police, she began to accept it as fact.[27]

In a similar fashion, the other eyewitness likely felt pressure to remember something for the police and lawyers, and after months of rehearsing an initially fuzzy memory, he could have firmly believed he saw Hennis walking down the driveway. Timothy Hennis was fortunate enough to receive a new trial and was found innocent due to a lack of physical evidence. Interestingly, while waiting on death row, he received several anonymous notes, thanking him for taking the rap and doing the time.

Pretty scary stuff! No one really knows how many people are sitting in a jail cell because of faulty eyewitness testimony. But consider the following. It's been estimated that every year in the United States there are over seventy-five thousand criminal trials that are decided on the basis of eyewitness testimony. In addition, a recent study analyzed forty cases where DNA evidence proved that the wrong person was imprisoned. Thirty-six of those cases, or 90 percent, involved erroneous eyewitness testimony.[28]

And yet, we place significant importance on eyewitness accounts. Elizabeth Loftus conducted a study where people, acting as jurors, heard a description of a robbery/murder, along with the prosecution and defense arguments. When the jurors heard only the circumstantial evidence in the case, 18 percent found the defendant guilty. However, when they heard the exact same evidence with one difference—the testimony from a single eyewitness—72 percent of the jurors found the defendant guilty. Such is the power of eyewitness testimony. As Loftus concluded, "Anyone in the world can be convicted of a crime he or she did not commit . . . based solely on the evidence of a witness that convinces a jury that his memory about what he saw is correct."[29]

Why is eyewitness testimony so powerful? As noted, many of us tend to think that our memories are permanently recorded, like nonerasable computer disks or videotapes. But as we have seen, our memory is not a literal copy or snapshot of an event; rather, it's a fragmentary and often-distorted representation of reality.[30] Unfortunately, we are particularly susceptible to misattribution errors in eyewitness accounts. Studies reveal, for example, that when people are shown pictures of two different faces, they later remember seeing a picture of a new face they had never seen before. Why? The new face had some of the characteristics of the two faces they did see. We make memory-conjunction errors, where we take attributes from different faces (e.g., eyes, nose, mouth) and combine them into a new face.[31]

In essence, we typically just get a general sense of familiarity of the facial features we see—which can be a recipe for disaster in eyewitness identification. Consider how police proceed in a criminal investigation. If you have some recollection of what a criminal looks like, you usually review a lineup or look through a set of photographs to make a positive ID. Psychologist Gary Wells has demonstrated that these common police procedures can actually promote misattribution, because witnesses are encouraged to rely on familiarity. Wells found that when witnesses see all the suspects and then have to identify the criminal (like in a lineup), they base their decision on relative judgments. That is, they pick the person who looks most like the suspect relative to the others in the lineup. The problem is, a witness will often select the person who looks most like the criminal even when the criminal isn't part of the lineup. One way to overcome this problem is to have witnesses make a "thumbs up or thumbs down" assessment on each suspect viewed individually. In fact, given these scientific findings, some police forces are incorporating such procedures in an effort to increase eyewitness accuracy.[32]

Eyewitness testimony is also powerful because eyewitnesses are often very confident in their identifications. As we've seen, however, confidence and accuracy do not necessarily coincide. In fact, confidence can be influenced by the mere suggestions of police and lawyers. For example, one study had subjects view a security video of a man entering a department store. They were told that the man murdered a security guard, and were asked to identify the person from a set of photos (the gunman was not in the set). Some of the people received confirming feedback—they were told they correctly identified the suspect. Others received disconfirming feedback or none at all. Those people receiving confirming feedback were more confident in their decisions, trusted their memories more, and said they actually had a better view of the gunman. Of course, they were wrong, but their confidence would play well in court. As psychologist Daniel Schacter says, "Eyewitness confidence bears at best a tenuous link to eyewitness accuracy: witnesses who are highly confident are frequently no more accurate than witnesses who express less confidence."[33]

WHERE DOES THIS LEAVE US?

Like our perception of the external world, our memory of past events is constructive. Memories can be influenced by suggestive and leading questions, and we can mix up past experiences to create new, reconstructed memories. As with perception, the memories we retrieve can also be biased by what we want and expect to believe. For example, one study showed people a picture of a white man and a black man talking in the subway. The white man had a straight razor in his hand. When later asked to recall the picture, half of the subjects said the razor was in the black man's hand. An erroneous memory was created because of what this group of people expected to see.[34] As psychologist Daniel Schacter states, "remembering the past is not merely a matter of activating or awakening a dormant trace or picture in the mind, but instead involves a far more complex interaction between the current environment, what one expects to remember, and what is retained from the past. Suggestive techniques tilt the balance among these contributors so that present influences play a much larger role in determining what is remembered than what actually happened in the past."[35]

Of course, it's impossible to discuss the many different ways our memories can go wrong here.[36] But I believe that the point is made. We can't just accept our memory for an event as reality. Even if we're very confident in a memory, we may still be very wrong. As with many of the topics we're exploring here, however, all is not bad. We often remember things quite well. In addition, as with decision heuristics, some of our memory problems are the result of rather useful strategies. If we remembered every detail of our past experiences, we would quickly reach information overload and have a difficult time functioning. For all its vices, our memory still allows us to function quite well. However, we have to be aware that our memories can be in error, and that those errors can have a significant influence on our beliefs and decisions.

CHAPTER 12: THE INFLUENCE OF OTHERS

If fifty million people say a foolish thing, it is still a foolish thing.

—Anatole France

You're seated in a small, windowless room. On the table in front of you is a large shock generator with a row of thirty switches arranged in a horizontal line. The switches are labeled from fifteen to four hundred fifty volts, indicating the level of voltage that would be administered if activated. They also have verbal descriptions that range from "Slight Shock" to "Danger: Severe Shock," with the last switch simply indicating "XXX." In the next room, a person is strapped to a chair with an electrode attached to his wrist. You can't see him, but you can hear him, and before being strapped in, he told you that he has a heart condition.

There's a man in a white lab coat standing over you. He says, "This is an experiment on the effects of punishment on learning. You will ask the person seated in the other room a number of multiple-choice questions. If he answers incorrectly, you are to give him an electric shock, starting with the lowest voltage, and increasing the charge after every successive incorrect answer." To give you an appreciation of the pain, the man in the lab coat gives you a forty-five volt shock. It jolts you a bit, and he says, "Although the shocks can be extremely painful, they cause no permanent tissue damage."

And so it begins. The person in the other room initially answers a few questions correctly, but then begins to make a number of errors. You start to increase the voltage on the shock generator after every wrong answer. At about seventy-five volts, he starts to grunt when you shock him. He gives a few more wrong answers, and at one hundred twenty volts he begins to shout, "Hey, these shocks are painful." At about one hundred fifty volts, he starts to plead with you, saying, "Stop! I refuse to continue." At that point, you turn to the man in a lab coat, but all he says is, "The experiment requires that you continue." Reluctantly, you continue to ask questions. At two hundred seventy volts, the person starts to scream loudly after he's shocked. You become very agitated and again turn to the man in the lab coat who tells you in a stern voice, "You have no choice; you must go on." Again, you continue. At three hundred volts, the person in the other room screams, "I can't answer any more!" The man standing over you says, "No answer is a wrong answer—you have to continue the shocks." You're getting very worried, and your hands start to shake as you pull the next switch. When you administer the higher voltages, you hear the person banging on the wall and begging to be let out. But you continue. Finally, there's no sound at all from the next room.

Now, you may say, "I would never do that. As soon as the person in the other room said they wanted out, I'd stop. How can you give those extreme shocks when he's crying out to stop? It's inhumane." But a wealth of research indicates that you're likely to do it. Psychologist Stanley Milgram conducted a series of classic experiments on obedience that followed the script given above.[1] Milgram first asked forty psychiatrists how far they thought people would go before they refused to shock any more. The psychiatrists thought that most everyone would stop around one hundred fifty volts, when the victim asked to be let out. In fact, the majority of people participating in the experiment, around 62 percent, continued to shock to the very end!

Were these people different from the rest of us? Not really. They weren't sadistic or insensitive to the victim. In fact, many of them began to sweat, tremble, and stutter when they were administering the shocks—but they continued. In addition, people from all walks of life have acted this way—men and women, blue-collar workers, white-collar professionals, and people with very different educational backgrounds.

Research has also found similar results in a number of other countries, including Australia, Jordan, Spain, and West Germany.[2]

Why do we act this way? We have an underlying tendency to obey authority figures. The initial studies by Milgram were conducted at Yale University. The school, the surroundings, and the experimenter (in his white lab coat) oozed authority. When similar studies were performed in a rundown commercial center, the number of subjects who were obedient dropped to 48 percent. Even more telling, when the experimenter wasn't an authority figure (e.g., when another person, arbitrarily substituted for the experimenter, came up with the idea to increase the shocks), only 20 percent of the participants shocked to the dire end.

Atrocities perpetuated by obedience, or in the name of obedience, have occurred throughout the world. We are quick to absolve ourselves of responsibility if we think we're carrying out the wishes of an authority figure. As one of Milgram's subjects said when asked why he continued to obey what seemed to be cruel orders, "I stopped, but [the experimenter] made me go on."

Our tendency to obey also affects the everyday decisions that we make in our professional lives. For example, one study had an unknown person place telephone calls to nurses in a hospital. The caller, who claimed to be a doctor at the hospital, told the nurses to give a patient twenty milligrams of a drug called Aspoten. The dose was twice as high as the maximum stated on the label, and there was a rule that a drug could not be given unless a doctor signed a prescription form. Yet, 95 percent of the nurses complied with the request. Such is the power of authority.[3]

Although we have the tendency to accept the claims of authority figures without question, we shouldn't. In fact, believing a claim just because a person is in a position of authority is a logical fallacy, called argument from authority. People in authority positions may just want to advance their own personal or political agenda. When President Nixon was running for reelection he argued that the country should elect him because he had a secret plan to end the Vietnam War—but he wouldn't give the details of the plan. Instead, we were to trust him because he had the authority of the presidency. Prior to the war with Iraq, many people (and countries) criticized President George W. Bush for not producing strong, credible evidence to support such a war. The attitude of the administration was, take our word for it. Millions were willing to go along just because the president said the war was necessary, irrespective of the evidence.

Authority figures can be flat out wrong. Remember the psychiatrist John Mack from Harvard, who believes in alien encounters? Should we believe such a bizarre claim because a professional in a position of authority believes it? Sometimes experts in one field make claims about another field. While it's certainly true that experts are more likely to be correct within their field of expertise, they may have no superior knowledge outside of that field. For example, Linus Pauling, an extremely intelligent individual who won two Nobel prizes, made a number of claims about the benefits of taking megadoses of vitamin C. He had no specific expertise or substantial research to back those claims, yet many people began taking large quantities of the vitamin on his recommendation.

Remember, small samples are open to a lot of variance. The beliefs of one, or a small number of experts, are more likely to be wrong as compared to the consensus view of a large number of experts. Thus, we should look to the consensus of experts in a field when setting our beliefs. Sometimes there will be little or no agreement among the experts, and thus no consensus view. This should tip us off that there's probably little evidence to support a very strong belief. The bottom line is, the larger the percentage of experts holding a certain belief, the more confident we can be in the accuracy of that belief.[4]

As can be seen, our beliefs and actions can be significantly influenced by authority figures. In fact, our tendency to obey and believe those in positions of authority can lead us to make many decisions that we may otherwise feel are inappropriate. Realizing that we have such a tendency is the first step in making more informed decisions in the presence of others. But obeying authority is not the only way that others can influence us. We also conform to our peers.

I'M DOING IT, WHY NOT YOU?

Take a look at the lines in Figure 11.[5] Is line A equal in length to line 1, 2, or 3? Most all of us see line 3 as equal to line A. But what if you were

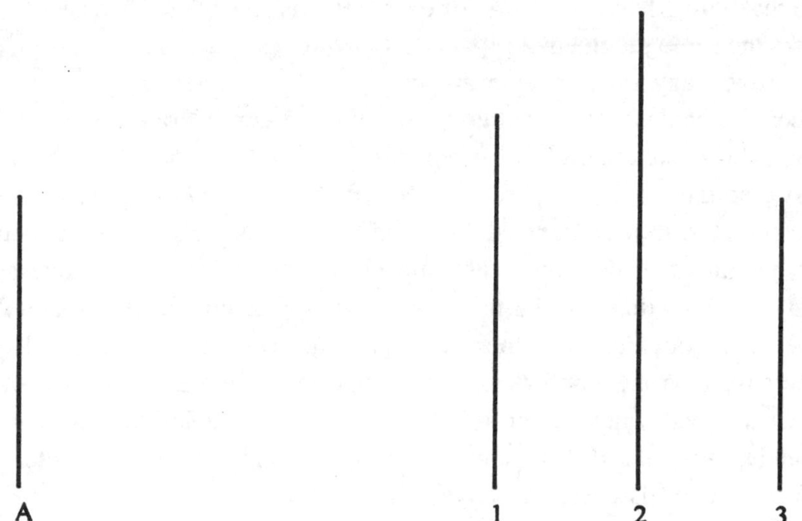

Figure 11. An example of conformity. Compare the length of the lines shown above. Is line A equal in length to line 1, 2, or 3? If a number of "confederates" say line A is equal to line 1, many people will agree.

in a room where seven other people said that line 1 was equal to line A? Would you start to think that lines 1 and A were similar? Most of us would say, "Of course not, it's obvious they're not equal. I don't care how many people say they are." However, we have a tendency to conform to others, especially when their views are unanimous.

To illustrate this point, psychologist Solomon Asch had seven to nine college students sit around a table and judge the length of lines, like those in figure 11. Interestingly, he was concerned only with the judgments of one student—the rest were confederates who were told what to say by Asch. The confederates gave their judgments first, and then the experimental subject responded. Sometimes the confederates' judgments were correct, while other times they unanimously made incorrect judgments. For example, in one instance they all agreed that a 3 inch line was the same as a 3¾ inch line. Asch found that, across a number of decisions, the experimental subjects conformed to the incorrect view in about one third of the cases, and that three fourths of them conformed at least once. We can make incorrect judgments for even obvious tasks, just because others make the same judgment.

How many other people are needed to get someone to conform? When the students were paired with only one confederate, they almost always answered correctly; when paired with two confederates, they answered incorrectly 13 percent of the time; and when paired with three confederates, they conformed 33 percent of the time. So just three incorrect judgments had a significant impact on subjects' decisions. Interestingly, the unanimity of the others' responses was crucial. For example, when one confederate in the group gave the right answer, and all the others were wrong, conformity to the majority view was only one fourth of what it was when the group was unanimous. A unanimous group of three had a greater impact than a majority of eight with one dissenter. In effect, a lone dissenter can have a major impact on the beliefs we set when we're with others.

Other experiments on conformity reveal similar effects. We tend to agree with others when they assert a number of amazing statements, such as most Americans are over sixty-five years old; the average American life expectancy is twenty-five years; or the average American eats six meals a day. In fact, conformity can even make us question one of our most fundamental rights—the right to free speech. Consider the following statement: Free speech being a privilege rather than a right, it is proper for society to suspend free speech whenever it feels itself threatened. Only 19 percent of people without peer pressure agreed with this statement, while 58 percent with peer pressure agreed.[6] This desire to conform can result in very costly decisions. Just consider the phenomenon of herd investing in the stock market. Investors often jump on the bandwagon, paying higher and higher prices for stocks they don't even know about, just because others are paying such prices.[7] Many people have lost their savings because of their willingness to go along with the herd.

As you can see, obedience and conformity can lead to a number of beliefs and decisions that have little evidence in their support. In fact, beliefs that may not otherwise be taken seriously often become credible if told by a person of authority or by several people at a time. Why? It may be that our tendency to conform is inborn. One way we form beliefs is by copying a model for our behavior—namely, our parents. If our parents or others in authority tell us at a very early age that angels, devils, heaven, and hell exist, we'll have a very strong predilection to agree with them. In fact, it may seem incomprehensible not to hold such beliefs later on in life. And, we would likely consider other competing beliefs, like reincarnation, to be quite bizarre. On the other hand, if our parents taught us that reincarnation is real, our beliefs concerning heaven and hell could easily be reversed.[8]

IT'S NOT MY JOB

It's late, and you're settled into bed. Just before falling off to sleep you hear a woman crying out for help. You go to the window and notice that a number of other people also turned on their lights because of the commotion. To your astonishment, you see an attacker repeatedly stabbing a woman on the street corner. You scream down "Let the girl alone!" and the assailant runs away. Thinking everything's OK, you go back to bed. A few minutes later, you hear the woman cry, "I'm dying! I'm dying!" You get up to find that the attacker has returned and is stabbing the girl once again. Lights go on all over the neighborhood and the attacker runs off a second time. Again, you go back to bed. The attacker returns for a third time—and kills the girl.

Would you go back to bed knowing that the girl needed help? Most everyone would say, "Of course not!" We like to think that if someone is in distress we'll come to her aid. But what if you knew that a number of other people were aware of the attack? Would that change your behavior? Most of us would say no—but research shows that it does. When we know others are present, we feel less responsible to act, a phenomenon known as diffusion of responsibility. In fact, the case presented above actually happened to a woman named Kitty Genovese in 1964. Kitty died after she was assaulted three times outside her apartment in New York City. The police investigation revealed that thirty-eight citizens saw the killing, but no one reported it during the attack. In fact, the first call was received thirty minutes after the assault began.[9]

Our behavior can drastically change if we think others are around to share the responsibility. As an interesting example, one study had students wait in a room either by themselves or with two other students (confederates put there by the researcher). While they were waiting, a stream of smoke started to pour in from a vent. When alone, 75 percent of the students reported the smoke within two minutes. However, when other people in the room remained inactive, only 10 percent of the students reported the smoke. They coughed, rubbed their eyes, and opened a window, but didn't report the incident.[10] Researchers in another study had a person drop pencils in an elevator to see if people would help pick them up—less help was offered as the number of people in the elevator increased. In fact, bystanders helped less when others were present in forty-eight out of fifty-six studies conducted on this issue. In general, individuals helped an average of 75 percent of the time when alone, and only 53 percent of the time when in a group. Interestingly, only one group appears immune to this effect—children under the age of nine.[11]

Research has also found that we often don't work as hard when we're in a group as when we're alone. One study found, for instance, that people pulled 47 percent harder on a rope when they were by themselves than when in a group of eight.[12] In addition, the presence of others can differentially affect our performance on simple versus complex tasks. For example, above average pool players make more successful shots when watched by others, while below average players make fewer successful shots. In fact, a review of over two hundred studies indicates that an audience impairs accuracy in complex tasks, and slightly improves accuracy in simple tasks.[13]

As you can see, our actions and decisions can change significantly because others are present. In some cases, our performance can improve, while in other cases it can decline. In addition, the presence of others can lead us to make decisions that we normally wouldn't make if we were by ourselves—even when we think those decisions are inappropriate.

AREN'T YOU ACCOUNTABLE?

Imagine that you have to make an important decision at the office. Now imagine that you'll have to justify the decision to your boss. Would your decision change? It turns out that being held accountable can have significant effects on our decision-making processes. Research indicates that accountable people tend to use more conscientious, complex, and analytical decision strategies than nonaccountable people when they don't know the views of the person to whom they are accountable.[14] For example, when subjects were told they would have to defend their loan and product marketing decisions to others, they selected more accurate and analytical decision strategies as compared to individuals who did not have to defend their position. Auditors who had to justify their bond rating decisions made more accurate and consistent decisions than auditors who did not have to justify.[15]

So accountability can produce a number of significant benefits for our decision making—but it also has a negative side. Detrimental effects can occur when we know the views and preferences of the person to whom we are accountable. As an example, psychologist Richard Tetlock had people report their thoughts on three controversial issues: affirmative action, capital punishment, and defense spending.[16] Some of the people were assigned to a "no accountability" group, and were told their responses would remain confidential. Three other groups were told they would have to justify their responses to either a person with liberal views, conservative views, or unknown views.

What happened? When an individual was accountable to someone with an unknown view, they were more likely to consider both sides of an issue and use a cognitively complex strategy. However, when an individual was accountable to a person with known views, they tended to shift their attitudes toward the views of that person. Once again, these results suggest that we tend to conform to people in authority positions. The moral of the story—if you want better quality and less biased work from your employees, don't let your views be known before the work is done.

THE RELIABILITY OF EVIDENCE RECEIVED FROM OTHERS

I never know how much of what I say is true.
—Bette Midler

As we've seen, our beliefs and decisions can be greatly influenced by others. In many cases, this is appropriate because other people can be an important source of information. We go to movies and read books that others say are good, and we're often glad we listened to them. However, problems can arise because the information we receive from others may not be the most reliable or unbiased. Why is that? We selectively expose ourselves to certain types of information and people. We typically read liberal magazines if we're liberal, and conservative magazines if we're conservative. We also tend to associate with liberals or conservatives depending upon our own political views. And so, the opinions that we receive from others can be biased toward our own beliefs, making it seem like there's overwhelming support for those beliefs. We're therefore less likely to question or change our point of view.[17]

In addition, we are storytellers, and we all have a desire to tell a good story. We want what we say to be informative and entertaining so that other people will listen to us. And since our audience wants to be entertained, they often give us the license to embellish the facts. As my friend Ron likes to say, "Never let the facts get in the way of a good story." As a result, misinformation is often passed on from one person to another. Just consider the urban legends that are told as if they were true. You may have heard that:

- Giant alligators live in the sewers of New York.
- George Washington had wooden teeth.
- A woman accidentally killed her poodle by drying it in a microwave.
- Paul McCartney died and was replaced by a look-alike.
- A flying saucer crashed in New Mexico and the Air Force is holding the alien bodies in a warehouse.
- Teenagers found a hook on their car door after a convict with a hook for a hand escaped from a local prison.[18]

None of these legends are true, but many people believe them because they heard the story from someone reputable. However, it's difficult to judge the reliability of a message. It may be told for the fourth or fifth time, with embellished details added every time it's passed on. Even if you hear a story from someone you trust, that person may have heard it from someone who isn't trustworthy. Also, a story's immediacy is usually enhanced to make it more entertaining and believable—an event that happened to someone in your friend's office is often relayed as happening to your friend. As a result, mere hearsay begins to take on a factual air.

In addition, we don't relay a message or a story verbatim—we relay the gist. The gist of a story gets the basic idea across, but the details are often lost, changed, and in many cases, made more extreme. Why? Extreme information is listened to more. My friend Dick was recently having some health problems. One morning, a mutual friend of ours told me that Dick was planning to see a specialist later in the day. One hour later, my friend Nelson informed me that Dick was in the hospital. I was amazed—was Dick so sick that he had to be rushed to the hospital in the last hour? No. It turned out that within the hour, the story had been passed around and significantly embellished. The gist of the story was correct—Dick was not feeling well—but the details got blown out of proportion. A story changes significantly as it's passed from one person to the next. Just put a few people around a table, whisper a story into one person's ear, and tell them to whisper it to the next person. What do you get? The last person tells a very different tale.

Our desire to be entertaining can lead to grossly distorted messages. Even national news organizations walk a fine line between objectivity and a desire to entertain. As Tom Brokaw said, "It's tricky, trying to generate understanding and insight while not ignoring the entertainment factor."[19] Cable TV and the national networks repeatedly cross that line when they air shows on UFOs, ESP, Bigfoot, and other pseudoscientific phenomenon. Just recently, ABC aired a primetime show called *Talking with the Dead*, where a psychic supposedly communicated with the dead relatives of celebrities, including the murdered wife of actor Robert Blake. The psychic communicator was interviewed, while a skeptic was not.

It's increasingly difficult to make appropriate decisions when we're exposed to a barrage of faulty information. The risk of AIDS for heterosexuals in the United States is a good example. What's your risk of contracting AIDS if you are a non-IV-drug-using heterosexual? In the 1980s we were told by the media: "Research studies now project that one in five heterosexuals could be dead from AIDS at the end of the next three years. That's by 1990. One in five. It is no longer just a gay disease"; "By 1991 one in ten babies may be AIDS victims"; and "The AIDS epidemic is the greatest threat to society, as we know it, ever faced by civilization—more serious than the plagues of past centuries."[20] If we believed these sensational accounts we'd stop having sex altogether.

What happened? News sources played up the accounts of heterosexual transmission, emphasizing that it's a heterosexual disease in Africa and Haiti. They typically failed to note that most heterosexual transmissions involve one partner from a high-risk group (e.g., gay, bisexual, intravenous drug user, hemophiliacs), and that public health practices in Africa and Haiti are so different from in the United States that they don't tell us much about the risk in the United States. But sensational stories get the ratings.

So how can we know whether to trust someone's information? Here are some hints.[21] Consider the source. With the AIDS issue, we have to look for the views of epidemiologists who try to understand and predict the spread of infectious diseases—not the views of sex therapists, actors, or talk show hosts. And, keep in mind that reporters can distort the views of the experts. Place more emphasis on past statistics instead of future projections. Even the experts have a hard time predicting future events, as we've seen. Be wary of anecdotal information. News magazines are notorious for reporting the problems of a single person, and since we are storytellers, we pay particular attention to that information. But as noted, personal accounts just don't provide good evidence to base our beliefs upon.

GROUP DECISION MAKING

So far we've seen how others can affect our beliefs and decisions. In all those cases, however, we still had to make our own individual judgment. What about group decision making? There are many situations where we're part of a group, and instead of making an individual decision, the group has to arrive at an overall judgment. What effect can group dynamics have on the final judgment reached? You know the old saying, "Two heads are better than one." But wait a minute, "Too many cooks spoil the broth." So which is it? As might be expected, groups can make more accurate decisions than individuals in some cases, but they can also exacerbate problems, which can lead to disastrous results.

Groupthink

When tightly cohesive groups are relatively isolated from outside dissenting viewpoints, they can fall prey to what psychologist Irving Janis called groupthink. As he states, groupthink is the "deterioration of mental efficiency, reality testing, and moral judgment that results from in-group pressures."[22] It's more likely to happen when groups are highly cohesive, the group members know and like each other, they are insulated from others because of the need for secrecy or some other reason, and they have a strong leader who states his or her opinion up front. The pressure to conform in such a group can be intense, and if a group leader gives his views up front, the result can be a bunch of yes-men chiming in agreement with little or no dissent. These types of groups usually exhibit an illusion of invulnerability which can lead to overoptimism and excessive risk taking. They also tend to believe in their own inherent morality, and, at the same time, stereotype their adversaries as evil, weak, or stupid.[23]

Groupthink can be seen in a number of disastrous decisions. For example, Albert Speer, one of Hitler's top advisors, described Hitler's inner circle as one of total conformity. In such a situation, atrocious acts can be carried out because no one offers dissenting views. The Nixon "palace guards" during the Watergate cover-up perjured themselves, offered bribes, and committed other crimes even though they knew better (many were lawyers). Why? They were circling the wagons around the president, who squelched dissenting views. One of the most famous examples of groupthink was the Bay of Pigs fiasco in 1961. President Kennedy recommended the invasion of Cuba, which was quickly wiped out by Cuba's armed forces. The United States was humiliated, leading Kennedy to ponder, "How could I have been so stupid to let them go ahead?"[24] NASA's decision to launch the *Challenger* in 1986 also suffered from groupthink. Their confidence was high from two dozen successful launches, and they had political and public pressures to launch. Even though data indicated that the O-rings could fail in low temperatures, and the launch date had near freezing temperatures, NASA officials, under pressure, didn't want to hear dissenting points of view.[25]

The same can be said for George W. Bush's decision to go to war with Iraq. Many Washington insiders and journalists maintain that the Bush

White House is the most secretive, closed, and uniform-thinking White House in recent memory. In fact, John Dean, a central figure in the Watergate scandal, argues that the Bush White House penchant for secrecy is "worse than Watergate."[26] When similar-thinking individuals insulate themselves from differing views, they're likely to take risky actions without adequately planning for other eventualities. The Bush team was convinced in the correctness of their beliefs—Bush actually told Bob Woodward that he does not "suffer doubt."[27] With such an unquestioning acceptance of one's belief, it's no wonder they thought the Iraqi people would welcome the United States with open arms. As a result, they did not appropriately plan for the war's aftermath, leading to the loss of thousands of lives and billions of dollars.

So how can we alleviate the problems of groupthink? One of the best ways is for group leaders to explicitly encourage dissenting viewpoints. A leader might even appoint a group member to be the devil's advocate and make it clear that their comments should be seriously considered. Leaders should not state their position at the outset. Following this recommendation, Japanese firms have the lowest-ranking executives at a meeting state their opinions first, so a subordinate doesn't have to worry about dissenting from a superior's opinion. Another group can be set up to investigate the same issue, and the two conclusions compared, or outside experts can be brought in and encouraged to challenge the consensus view.[28] Without such measures, our natural tendency to conform will become exacerbated when we're in a closely knit group.

Group Polarization

What if your friend came up to you one day and said, "Can I get your opinion on something? My doctor just told me I have a severe heart problem, and if I don't get an operation, I'll have to quit my career, change my diet, and give up most of my favorite sports. What do you think—should I get the operation?" If successful, the operation would correct his heart condition. But success is not guaranteed, and the operation may actually prove fatal. What if the doctor said that the chance of success was 90 percent? What if it was 80 percent, 70 percent, 60 percent, or 50 percent? What's the lowest probability that you would accept and still recommend the operation?[29]

Let's assume that you're a risk taker and you said 60 percent. Do you think your decision would change if you were in a group with other risk takers? Research suggests that it would. If you're in a group with other like-minded individuals, the group's final decision will likely be more extreme than the members' individual judgments. If you're discussing the issue with other risk takers, the group's decision may be to accept a 50 percent, or even a 40 percent, chance of success. In effect, polarization will occur—the group's discussion will amplify the existing inclinations of the group members.

For example, one study had people first respond individually to twelve hypothetical risk scenarios like the one presented above.[30] They were then put in groups of about five members and asked to arrive at a consensus judgment. Group discussion often led to greater risk taking when the members were riskier individuals, and more caution when the members were cautious. Highly prejudiced students have also been found to be more prejudiced after discussing racial issues with each other, while less prejudiced students became even less prejudiced after talking with one another.[31] Mock juries were more lenient after group discussion when given weak incriminating evidence, and more harsh after discussing strong evidence. Thus, initial positions become polarized by group discussion.[32]

The idea of group polarization is surprising to many because we think that group discussion will moderate extreme views. This will happen when two powerful factions argue pro and con. However, if there's an initial leaning one way or the other by a majority of members, the group's judgment will likely lean even more strongly in that direction. Why? Arguments in favor of that view tend to get more consideration, and an individual's responsibility for the decision is diffused. One just has to consider mob lynchings to appreciate the disastrous consequences of group polarization.[33]

IT'S NOT ALL BAD

We make many decisions in groups, and they're obviously not all bad. In fact, group decision making is often more accurate than individual decision making. Consider the following problem.[34]

> A man bought a horse for $60 and sold it for $70. He then bought it back for $80 and again sold it for $90. How much money did he make in the horse business?

The correct answer is $20, but many people get it wrong. You can solve the problem a couple of ways. The man started with $60 and ended up with $90, a difference of $30. However, he had to put in $10 more when he bought the horse back, leaving him with $20. Or think about the transactions as involving two separate horses, each netting $10, for a total profit of $20.

When working alone, college students answered the problem correctly only 45 percent of the time. However, when the students worked in groups of five or six, they were accurate 72 percent of the time with an inactive leader (who just sat there) and 84 percent of the time with an active leader (who encouraged all the members to participate). Active leaders were especially useful when only one member of the group initially arrived at the correct answer. In this case, 36 percent of the groups with inactive leaders answered correctly, while 76 percent of the groups with active leaders were correct. As we found with groupthink, one of the best ways to increase group decision accuracy is to have a leader encourage dissenting opinions.

To further examine group decision making, psychologist Reid Hastie compared groups and individuals on three different types of judgments: general knowledge, brain teasers (e.g., the horse trading problem given above), and judgments of quantities (e.g., how many beans are in a jar). Across all three tasks, groups made more accurate judgments than the average individual in the group—but the best individual in a group outperformed the group judgment. That is, groups generally outperform individuals, but the best member of a group does better than the group when she works alone. This conclusion has been supported by over fifty years of research on group decision making.[35]

And so, group judgments are often more accurate than the judgments of many individuals, but not all individuals. The accuracy of groups depends on many factors, such as task difficulty, competence of group members, and group member interaction. Given all the variables that can affect a group's judgment, it's difficult to make sweeping conclusions about the benefits of group decision making. In general, it's often good to pool the resources of different individuals—but that doesn't guarantee success. And, of course, we have to be aware, and try to prevent, the particular problems that arise through group dynamics, such as groupthink and group polarization.

EPILOGUE: SOME FINAL THOUGHTS

Our knowledge can only be finite, while our ignorance must necessarily be infinite.

—Karl Popper

The fundamental cause of trouble in the world today is that the stupid are cocksure while the intelligent are full of doubt.

—Bertrand Russell

So there you have it. Our journey through the minefields of thinking and deciding is just about over. As we've seen, we have a number of cognitive tendencies that lead us to form incorrect beliefs and make erroneous decisions. Of course, it's not all bad. We've done pretty well at surviving on this rotating ball we call home—but we could do much better. Let's take a few minutes to revisit the six major mistakes that often get us into trouble.

We prefer stories to statistics. Since we have evolved as storytelling creatures, our mind naturally gravitates toward stories and away from statistics. As a result, we overemphasize anecdotal information when forming beliefs and making decisions. Our preference for anecdotal data cannot be overestimated. In fact, you may have noticed that I've discussed a number of personal stories in this book. Knowing that we pay more attention to anecdotes, I thought they would be the best way to get the main points across. Of course, the conclusions reached here are backed by rigorous scientific investigation. The problem is, when we rely purely on anecdotal information in our everyday decision making, we typically disregard the statistics that may conflict with the anecdotes. Our failure to rely on the statistics of science leads us to believe in homeopathic remedies, dowsing, facilitated communication, and a host of other weird and/or erroneous claims.

We seek to confirm. In order to make balanced and informed decisions, we should pay attention to both supporting and contradictory information. But we don't. Instead, we emphasize information that confirms our existing beliefs and expectations, and disregard or reinterpret information that contradicts them. In essence, once we develop a preference or expectation, we have an ingrained tendency to interpret new information in a way that supports what we expect or want to believe. As we've seen, this biased evaluation of evidence is a main contributor to holding countless faulty beliefs.

We rarely appreciate the role of chance and coincidence in life. We are causal-seeking animals. From an evolutionary standpoint, this tendency has served us well, because when we discover the cause for something, our knowledge increases, as does our chance of survival. However, our penchant to look for causes is so overpowering that we see associations when none exists—we begin to see causes for things that are random or simply the result of coincidence. We consequently believe that a hot hand can affect the outcome of a basketball game, that an evaluation of past stock prices allows us to predict future prices, and that superstitious behavior can affect our performance.

We can misperceive our world. We like to think that we perceive the world as it actually is, but our senses can be deceived. We can see and hear things that don't really exist. A considerable amount of research indicates that our perceptions are greatly influenced by what we expect to see and what we want to see. And so, our biases can result in hallucinations—if we believe in ghosts or aliens, we're more likely to see them. Misperceiving the world is one of the main reasons why anecdotal data can lead us astray.

We oversimplify. Since we lead very complex lives, we're constantly on the lookout for ways to simplify things. This also happens in our decision making. We use a number of simplifying heuristics when we make decisions, and while those heuristics often serve us well, they can also lead to serious errors. When we base our decisions on similarity assessments, for example, we ignore other relevant information, like the impact of base rates, sample size, and regression to the mean. When we rely on what comes easily to mind, we overestimate the likelihood of sensational events. As a result, our beliefs and decisions can be greatly influenced by unreliable information, and insufficiently influenced by relevant and reliable data.

We have faulty memories. Although we often complain about our forgetfulness, we tend to think that the things we mange to remember are recalled quite accurately, especially if we have confidence in the memory. But research indicates that our memories can be very wrong, even when we're very confident. This even occurs in regard to sensational and tragic events. How did you hear about the World Trade Center disaster? Your answer may be quite different if asked the question in three years, as compared to three days, after the tragedy occurred. Current beliefs, expectations, and even suggestive questioning can affect our memories. In effect, we may reconstruct our memories, and with each successive reconstruction, memories can get further and further from the truth. Given that much of the information we use in our thinking and deciding is retrieved from memory, those faulty memories can have a major impact on our forming erroneous beliefs and decisions.

Of course, we've talked about a number of other pitfalls in our thinking, but the six listed above are the main categories. As I've tried to stress, you shouldn't feel bad if you make these mistakes—everybody I know makes them. Why? Most of the problems are the result of our evolutionary development or our desire—and need—to simplify our thinking. We can't pay attention to all the information which barrages us every day. Fortunately, our simplifying strategies work well in many cases—they give us decisions that are good enough. The problem is, we start to rely on them when we shouldn't, leading to grossly inaccurate beliefs and decisions that can lead to disasters.

One other point must be kept in mind. Knowledge of these pitfalls is the first step to improving our beliefs and decisions. But that knowledge doesn't ensure that our decisions will yield the best possible outcomes. As we've seen, chance has an important influence on our lives, so even if we follow the best possible decision strategy, the outcomes of our decisions can still go horribly wrong. To see what I mean, consider the current interest in high-stakes poker, played almost every night on ESPN, Bravo, and the Travel Channel. On a recent show, the announcer evaluated the hands of two players, Mark and Steve, and said, "At this point, Mark is a 90 percent favorite to win the hand." How did he know? Mark had a strong winning hand at the time, and Steve's only chance to beat him was to draw to an inside straight, a very unlikely event. Accordingly, Mark bet big. Steve decided to stay in and, amazingly, filled the straight to win the hand. Was Mark's decision to bet big a bad one because he lost the hand? Not at all. Given the information at the time, his decision was right, even though the outcome was bad. So it is with many decisions in life. When judging if someone is a good decision maker, we have to judge the quality of his decision process (how did he go about making the decision?), not the quality of the decision outcome.

I've tried to emphasize that the best way to improve our thinking and deciding is to take a skeptical and critical approach. Unfortunately, we are quick to believe things on the basis of incomplete or inappropriate evidence—critical thinking does not come naturally to us. As psychologist Alfred Mander stated back in 1947, "Thinking is skilled work. It is not true that we are naturally endowed with the ability to think clearly and logically—without learning how, or without practicing....People with untrained minds should no more expect to think clearly and logically than people who have never learned and never practiced can expect to find themselves good carpenters, golfers, bridge-players, or pianists."[1]

One thing, above all, must be kept in mind. We humans are believing creatures—we want to believe things. But as Theodore Schick and Lewis Vaughn noted, if we have a good reason to question a belief, we can't accept it as true. Wanting something to be true will not make it true, no matter how hard we try. The best we can do is proportion the extent of our belief to the extent of the evidence for that belief. And if the evidence doesn't strongly support a belief, a leap of faith will never help us know that the belief is true.[2] Amazingly, one of the paradoxes of human nature is that we hold some of our strongest beliefs in areas that we know the least about.

We want to believe things because we want certainty in life. But life can be very complex and unpredictable. While we might find it more comfortable to be certain in our beliefs—to think in terms of black and white—we must learn to accept how much we don't know. Sometimes we have to live with the various shades of gray in our knowledge. This is particularly significant because erroneous beliefs can cause more problems than not believing at all. As psychologist Tom Gilovich said, "Sometimes it's not the things we don't know that get us into trouble; it's the things we know that just ain't so."[3] We have to be, therefore, stingy with our beliefs—to withhold a belief in something until compelling evidence exists in its support. While this may go against our deeply ingrained predispositions, it is, without a doubt, one of the most important things we can do. On a personal level, and as a society, we will benefit from this skeptical stance, and make more informed judgments and decisions.

NOTES

INTRODUCTION: A SIX PACK OF PROBLEMS

1. See B. Malkiel, *A Random Walk Down Wall Street* (New York: Norton, 2003), p. 187; and W. Sherden, *The Fortune Sellers: The Big Business of Buying and Selling Predictions* (New York: John Wiley and Sons, 1998), p. 85, for research on the unpredictability of the stock market. While some people say that the experts have outperformed the darts in more instances, Malkiel notes that this is not the case when you factor in the market impact of the experts' recommendations.

2. See M. Shermer, "Why Smart People Believe Weird Things," *Skeptic* 10, no. 2 (2003): 62, for a discussion of these influences.

3. S. Vyse, *Believing in Magic: The Psychology of Superstition* (New York: Oxford University Press, 1997), p. 24.

4. Skeptic News, "Prayer an Issue in Death," *Skeptic* 5, no. 3 (1997): 25.

5. B. Glassner, *The Culture of Fear* (New York: Basic Books, 1999), p. xxvi.

6. Michael Shermer, head of the Skeptics Society and editor in chief of *Skeptic* magazine, has effectively made this point. See M. Shermer, "The Belief Module," *Skeptic* 5, no. 4 (1997): 78.

7. C. Sagan, *The Demon-Haunted World* (New York: Random House, 1995), p. 214. Half will be below average assuming no extreme cases.

8. This event actually happened. See A. Harter, "Bigfoot," *Skeptic* 6, no. 3 (1998): 97.

9. A. Hastorf and H. Cantril, "They Saw a Game: A Case Study," *Journal of Abnormal and Social Psychology* 49 (1954): 129.

10. R. Bartholomew, "Penis Panics: The Psychology of Penis Shrinking Mass Hysterias," *Skeptic* 7, no. 4 (1999): 45.

11. See E. Loftus and K. Ketcham, *The Myth of Repressed Memory: False Memories and Allegations of Sexual Abuse* (New York: St. Martin's, 1994), for a number of compelling cases.

12. E. Loftus and G. Loftus, "On the Performance of Stored Information in the Human Brain," *American Psychologist* 35, no. 5 (1980): 409.

CHAPTER 1: WEIRD BELIEFS AND PSEUDOSCIENTIFIC THINKING

1. M. Gardner, "The Magic of Therapeutic Touching," *Skeptical Inquirer* 24, no. 6 (2000): 48; Committee for the Scientific Investigation of Claims of the Paranormal, "'Therapeutic Touch' Fails a Rare Scientific Test," *Skeptical Inquirer* 22, no. 3 (1998): 6; and D. Swenson, "Thought Field Therapy," *Skeptic* 7, no. 4 (1999): 60.

2. T. Schick and L. Vaughn, *How to Think about Weird Things* (New York: McGraw-Hill, 2002), p. 276; L. Rosa et al., "A Close Look at Therapeutic Touch," *Journal of the American Medical Association* 279, no. 13 (April 1998): 1005; and J. Enright, "Testing Dowsing: The Failure of the Munich Experiments," *Skeptical Inquirer* 23, no. 1 (1999): 39.

3. Study reported in M. Gardner, "Facilitated Communication: A Cruel Farce," *Skeptical Inquirer* 25, no. 1 (2001): 17. Also see G. Green, "Facilitated Communication: Mental Miracle or Sleight of Hand," *Skeptic* 2, no. 3 (1994): 73.

4. Ibid.

5. Gallup poll, June 2005, http://www.gallup. com/poll/releases/pr010608.asp (accessed August 29, 2005). Also see *Skeptical Inquirer* 29, no. 5 (2005): 5.

6. There are more shipping lanes in the area known as the Bermuda Triangle than in the surrounding areas, so accidents are more likely to happen. See M. Shermer, *Why People Believe Weird Things* (New York: Freeman, 1997), p. 55. Also see L. Kusche, *The Bermuda Triangle Mystery—Solved* (New York: Harper and Row, 1975), for explanations of the "mysterious" disappearances in the Bermuda Triangle.

7. For example, $355,255 was given to the University of Alabama Birmington Burn Center to test therapeutic touch. See Schick and Vaughn, *How to Think about Weird Things*, for a more detailed account of the money spent on extraordinary phenomena.

8. Ben-Shakhar et al., "Can Graphology Predict Occupational Success?

Two Empirical Studies and Some Methodological Ruminations," *Journal of Applied Psychology* 71, no. 4 (1986): 645; S. Sutherland, *Irrationality: Why We Don't Think Straight* (New Brunswick, NJ: Rutgers University Press, 1992), p. 167.

9. D. Regan, *For the Record* (San Diego: Harcourt Brace Jovanovich, 1988), p. 3, reported in S. Vyse, *Believing in Magic: The Psychology of Superstition* (New York: Oxford University Press, 1997), p. 24. While many of Reagan's actions were influenced by an astrologer, the extent of his belief is unclear. A main reason for astrology's influence on the presidency was the president's wife, Nancy.

10. T. Gilovich, *How We Know What Isn't So* (New York: Free Press, 1991), p. 2; Vyse, *Believing in Magic: The Psychology of Superstition* (New York: Oxford University Press, 1997), p. 16; and M. Gardner, in foreword to Schick and Vaughn, *How to Think about Weird Things*, p. vii.

11. J. Mack, *Abduction: Human Encounters with Aliens* (New York: Maxwell Macmillan International, 1994).

12. See, for example, J. Randi, *Flim-Flam* (Amherst, NY: Prometheus Books, 1982); J. Nickell, *Real-Life X-Files* (Lexington: University Press of Kentucky, 2001); and M. Gardner, *Science: Good, Bad, and Bogus* (Amherst, NY: Prometheus Books, 1989), for detailed investigations of haunted mansions, clairvoyance, alien abduction, and a host of other extraordinary beliefs.

13. Data on violent crime obtained from http://www.fbi.gov/ucr/cius_03/xl/03tb101.xls (accessed 9/8/05). Also see B. Glassner, *The Culture of Fear* (New York: Basic Books, 1999).

14. B. Bushman and R. Baumeister, "Threatened Egotism, Narcissism, Self-Esteem, and Direct and Displaced Aggression: Does Self-Love or Self-Hate Lead to Violence," *Journal of Personality and Social Psychology* 75, no. 1 (1996): 219.

15. See K. Stanovich, *How to Think Straight about Psychology* (Boston: Allyn and Bacon, 2001); and B. Glassner, *The Culture of Fear*, for listings of numerous beliefs that research demonstrates are false. Also see W. Niemeyer and I. Starlinger, "Do the Blind Hear Better?" *Audiology* 20 (1981): 503; R. Paloutzian, *Invitation to the Psychology of Religion* (Glenview, IL: Scott, Foresman, 1983); D. Buss, "Human Mate Selection," *American Scientist* 73, no. 1 (1985): 47; and E. Lawler, *Motivation in Work Organizations* (Monterey, CA: Brooks/Cole, 1973).

16. Stanovich, *How to Think Straight about Psychology*, p. 19.

17. In fact, if you believe the ads, you, too, can become a remote viewer. As an ad in the magazine *Psychology Today* (December 2000, p. 63) said, "Discover

the amazing power of your unconscious mind to travel anywhere in the universe. To retrieve accurate data about people, things or events. Defy boundaries of time and space." It goes on to say, "until recently this technology was classified top-secret by the Pentagon. . . . Both the CIA and U.S. Army had remote viewing units that operated successfully for more than a decade doing secret missions like locating the American hostages held in Iran, discovering hidden nuclear and biological weapons, [and] determining the cause of aircraft disasters. . . . Now, you can learn step-by-step the same remote viewing protocols." All you need to attain such power is $279.95, the cost of the tapes.

18. Committee for the Scientific Investigation of Claims of the Paranormal, "Science Indicators 2000: Belief in the Paranormal or Pseudoscience," *Skeptical Inquirer* 25, no. 1 (2001): 12; G. Sparks, T. Hansen, and R. Shah, "Do Televised Depictions of Paranormal Events Influence Viewers' Beliefs?" *Skeptical Inquirer* 18, no. 4 (1994): 386; K. Parejko, "A Biologist's View of Belief," *Skeptic* 7 no. 1 (1999): 37; and G. Sparks, "Paranormal Depictions in the Media: How Do They Affect What People Believe?" *Skeptical Inquirer* 22, no. 4 (1998): 35.

19. R. Ehrlich, "Are People Getting Smarter or Dumber?" *Skeptic* 10, no. 3 (2003): 50.

20. C. MacDougall, *Superstition and the Press* (Amherst, NY: Prometheus Books, 1983), p. 558; Stanovich, *How to Think Straight about Psychology*, p. 203. This problem is exacerbated when programs that run well-researched stories also cover fringy pseudoscientific topics. For example, psychics have been featured on CNN's *Larry King Live*, NBC's *Dateline* and *The Today Show*, and CBS's *Early Show*.

21. Data is from the National Science Board's report, *Science and Engineering Indicators 2000*, in a section titled "Belief in the Paranormal or Pseudoscience," reported in *Skeptical Inquirer* (January/February 2001): 12.

22. K. Feder, "Trends in Popular Media: Credulity Still Reigns," *Skeptical Inquirer* 12, no. 2 (1988): 124.

23. Glassner, *The Culture of Fear*, p. xxi; K. Frost et al., "Relative Risk in the News Media," *American Journal of Public Health* 87 (1997): 842.

24. Glassner, *The Culture of Fear*, p. xxi.

25. D. Fan, "News Media Framing Sets Public Opinion That Drugs Is the Country's Most Important Problem," *Substance Use and Misuse* 31 (1996): 1413–21; Glassner, *The Culture of Fear*, p. 133.

26. Glassner, *The Culture of Fear*, p. xxii.

27. Ibid.

28. Ibid., p. xiv.

29. Ibid.

30. S. Gabriel et al., "Risk of Connective-Tissue Diseases and Other Disorders after Breast Implantation," *New England Journal of Medicine* 330, no. 24 (1994): 1748.

31. See, for example, J. Sanchez-Guerrero et al., "Silicone Breast Implants and the Risk of Connective-Tissue Diseases and Symptoms," *New England Journal of Medicine* 332 (1995): 1666; and C. Burns et al, "The Epidemiology of Scleroderma among Women: Assessment of Risk from Exposure to Silicone and Silica," *Journal of Rheumatology* 119 (1996): 1940.

32. M. Angell, "Evaluating the Health Risks of Breast Implants," *New England Journal of Medicine* 335, no. 15 (1996): 1154; M. Angell, *Science on Trial: The Clash of Medical Evidence and the Law in the Breast Implant Case* (New York: Norton, 1996), pp. 21–23, 101–102; and Glassner, *The Culture of Fear*, pp. 164–74.

33. Stanovich, *How to Think Straight about Psychology*, p. 65.

34. E. Borgida and R. Nisbett, "The Differential Impact of Abstract vs. Concrete Information on Decisions," *Journal of Applied Social Psychology* 7, no. 3 (1977): 258.

35. J. Randi, "The Project Alpha Experiment: 1. The First Two Years," *Skeptical Inquirer* 7 (1983): 24; Stanovich, *How to Think Straight about Psychology*, p. 69.

36. In fact, I'm using a number of personal stories in this book to make a variety of points, realizing that we naturally pay attention to such accounts. Of course, the points made here are typically backed up by considerable research, as referenced throughout the book.

37. Shermer, *Why People Believe Weird Things*, p. 33.

38. C. Sagan, *The Demon-Haunted World* (New York: Random House, 1995), p. 43.

39. S. Carey, *A Believer's Guide to the Scientific Method* (New York: Wadsworth, 1998), p. 94.

40. See Schick and Vaughn, *How to Think about Weird Things*; and P. Kurtz, "The New Paranatural Paradigm: Claims of Communicating with the Dead," *Skeptical Inquirer* 26, no. 6 (2000): 27.

41. S. Blackmore, "What Can the Paranormal Teach Us about Consciousness?" *Skeptical Inquirer* 25, no. 2 (2001): 24.

42. Stanovich, *How to Think Straight about Psychology*, p. 197.

43. Sagan, *The Demon-Haunted World*, p. 14.

44. For example, many of the books in the research library are about Cayce and his prophecies. Known as the "sleeping prophet," he would sit in a chair, close his eyes, and talk about angels and archangels, astrological influences on earth experiences, the missing years of Jesus, reincarnation, and so on.

45. Sagan, *The Demon-Haunted World*, p. 4.

46. K. Dillion, "Facilitated Communication, Autism, and Ouija," *Skeptical Inquirer* 17 (Spring 1993): 281; Stanovich, *How to Think Straight about Psychology*, p. 95.

47. These examples of erroneous beliefs are from Glassner, *The Culture of Fear*, pp. 27, 30, 40, and 76.

48. Glassner, *The Culture of Fear*, p. 210.

CHAPTER 2: A GREMLIN ON MY SHOULDER

1. Recent research suggests that a number of eerie feelings (e.g., chills down a spine, shivering, and feelings of revulsion and fear) often interpreted as indicating a ghostly presence can occur from low-frequency sounds (10–20 Hz). This infrasound, which can exist at "haunted" sites, can't be heard, but can be felt. See Skeptic News, "Infrasound as a Possible Source of Sensations of the Paranormal," *Skeptic* 10, no. 3 (2003): 10.

2. Interestingly, many people believe in ghosts because they think we have an "energy field" that carries on long after our physical bodies die off. However, you have to ask, Why would such an energy field apply to our clothes? Ghosts are practically never seen to be naked. Where do the clothes come from? Why would they carry over to the other side? Perhaps a better explanation is that people are seeing what they expect to see; fully clothed spirits often dressed in "ghostly" white flowing gowns.

3. C. Sagan, *The Demon-Haunted World* (New York: Random House, 1995), p. 109.

4. T. Schick and L. Vaughn, *How to Think about Weird Things* (New York: McGraw-Hill, 2002), p. 15.

5. Some people believe in things not because of the evidence supporting a claim, but because of the lack of evidence against it. They take the position that if you can't prove it's false, it must be true. However, this is a logical fallacy called appeal to ignorance. For example, since no one has proven that there aren't alien encounters, some people say that they must be occurring. But if we set our beliefs in this way, we would have to believe all sorts of crazy things, like fairies, elves, and my little gremlin.

6. See M. Shermer, *Why People Believe Weird Things* (New York: Freeman, 1997); and "What Is a Skeptic?" *Skeptic* 11, no. 4 (2005): 5.

7. Psychologist Terence Hines makes an excellent point when he argues that believers in the paranormal, rather than being open-minded, are, in fact,

extremely closed-minded. As he indicates, scientists specify the exact type of evidence they would need to accept the reality of astrology, ESP, or alien visitation. If the evidence is there, they're willing to change their minds and accept the existence of the phenomenon. On the other hand, believing in these phenomena without credible evidence (or with a plethora of disconfirming evidence) is true closed-mindedness. Why? Believers are, in effect, saying, "There is no conceivable piece of evidence that will cause me to change my mind!" See T. Hines, *Pseudoscience and the Paranormal* (Amherst, NY: Prometheus Books, 2003), p. 15.

8. C. Sagan, "The Burden of Skepticism," Pasadena lecture, 1987, in Shermer, *Why People Believe Weird Things*, p. vi.

9. Keep in mind that a claim isn't untrue just because there's presently no credible evidence for it. A lack of evidence doesn't mean we should end up at the left end of the continuum, with a strong disbelief. It just means that we shouldn't move away from the midpoint.

10. Schick and Vaughn, *How to Think about Weird Things*, p. 252.

11. K. Popper, *The Logic of Scientific Discovery* (New York: Harper and Row, 1968).

12. C. Sagan, *The Demon-Haunted World*, p. 171. As a further example, the hypothesis "God created the universe" can't be tested. That doesn't mean that there's no God. It just means that there's no way we can test to see if a God exists. On the other hand, the hypothesis "Praying to God can cure illness" can be tested, because we can conduct controlled experiments to see if people get better after they were prayed for. We can't test whether God created the universe, but we can test whether he created it ten thousand years ago, as some creationists maintain. In effect, we're talking here about critical thinking surrounding claims that can be tested.

13. Schick and Vaughn, *How to Think about Weird Things*, p. 179.

14. Or consider, once again, my little gremlin. We already know from neurobiological research that our thoughts originate from electrochemical activity in the brain. In fact, if certain sections of our brain are injured, our thought processes can be severely impaired. As a consequence, the hypothesis that a gremlin is originating all my thoughts is poor because it requires that we assume a gremlin is needed for thinking, while thinking can be explained by neural firings.

15. W. Jarvis, "Homeopathy: A Position Statement by the National Council against Health Fraud," *Skeptic* 3, no. 1 (1994): 50; V. Mornstein, "Alternative Medicine and Pseudoscience: Comments by a Biophysicist," *Skeptical Inquirer* 26, no. 6 (2002): 40; and P. Stevens, "Magical Thinking in Complementary and Alternative Medicine," *Skeptical Inquirer* 25, no. 6 (2001): 32.

16. Ibid. Don't be fooled into thinking that homeopathic remedies are like vaccines, where a small amount of a sickness agent builds a person's immunity to a disease. With homeopathy's law of infinitesimals, the smaller the dose, the more powerful the effect. This is not how a vaccine works. You cannot cut a vaccine's recommended dose in half and get a more powerful effect, which is what the law of infinitesimals would predict. So why did homeopathic medicine gain a following? Remember that early in our medical history we used bleeding, leeches, and often poisonous potions for cures. Since about 85 percent of our maladies are self-limiting, it was, in fact, better not to go to the doctor. So when Samuel Hahnemann founded the school of homeopathic medicine in the 1800s, his approach actually was better than what was available at the time because his treatments were so diluted they did nothing, and therefore allowed patients to get better on their own.

17. Schick and Vaughn, *How to Think about Weird Things,* p. 255, discuss two more criteria for judging the appropriateness of hypotheses: fruitfulness and scope. Fruitfulness asks, Does the hypothesis give us predictions that explain new phenomenon? Does it open new lines of inquiry, or predict previously unknown phenomenon? If so, it's fruitful. For example, Einstein's theory of relatively predicted that light rays will appear to be bent around massive objects because the space around them is curved. Future testing revealed this to be the case. Scope asks the question, How many different phenomena can the hypothesis explain? The more a hypothesis explains, the more evidence it has in its favor, and therefore the more likely it is to be correct. Einstein's theory of relativity is preferred over Newton's theories of gravitation and motion because Einstein's theory has a greater scope. While these are important criteria for the advancement of science, I simplified the discussion to those questions that I think are most important in setting our everyday beliefs.

18. For example, the US Department of Health and Human Services gave $200,000 to a Buffalo nursing center for research on therapeutic touch, while the Department of Defense gave $355,225 to the University of Alabama to study how therapeutic touch works on burn patients. While it's good to test the claims of alternative medicine, it turns out that much of the time the tests rely on anecdotal evidence as opposed to scientifically controlled experiments. We also have to question whether considerable sums should be spent to investigate claims that are contradicted by strongly supported scientific knowledge.

19. L. Rosa et al., "A Close Look at Therapeutic Touch," *Journal of the American Medical Association* 279, no. 13 (April 1998): 1005. Also see L. Rosa, "Therapeutic Touch," *Skeptic* 3, no. 1 (1994): 40; and M. Gardner, "The Magic of Therapeutic Touching," *Skeptical Inquirer* 24, no. 6 (2000): 48.

20. J. Dodes, "The Mysterious Placebo," *Skeptical Inquirer* 21, no. 1 (1997): 44; W. G. Thompson, *The Placebo Effect and Health* (Amherst, NY: Prometheus Books, 2005).

21. N. Postman, *Conscientious Objectives* (New York: Vintage Books, 1988), p. 96; K. Stanovich, *How to Think Straight about Psychology* (Boston: Allyn and Bacon, 2001), p. 59.

22. A. Roberts et al., "The Power of Nonspecific Effects in Healing: Implications for Psychosocial and Biological Treatments," *Clinical Psychology Review* 13, no. 5 (1993): 375; J. Turner, R. Gallimore, and C. Fox-Henning, "An Annotated Bibliography of Placebo Research (Ms. No. 2063)," *JSAS Catalog of Selected Documents in Psychology* 10, no. 2 (1980): 22; and L. White, B. Tursky, and G. Schwartz, "Placebo in Perspective," in *Placebo Theory, Research and Mechanisms*, ed. L. White, B. Tursky, and G. Schwartz (New York: Guilford, 1985), p. 3.

23. Stanovich, *How to Think Straight about Psychology*, p. 59.

24. S. Vyse, *Believing in Magic: The Psychology of Superstition* (New York: Oxford University Press, 1997), p. 112.

25. Schick and Vaughn, *How to Think about Weird Things*, p. 257.

26. D. Eisenberg et al., "Unconventional Medicine in the United States: Prevalence, Costs, and Patterns of Use," *New England Journal of Medicine* 328, no. 4 (1993): 246; US Congress House Select Committee on Aging, *Quackery: A $10 Billion Scandal* (Washington DC: US Government Printing Office, May 31, 1984); and Stanovich, *How to Think Straight about Psychology*, p. 219.

27. The relevance of double-blind studies and control groups will be discussed later.

28. K. Atwood, "The Ongoing Problem with the National Center for Complementary and Alternative Medicine," *Skeptical Inquirer* (September/October 2003): 23; S. Green, "Stated Goals and Grants of the Office of Alternative Medicine/National Center for Complementary and Alternative Medicine," *Scientific Review of Alternative Medicine* 5, no. 4 (2001): 205; and L. Jaroff, "The Solution Is Not in the Solution: Homeopathy and the Office of Alternative Medicine," *Skeptic* 5, no. 3 (1997): 51.

29. M. Shermer, "The Knowledge Filter," *Skeptic* 7, no. 1 (1999): 67. I'm not implying that all "alternative medicine" is bunk; only that it should be tested with the same rigor as more traditional medicine. If a technique is shown to be useful, it should be part of medicine—there is no need for the "alternative" distinction. Either something works, and it's medicine, or it doesn't, and it's nonsense.

30. R. Carroll, *The Skeptic's Dictionary* (Hoboken, NJ: John Wiley and Sons, 2003), p. 146.

31. Shermer, *Why People Believe Weird Things*, p. 4.

32. R. Hyman, "Cold Reading: How to Convince Strangers That You Know All about Them," *Zetetic,* now *Skeptical Inquirer* (Spring/Summer 1977): 18.

33. J. Randi, "John Edward and the Art of Cold Reading," *Skeptic* 8, no. 3 (2000): 6. Also see J. Nickell, "John Edward: Hustling the Bereaved," *Skeptical Inquirer* 25, no. 6 (2001): 19, for a discussion of warm reading.

CHAPTER 3: THINKING LIKE A SCIENTIST

1. The ad is in *Psychology Today*, April 2001, p. 91. Interestingly, the ad notes that many subliminal tapes don't work (perhaps to counter credible research which indicates the uselessness of subliminal tapes). However, it goes on to say that with a new technological breakthrough, these particular tapes work. Of course, there's no mention of what the breakthrough is.

2. A. Greenwald et al., "Double-Blind Tests of Subliminal Self-Help Audiotapes," *Psychological Science* 2, no. 2 (1991): 119.

3. K. Stanovich, *How to Think Straight about Psychology* (Boston: Allyn and Bacon, 2001), p. 102.

4. National Science Board, *Science and Engineering Indicators* (2004), p. 7–3.

5. Much of the discussion of science in this chapter is based upon the excellent work of Stanovich, *How to Think Straight about Psychology*; C. Sagan, *The Demon-Haunted World* (New York: Random House, 1995); and M. Shermer, *Why People Believe Weird Things* (New York: Freeman, 1997). I strongly recommend each of these books for those who want a more detailed discussion of science and its benefits.

6. K. Frazier, "Science and Religion 2001: Introductory Thoughts," *Skeptical Inquirer* 25, no. 5 (2001): 23.

7. M. Shermer, "The Unlikeliest Cult in History," *Skeptic* 2, no. 2 (1993): 81.

8. Sagan, *The Demon-Haunted World*, p. 27.

9. Stanovich, *How to Think Straight about Psychology*, p. 33.

10. Ibid. In fact, it's better to have evidence from many different studies, than from one large study, because different studies are unlikely to have similar weaknesses, so competing explanations will more likely be accounted for.

11. Creationism, on the other hand, makes a number of assertions that are untenable given our knowledge of the world (e.g., many strict creationists believe that the Earth is only six to ten thousand years old, a belief that is clearly

contradicted by scientific evidence). To overcome such inconsistencies, the theory of intelligent design has recently been formulated. Proponents of intelligent design usually maintain that, while evolution has occurred, life is so complex that it must have been created by a powerful entity. This assertion, however, is essentially untestable, and therefore does not belong in a science classroom.

12. There are other limits to the knowledge we gain from science. Science only tells us about our natural world. It can't tell us if something is moral, just, or beautiful.

13. T. Kuhn, *The Structure of Scientific Revolutions* (Chicago: University of Chicago Press, 1970).

14. Stanovich, *How to Think Straight about Psychology*, p. 37. Also see I. Asimov, "The Relativity of Wrong," *Skeptical Inquirer* 14 (1989): 35.

15. See "The Hamster: Think Progress 'Interviews' Jerry Falwell," www.thehamster.com (accessed September 8, 2005).

16. M. McClosky, "Intuitive Physics," *Scientific American* 248 (1983): 122.

17. Ibid.

18. Also see Stanovich, *How to Think Straight about Psychology*, p. 99.

19. See A. Kohn, *You Know What They Say—The Truth about Popular Beliefs* (New York: HarperCollins, 1990); and S. Della Sala, ed., *Mind Myths: Exploring Popular Assumptions about the Mind and Brain* (West Sussex, UK: John Wiley and Sons, 1999).

20. Stanovich, *How to Think Straight about Psychology*, p. 101.

21. Ibid., p. 101; Sagan, *The Demon-Haunted World*, p. 290.

22. Stanovich, *How to Think Straight about Psychology*, p. 144.

23. Ibid., p. 138.

24. Ibid., p. 139; I. Lazar et al., "Lasting Effects of Early Education: A Report from the Consortium of Longitudinal Studies," *Monographs of the Society for Research in Child Development* 47 (1982); and S. Ramey, "Head Start and Preschool Education: Toward Continued Improvement," *American Psychologist* 54, no. 5 (1999): 344.

25. See Sagan, *The Demon-Haunted World*, p. 20, for a more involved discussion of these differences.

26. Ibid., p. 31.

27. S. Vyse, *Believing in Magic: The Psychology of Superstition* (New York: Oxford University Press, 1997), p. 211.

28. S. Thompson, "Penn and Teller Part 2," Onion A. V. Club (June 4, 1998), http://avclub.com/content/node/23184 (accessed September 18, 2005).

29. T. Schick and L. Vaughn, *How to Think about Weird Things* (New York: McGraw-Hill, 2002), p. 251.

CHAPTER 4: THE ROLE OF CHANCE AND COINCIDENCE

1. M. Shermer, "The Belief Module," *Skeptic* 5, no. 4 (1997): 78; see also Shermer, *Why People Believe Weird Things* (New York: Freeman, 1997).

2. E. Langer, "The Illusion of Control," *Journal of Personality and Social Psychology* 32 (1975): 311; C. Wortman, "Some Determinants of Perceived Control," *Journal of Personality and Social Psychology* 31 (1975): 282; and S. Plous, *The Psychology of Judgment and Decision Making* (New York: McGraw-Hill, 1993), p. 171.

3. Shermer, *Why People Believe Weird Things*; also see Shermer, "Deviations," *Skeptic* 1, no. 3 (1992): 12.

4. Shermer, *Why People Believe Weird Things*, p. 70.

5. S. Blackmore, "Belief in the Paranormal: Probability Judgments, Illusion of Control, and the Chance Baseline Shift," *British Journal of Psychology* 76 (1985): 459; S. Vyse, *Believing in Magic: The Psychology of Superstition* (New York: Oxford University Press, 1997), p. 102.

6. In fact, the results of previous spins are prominently displayed next to the roulette wheel so that gamblers can keep track of the prior numbers.

7. T. Gilovich, R. Vallone, and A. Tversky, "The Hot Hand in Basketball: On the Misperception of Random Sequences," *Cognitive Psychology* 17 (1985): 295.

8. Ibid.

9. You might say, wait a minute, the hot hand doesn't happen all the time, it's just every once in a while, so the overall probabilities may not change much. But with that view, the theory of the hot hand is unfalsifiable. You'd be saying that it happens only sometimes after a player makes a few baskets, but not at other times, and that we don't know when it's going to happen. If that's so, the hot hand hypothesis can't be tested, and is therefore similar to the reasoning of psychics who say that psychic ability can't be demonstrated under controlled conditions because of the negative energy given off by researchers. It's just after-the-fact theorizing.

10. Gilovich, Vallone, and Tversky, "The Hot Hand in Basketball," p. 295; T. Gilovich, *How We Know What Isn't So* (New York: Free Press, 1991), p. 16; and Plous, *The Psychology of Judgment and Decision Making*, p. 114.

11. Gilovich, Vallone, and Tversky, "The Hot Hand in Basketball."

12. G. Belsky and T. Gilovich, *Why Smart People Make Big Money Mistakes* (New York: Simon and Schuster, 1999), p. 116.

13. K. Stanovich, *How to Think Straight about Psychology* (Boston: Allyn and Bacon, 2001), p. 99.

14. W. Weaver, *Lady Luck: The Theory of Probability* (New York: Dover, 1982); S. Plous, *The Psychology of Judgment and Decision Making*, p. 153.

15. R. Blodgett, "Against All Odds," *Games* (November 1983): 14; Plous, *The Psychology of Judgment and Decision Making*, p. 155.

16. See, for example, Plous, *The Psychology of Judgment and Decision Making*, p. 153, for a discussion of this case.

17. Penn Jillette, quoted in "The Fearful Angels of Our Nature" by M. Shermer, in *Skeptic* 7, no. 3 (1999): 94.

18. Shermer, *Why People Believe Weird Things*, p. 72.

19. Vyse, *Believing in Magic: The Psychology of Superstition*, p. 3.

20. D. Albas and C. Albas, "Modern Magic: The Cases of Examinations," *Sociology Quarterly* 30 (1989): 603; Vyse, *Believing in Magic: The Psychology of Superstition*, p. 30.

21. See M. Shermer, "The Belief Module," *Skeptic* 5, no. 4 (1997): 83.

22. Vyse, *Believing in Magic: The Psychology of Superstition*, p. 199.

23. B. F. Skinner, "'Superstition' in the Pigeon," *Journal of Experimental Psychology* 38 (1948): 168; Vyse, *Believing in Magic: The Psychology of Superstition*, p. 70.

24. Vyse, *Believing in Magic: The Psychology of Superstition*, p. 27.

25. Ibid., p. 137.

CHAPTER 5: SEEING THINGS THAT AREN'T THERE

1. See, for example, V. S. Ramachandran and S. Blakeslee, *Phantoms in the Brain* (New York: Quill-William Morrow, 1998), p. 67.

2. S. Coren and J. Miller, "Size Contrast as a Function of Figural Similarity," *Perception and Psychophysics* 16 (1974): 355. A sports announcer doesn't really change when he's standing next to a large racehorse, so the contrast effect seems to occur mostly when items are similar. Contrast effects also occur in our judgments. We judge the honesty of someone we know relative to the other individuals we know. Even happiness is dependent on context. It's been found that lottery winners received less pleasure from a variety of daily tasks, such as watching TV, talking with friends, eating breakfast, etc., as compared to non–lottery winners. See P. Brickman, D. Coates, and R. Janoff-Bulman, "Lottery Winners and Accident Victims: Is Happiness Relative?" *Journal of Personality and Social Psychology* 36 (1978): 917. By comparison, these activities don't match the thrill of winning.

3. S. Sutherland, *Irrationality: Why We Don't Think Straight* (New Brunswick, NJ: Rutgers University Press, 1992), p. 135.

4. J. Bruner and L. Postman, "On the Perception of Incongruity: A Paradigm," *Journal of Personality* 18 (1949): 206. In some cases, we get confused when our perception doesn't match our expectations, and so we take a compromise position. For example, a red six of spades is sometimes seen as a purple six of spades or hearts.

5. L. Zusne and W. Jones, *Anomalistic Psychology: A Study of Extraordinary Phenomena of Behavior and Experience* (Hillsdale, NJ: Erlbaum Associates, 1982).

6. T. Schick and L. Vaughn, *How to Think about Weird Things* (New York: McGraw-Hill, 2002), p. 37.

7. A. Harter, "Bigfoot," *Skeptic* 6, no. 3 (1998): 97.

8. Schick and Vaughn, *How to Think about Weird Things*, p. 57; I. Kelly, J. Rotton, and R. Culver, "The Moon Was Full and Nothing Happened," in *The Hundredth Monkey*, ed. K. Frazier (Amherst, NY: Prometheus Books, 1991), p. 31.

9. S. Asch, "Forming Impressions of Personality," *Journal of Abnormal and Social Psychology* 41 (1946): 258.

10. H. Kelly, "The Warm Cold Variable in First Impressions of Persons," *Journal of Personality* 18 (1950): 431; E. Thorndike, "A Constant Error in Psychological Ratings," *Journal of Applied Psychology* 4 (1920): 25–29; K. Dion, E. Berscheid, and E. Walster, "What Is Beautiful Is Good," *Journal of Personality and Social Psychology* 24 (1972): 285; and D. Landy and H. Sigall, "Beauty Is Talent: Task Evaluation as a Function of the Performer's Physical Attractiveness," *Journal of Personality and Social Psychology* 29 (1974): 299.

11. C. Ross, "Rejected," *New West* 12 (February 1979): 39.

12. M. Frank and T. Gilovich, "The Dark Side of Self and Social Perception: Black Uniforms and Aggression in Professional Sports," *Journal of Personality and Social Psychology* 54, no. 1 (1988): 74.

13. Frank and Gilovich, "The Dark Side of Self and Social Perception," also found evidence to suggest that wearing black can actually cause aggressive behavior.

14. L. Egbert et al., "Reduction of Postoperative Pain by Encouragement and Instruction of Patients," *New England Journal of Medicine* 270 (1964): 825; Sutherland, *Irrationality*, p. 180.

15. I. Kirsch and L. Weixel, "Double-Blind versus Deceptive Administration of a Placebo," *Behavioral Neuroscience* 102 (1988): 319.

16. S. Vyse, *Believing in Magic: The Psychology of Superstition* (New York: Oxford University Press, 1997), p. 136.

17. A. Hastorf and H. Cantril, "They Saw a Game: A Case Study," *Journal of*

Abnormal and Social Psychology 49 (1954): 129. Also see S. Plous, *The Psychology of Judgment and Decision Making* (New York: McGraw-Hill, 1993), p. 18.

18. R. Vallone, L. Ross, and M. Lepper, "The Hostile Media: Biased Perception and Perceptions of Media Bias in Coverage of the Beirut Massacre," *Journal of Personality and Social Psychology* 49, no. 3 (1985): 577.

19. D. Russell and W. Jones, "When Superstition Fails: Reactions to Disconfirmation of Paranormal Beliefs," *Personality and Social Psychology Bulletin* 6, no. 1 (1980): 83.

20. Skeptic News, "Virgin Ice Cream," *Skeptic* 8, no. 1 (2000): 16.

21. C. Gonzalez, "Crowds Report Visions of Mary," *Springfield (MA) Sunday Republican*, September 12, 1999, p. A25.

22. Schick and Vaughn, *How to Think about Weird Things*, p. 38.

23. T. Gilovich, *How We Know What Isn't So* (New York: Free Press, 1991), p. 77.

24. P. Cross, "Not *Can* but *Will* College Teaching Be Improved?" *New Directions for Higher Education* 17 (Spring 1977): 1; N. Weinstein, "Unrealistic Optimism about Future Life Events," *Journal of Personality and Social Psychology* 39 (1980): 806; and N. Weinstein, "Unrealistic Optimism about Susceptibility to Health Problems," *Journal of Behavioral Medicine* 5 (1982): 441.

25. P. Glick and D. Gottesman, "The Fault Is Not in the Stars: Susceptibility of Skeptics and Believers in Astrology to the Barnum Effect," *Personality and Social Psychology Bulletin* 15 (1989): 572; Vyse, *Believing in Magic: The Psychology of Superstition*, p. 135.

26. C. Sagan, *The Demon-Haunted World* (New York: Random House, 1995), p. 104.

27. Skeptic News, "A Skeptic in the Trenches," *Skeptic* 7, no. 3 (1999): 11. Joe Nickell reports that other evidence suggests that these hallucinations may be the result of subject suggestibility as opposed to magnetic stimulation. See J. Nickell, "Mystical Experiences: Magnetic Fields or Suggestibility?" *Skeptical Inquirer* 25, no. 5 (2005): 14.

28. Ramachandran and Blakeslee, *Phantoms in the Brain*, p. 188.

29. P. McKellar, *Imagination and Thinking* (New York: Basic Books, 1957), p. 29. Hypnagogic and hypnopompic imagery can be visual, auditory, or tactile, and some may pass quickly. As McKellar states, however, the distinction between "images" and vivid hallucinations is fuzzy. In some cases, images can be quite vivid and may be termed hallucinations.

30. S. Wilson and T. Barber, "The Fantasy-Prone Personality: Implications for Understanding Imagery, Hypnosis, and Parapsychological Phenomena," in *Imagery: Current Theory, Research in Application*, ed. A. Sheikh (New York: John Wiley and Sons, 1983); K. Basterfield and R. Bartholomew, "Abductions:

The Fantasy Prone Personality Hypothesis," *International UFO Review* 13, no. 3 (1988): 9.

31. L. Zusne and W. Jones, *Anomalistic Psychology: A Study of Extraordinary Phenomena of Behavior and Experience* (Hillsdale, NJ: Erlbaum Associates, 1982).

32. R. Bartholomew and E. Goode, "Phantom Assailants and the Madness of Crowds: The Mad Gasser of Botetourt County," *Skeptic* 7, no. 4 (1999): 50.

33. R. Bartholomew, "Monkey Man Delusion Sweeps India," *Skeptic* 1, no. 9 (2001): 13.

34. R. Bartholomew, "Penis Panics: The Psychology of Penis Shrinking Mass Hysterias," *Skeptic* 7, no. 4 (1999): 45.

35. R. Bartholomew and E. Goode, "Mass Delusions and Hysterias Highlights from the Past Millennium," *Skeptical Inquirer* 24, no. 3 (2000): 20.

36. Ramachandran and Blakeslee, *Phantoms in the Brain*, p. 72.

37. Ibid.

38. Ibid., pp. 106–109.

39. O. Sacks, *The Man Who Mistook His Wife for a Hat* (New York: Summit Books, 1985), p. 10. Interestingly, a map on the brain's surface corresponds to different body areas. When a certain brain surface is stimulated, you can feel it in your hand, foot, etc. Sometimes when an injury occurs, adjacent brain areas can commingle. For example, the foot is beside the genitals on the brain's map. If a person loses a leg, and is stimulated in the genitals, the person will often experience sensations in the phantom leg. One of Dr. Ramachandran's patients said, "Doctor, every time I have sexual intercourse, I experience sensations in my phantom foot. You see, I actually experience my orgasm in my foot." Ramachandran said a colleague suggested he name his book "The Man Who Mistook His Foot for a Penis." See Ramachandran and Blakeslee, *Phantoms in the Brain*, p. 36.

40. Ramachandran and Blakeslee, *Phantoms in the Brain*, p. 162.

41. R. Restak, *The Brain: The Last Frontier* (New York: Warner Books, 1979).

42. Ibid.

43. Ramachandran and Blakeslee, *Phantoms in the Brain*, p. 47.

44. Zusne and Jones, *Anomalistic Psychology*.

45. R. Abelson, "Beliefs Are Like Possessions," *Journal for the Theory of Social Behaviour* 16 (1986): 222.

46. Plous, *The Psychology of Judgment and Decision Making*, p. 21.

CHAPTER 6: SEEING ASSOCIATIONS THAT AREN'T THERE

1. B. Malkiel, *A Random Walk Down Wall Street* (New York: Norton, 2003), p. 136. A typical chart for a company produces a vertical line, with the top indicating the stock's high price for the day and the bottom indicating the low price. A small line is marked horizontally to indicate where the price closed for the day.

2. Ibid., p. 130.

3. Ibid., p. 150.

4. A. Moore, "Some Characteristics of Changes in Common Stock Prices," in *The Random Characteristics of Stock Market Prices*, ed. Paul H. Cootner (Cambridge, MA: MIT Press, 1964), p. 139; E. Fama, "The Behavior of Stock Market Prices," *Journal of Business* 38, no. 1 (1965): 34; and W. Sherden, *The Fortune Sellers: The Big Business of Buying and Selling Predictions* (New York: John Wiley and Sons, 1998), p. 86.

5. Malkiel, *A Random Walk Down Wall Street*, p. 166.

6. The diagnosis is made by using some type of scoring system. Although many scoring schemes have been developed, the Exner Comprehensive System has recently gained the most acceptance (see J. Exner, *The Rorschach: A Comprehensive System* [New York: John Wiley and Sons, 1986]).

7. L. Chapman and J. Chapman, "Illusory Correlation as an Obstacle to the Use of Valid Psychodiagnostic Signs," *Journal of Abnormal Psychology* 74 (1969): 271.

8. Ibid.

9. Ibid.

10. In some cases, we don't see a correlation when one exists (i.e., invisible correlation) because we don't expect one to exist. For example, we didn't see a correlation between smoking and lung cancer for many years.

11. For example, research indicates that the Exner Comprehensive System, used to score the Rorschach, cannot reliably predict mental health problems. Fourteen studies tested whether the system's depression index accurately predicts a depression diagnosis. There was no significant relation in eleven studies, mixed results in two, and positive results in only one. Also, the test overpathologizes. That is, research suggests that it erroneously identifies about 75 percent of normal individuals as being emotionally disturbed. J. Wood et al., *What's Wrong with the Rorschach?* (San Francisco: Jossey-Bass, 2003); J. Wood et al., "The Rorschach Inkblot Test, Fortunetellers and Cold Reading," *Skeptical Inquirer* (August 2003): 29; T. Hines, *Pseudoscience and the Paranormal*

(Amherst, NY: Prometheus Books, 2003), p. 188; and S. Lilienfeld, "Projective Measures of Personality and Psychopathology: How Well Do They Work?" *Skeptical Inquirer* 23, no. 5 (1999): 32.

12. J. Wood et al., *What's Wrong with the Rorschach?*

13. L. Chapman and J. Chapman, "Genesis of Popular but Erroneous Psychodiagnostic Observations," *Journal of Abnormal Psychology* 72 (1967): 193, also gave randomly paired patient drawings and descriptions to college students who never heard of the draw-a-person test. Students reported the same illusory correlations as the clinicians (e.g., most thought suspicious patients would draw atypical eyes).

14. L. Chapman and J. Chapman, "Test Results Are What You Think They Are," *Psychology Today* (1971): 18.

15. G. Ben-Shakhar et al., "Can Graphology Predict Occupational Success? Two Empirical Studies and Some Methodological Ruminations," *Journal of Applied Psychology* 71, no. 4 (1986): 645.

16. S. Sutherland, *Irrationality: Why We Don't Think Straight* (New Brunswick, NJ: Rutgers University Press, 1992), p. 167.

17. T. Gilovich, *How We Know What Isn't So* (New York: Free Press, 1991), p. 3.

18. J. Smedslund, "The Concept of Correlation in Adults," *Scandinavian Journal of Psychology* 4 (1963): 165.

19. M. Matlin, *Cognition* (Chicago, IL: Holt, Rinehart and Winston, 1998), p. 413.

20. The mathematics of the calculation can be found in any introductory statistics book.

21. Much of the discussion in the following sections is based upon K. Stanovich, *How to Think Straight about Psychology* (Boston: Allyn and Bacon, 2001), a book I highly recommend for those who want a more involved discussion of these topics.

22. R. Dawes, *House of Cards, Psychology and Psychotherapy Built on Myth* (New York: Free Press, 1994), p. 246; J. Kahne, "The Politics of Self-Esteem," *American Educational Research Journal* 33 (1996): 3; and Stanovich, *How to Think Straight about Psychology*, p. 82.

23. Stanovich, *How to Think Straight about Psychology*, p. 79.

24. Advanced statistical techniques, like regression and path analysis, have been developed which can indicate the strength of an association when other variables are removed or factored out.

25. E. Page and T. Keith, "Effects of U.S. Private Schools: A Technical Analysis of Two Recent Claims," *Educational Researcher* 10, no. 7 (1981): 7; D.

Berliner and B. Biddle, *The Manufactured Crisis: Myths, Fraud, and the Attack on America's Public Schools* (Reading, MA: Addison-Wesley Publishing Company, 1995); C. Jencks, "How Much Do High School Students Learn?" *Sociology of Education* 58 (1985): 128; and Stanovich, *How to Think Straight about Psychology*, p. 79.

26. J. Finn and C. Achilles, "Tennessee's Class Size Study: Findings, Implications, Misconceptions," *Educational Evaluation and Policy Analysis* 21 (1999): 97.

27. Example is from Stanovich, *How to Think Straight about Psychology*, p. 83.

28. B. Powell and L. Steelman, "Bewitched, Bothered, and Bewildering: The Use and Misue of State SAT and ACT Scores," *Harvard Educational Review* 66, no. 1 (1996): 27; Stanovich, *How to Think Straight about Psychology*, p. 83.

29. Powell and Steelman, "Bewitched, Bothered, and Bewildering."

30. B. Powell, "Sloppy Reasoning, Misused Data," *Phi Delta Kappan* 75, no. 4 (1993): 283; Stanovich, *How to Think Straight about Psychology*, p. 84.

31. Powell and Steelman, "Bewitched, Bothered, and Bewildering."

CHAPTER 7: PREDICTING THE UNPREDICTABLE

1. W. Sherden, *The Fortune Sellers: The Big Business of Buying and Selling Predictions* (New York: John Wiley and Sons, 1998), p. 2.

2. E. Marshall, "Police Science and Psychics," *Science* 210 (1980): 994.

3. M. Yafeh and C. Heath, "Nostradamus's Clever 'Clairvoyance,'" *Skeptical Inquirer* (September/October 2003): 38.

4. Ibid.

5. Ibid.

6. T. Schick and L. Vaughn, *How to Think about Weird Things* (New York: McGraw-Hill, 2002), p. 61.

7. S. Madey and T. Gilovich, "Effects of Temporal Focus on the Recall of Expectancy-Consistent and Expectancy-Inconsistent Information," *Journal of Personality and Social Psychology* 65, no. 3 (1993): 458.

8. B. Holland, "You Can't Keep a Good Prophet Down," *Smithsonian Magazine* (April 1999): 69.

9. J. Dixon, *My Life and Prophecies* (New York: Morrow, 1969).

10. Predictions were listed in http://www.sylviabrown.com (accessed April 15, 2002). People often say, "What about psychic detectives? The police wouldn't enlist their help if they didn't work." But remember, we all fall prey to

biases in our thinking, including the police. When examined closely, the data reveal that psychic detectives are of no value. See T. Hines, *Pseudoscience and the Paranormal* (Amherst, NY: Prometheus Books, 2003), p. 73; and W. Rowe, "Psychic Detectives: A Critical Examination," *Skeptical Inquirer* 17 (1993): 159.

11. H. Johnson, *Sleepwalking through History: America in the Reagan Years* (New York: Anchor Books, 1991); K. Stanovich, *How to Think Straight about Psychology* (Boston: Allyn and Bacon, 2001), p. 71.

12. W. Eng, *The Technical Analysis of Stocks, Options and Futures* (Chicago: Probus, 1988); Sherden, *The Fortune Sellers*, p. 89.

13. S. Carlson, "A Double-Blind Test of Astrology," *Nature* (1985): 318. The profiles were based upon the California Personality Profile.

14. B. Forer, "The Fallacy of Personal Validation: A Classroom Demonstration of Gullibility," *Journal of Abnormal and Social Psychology* 44 (1949): 118; Schick and Vaughn, *How to Think about Weird Things*, p. 59.

15. M. Gauquelin, *Astrology and Science* (London: Peter Davies, 1969), p. 149; Schick and Vaughn, *How to Think about Weird Things*, p. 128.

16. Much of the discussion in this chapter is based upon the excellent books by W. Sherden, *The Fortune Sellers*, and B. Malkiel, *A Random Walk Down Wall Street* (New York: Norton, 2003).

17. Example is based on Stanovich, *How to Think Straight about Psychology*, p. 175.

18. M. Fridson, *Investment Illusions* (New York: Wiley, 1993), p. 67. This is exacerbated when the advertisements are misleading. For example, one fund advertised that it ranked #1 in performance over eleven presidential elections. However, the ad's fine print stated that the fund only outperformed other funds over a specific three-month period, and only for certain asset values (Malkiel, *A Random Walk Down Wall Street*, p. 373). If you look hard enough, you'll find something that looks like superior performance.

19. Investment Company Institute, *Investment Company Fact Book* (Investment Company Institute, 2005), p. 3.

20. M. Jensen, "Problems in Selection of Security Portfolios: The Performance of Mutual Funds in the Period 1945–1964," *Journal of Finance* 23, no. 2 (1968): 389; Sherden, *The Fortune Sellers*, p. 107. "Buy the market and hold" refers to buying a large number of stocks to represent the market, and then just holding on to them, as opposed to actively trading them.

21. See Sherden, *The Fortune Sellers*, p. 108; and Malkiel, *A Random Walk Down Wall Street*, pp. 187–90.

22. Malkiel, *A Random Walk Down Wall Street*, pp. 187, 189, 190.

23. Figure is from Sherden, *The Fortune Sellers*, p. 108.

24. Malkiel, *A Random Walk Down Wall Street*, p. 373.

25. Ibid.

26. Ibid., p. 187.

27. Ibid., p. 192.

28. Sherden, *The Fortune Sellers*, pp. 6, 99.

29. Ibid., p. 103.

30. J. Kim, "Watch Out for Investing Newsletters Luring You with Outdated Returns," *Money Magazine* (September 1994): 12.

31. G. Belsky and T. Gilovich, *Why Smart People Make Big Money Mistakes* (New York: Simon and Schuster, 1999), p. 178.

32. The typical investor today holds on to a fund for less than seven years, while the average holding period was more than sixteen years in 1970.

33. Belsky and Gilovich, *Why Smart People Make Big Money Mistakes*.

34. T. Odean and B. Barber, "Trading Is Hazardous to Your Wealth: The Common Stock Investment Performance of Individual Investors," *Journal of Finance* 55, no. 2 (2000): 773. The individuals in the top 20 percent turned over about 10 percent of their portfolios each month, compared to only 6.6 percent for the other individuals.

35. See Sherden, *The Fortune Sellers*, p. 94, for a description of market efficiency.

36. Malkiel, *A Random Walk Down Wall Street*, p. 200.

37. Belsky and Gilovich, *Why Smart People Make Big Money Mistakes*, p. 60, based on an article by H. Seyhun, "Stock Market Extremes and Portfolio Performance," http://www.towneley.com (accessed September 2005).

38. Sherden, *The Fortune Sellers*, p. 116.

39. Ibid., p. 118.

40. See Malkiel, *A Random Walk Down Wall Street*, p. 197, for a discussion of the random-walk theory in finance.

41. Sherden, *The Fortune Sellers*, p. 91.

42. Malkiel, *A Random Walk Down Wall Street*, p. 196.

43. Ibid., p. 198.

44. Sherden, *The Fortune Sellers*, p. 61.

45. We seem to think that the economy has regular business cycles. However, statistical evidence does not support this myth. For example, an analysis of the turning points in the US economy between 1969 and 1991 shows that the time between officially declared turning points was as little as six months to as much as ninety-one months. See Sherden, *The Fortune Sellers*, p. 72.

46. Sherden, *The Fortune Sellers*, p. 55.

47. Ibid., p. 64.

48. Ibid., p. 66.

49. Ibid., p. 68. Our ability to forecast the economy also has not improved over the last three decades. While some forecasting organizations have stated that their forecasting skill is improving, it turns out that naive models' error rates have declined more than the forecasting organization's error rates.

50. Ibid., p. 61.

51. Ibid., p. 77.

52. "Pick a Number," *Economist* (June 13, 1992): 18.

53. Sherden, *The Fortune Sellers*, p. 36.

54. Ibid., p. 31. In fact, the American Meteorological Society proclaimed that it is theoretically impossible to predict the weather beyond ten to fourteen days. Even if it's theoretically possible, it may be economically impossible to go that far out.

55. Ibid., p. 37.

56. Ibid., p. 44.

57. Ibid., p. 49.

58. Ibid., pp. 169, 176; S. Schnaars, *Megamistakes: Forecasting and the Myth of Rapid Technological Change* (New York: Free Press, 1989), p. 9; and H. Kahn and A. Wiener, *The Year 2000: A Framework for Speculation on the Next Thirty-three Years* (New York: Macmillan, 1967).

59. Sherden, *The Fortune Sellers*, p. 185.

60. Ibid., pp. 190, 170, 174–75.

61. Ibid., p. 18.

62. Ibid., pp. 11–12.

63. Ibid., pp. 69–70. Complexity is the main reason it's difficult to predict human behavior. There are many interacting variables that have an impact on human behavior. As a consequence, psychological research allows us to make predictions about general tendencies in a group of individuals, but we can't predict what one individual will do. So it is with the stock market. We can look at the overall market and predict that, in the long run, it will likely go up as opposed to down. But given the complexity of the system, we can't predict what will happen to an individual stock.

64. Ibid., pp. 6–7.

CHAPTER 8: SEEKING TO CONFIRM

1. This example is based upon S. Sutherland, *Irrationality: Why We Don't Think Straight* (New Brunswick, NJ: Rutgers University Press, 1992), p. 131; and I. Janis and L. Mann, *Decision Making: A Psychological Analysis of Conflict, Choice and Commitment* (New York: Free Press, 1977).

2. D. Russell and W. Jones, "When Superstition Fails: Reactions to Disconfirmation of Paranormal Beliefs," *Personality and Social Psychology Bulletin* 6, no. 1 (1980): 83.

3. See R. Clarke, *Against All Enemies* (New York: Free Press, 2004); B. Woodward, *Plan of Attack* (New York: Simon and Schuster, 2004); and transcripts of the 9/11 commission hearings for an in-depth discussion of this issue.

4. T. Gilovich, *How We Know What Isn't So* (New York: Free Press, 1991), p. 50.

5. C. Lord, L. Ross, and M. R. Lepper, "Biased Assimilation and Attitude Polarization: The Effects of Prior Theories on Subsequent Considered Evidence," *Journal of Personality and Social Psychology* 37 (1979): 2098. Our preferences for what we want to believe affect not only the kind of data we look at but also the amount of data we search for. If the initial data we observe is consistent with what we want to believe, we are often satisfied and end the search. However, if the initial data we see is inconsistent, we often search for more data until we find something in support.

6. M. Shermer, "Why Smart People Believe Weird Things," *Skeptic* 10, no. 2 (2003): 63.

7. T. Gilovich, "Biased Evaluation and Persistence in Gambling," *Journal of Personality and Social Psychology* 44, no. 6 (1983): 1110; R. Lau and D. Russell, "Attributions in the Sports Pages," *Journal of Personality and Social Psychology* 39 (1980): 29; M. Davis and W. Stephan, "Attributions for Exam Performance," *Journal of Applied Social Psychology* 10 (1980): 235; P. Tetlock, "Explaining Teacher Explanations for Pupil Performance: An Examination of the Self-Presentation Interpretation," *Social Psychology Quarterly* 43 (1980): 283; and M. Wiley, K. Crittenden, and L. Birg, "Why Rejection? Causal Attribution of a Career Achievement Event," *Social Psychology Quarterly* 42 (1979): 214.

8. M. Snyder and W. Swann, "Hypothesis-Testing Processes in Social Interaction," *Journal of Personality and Social Psychology* 36 (1978): 1202.

9. Also see M. Snyder and N. Cantor, "Testing Hypotheses about Other People: The Use of Historical Knowledge," *Journal of Personality and Social Psychology* 15 (1979): 330.

10. M. Snyder, "Seek and Ye Shall Find: Testing Hypotheses about Other People," in *Social Cognition: The Ontario Symposium on Personality and Social Psychology*, ed. E. Higgins, D. Herman, and M. Zanna (Hillsdale, NJ: Lawrence Erlbaum, 1981), p. 277.

11. This can occur even if a lie detector is done in good faith because the data gathering can be unknowingly biased. If the tone of the polygrapher is more cold or hostile, the suspect may be more uneasy, which can result in a more

incriminating chart. See G. Ben-Shakhar et al., "Seek and Ye Shall Find: Test Results Are What You Hypothesize They Are," *Journal of Behavioral Decision Making* 11 (1998): 235, for dysfunctional consequences of confirming strategies when clinicians diagnose patients with the Rorschach and draw-a-person projective tests.

12. J. Greenberg, K. Williams, and M. O'Brien, "Considering the Harshest Verdict First: Biasing Effects on Mock Juror Verdicts," *Personality and Social Psychology Bulletin* 12, no. 1 (1986): 41.

13. P. Wason, "On the Failure to Eliminate Hypotheses in a Conceptual Task," *Quarterly Journal of Experimental Psychology* 12 (1960): 129.

14. It should be noted that positive hypothesis testing can reveal errors in a hypothesis in some cases. See J. Klayman, "Varieties of Confirmation Bias," in *Decision Making from a Cognitive Perspective*, ed. J. Busemeyer, R. Hastis, and D. Medin (San Diego: Academic Press, 1995), p. 385, for a detailed discussion of this issue.

15. This example is from P. Wason and P. Johnson-Laird, *Psychology of Reasoning: Structure and Content* (Cambridge, MA: Harvard University Press, 1972).

16. R. Dawes, "The Mind, the Model and the Task," in *Cognitive Theory*, vol. 1, ed. F. Restle et al. (Hillsdale, NJ: Erlbaum, 1975), p. 119.

17. R. Rosenthal and L. Jacobson, *Pygmalion in the Classroom: Teacher Expectations and Pupils' Intellectual Development* (New York: Holt, Rinehart, and Winston, 1968); C. Word, M. Zanna, and J. Cooper, "The Nonverbal Mediation of Self-Fulfilling Prophecies in Interracial Interaction," *Journal of Experimental Social Psychology* 10 (1974): 109.

18. Gilovich, *How We Know What Isn't So*, p. 33. Of course, one problem in attending to all the relevant data is that we don't always have all the data. For example, when evaluating a firm's hiring practices, we know how the people we hired turned out, but we typically don't know about those rejected.

19. J. Holt, *How Children Fail* (New York: Delacorte Press/Seymour Lawrence, 1982).

20. C. Mynatt, M. Doherty, and R. Tweney, "Confirmation Bias in a Simulated Research Environment: An Experimental Study of Scientific Inference," *Quarterly Journal of Experimental Psychology* 29 (1977): 85.

21. J. Russo and P. Schoemaker, *Decision Traps: Ten Barriers to Brilliant Decision Making and How to Overcome Them* (New York: Simon and Schuster, 1989), p. xiv. Another possibility may be to first treat a task as a fact-gathering mission as opposed to testing a specific hypothesis. See Snyder, "Seek and Ye Shall Find."

CHAPTER 9: HOW WE SIMPLIFY

1. Most of the discussion in this chapter is based upon the seminal work of two psychologists, Amos Tversky and Daniel Kahneman. In fact, Dan Kahneman recently received the Nobel Prize in economics for his work in this area (unfortunately, Amos Tversky recently died, and was therefore ineligible). Our debt to these and other researchers investigating decision making cannot be overestimated.

2. A. Tversky and D. Kahneman, "Judgment under Uncertainty: Heuristics and Biases," *Science* 185 (1974): 1124.

3. T. Schick and L. Vaughn, *How to Think about Weird Things* (New York: McGraw-Hill, 2002), p. 145.

4. S. Sutherland, *Irrationality: Why We Don't Think Straight* (New Brunswick, NJ: Rutgers University Press, 1992), p. 183.

5. Discussion of similar examples can be found in J. Paulos, *Innumeracy: Mathematical Illiteracy and Its Consequences* (New York: Vintage Books, 1988), p. 89; Sutherland, *Irrationality*, p. 208; and K. Stanovich, *How to Think Straight about Psychology* (Boston: Allyn and Bacon, 2001), p. 161.

6. W. Casscells, A. Schoenberger, and T. Graboys, "Interpretation by Physicians of Clinical Laboratory Results," *New England Journal of Medicine* 299 (1978): 999.

7. In the actual calculation, this diagnosticity ratio is multiplied by the base rate of having the virus over not having the virus. That is, (1.00 / 0.05) X (0.002 / 0.998) = 0.04008. This indicates that the odds of having the virus are 0.04008 to 1. To convert the odds to a probability, take the number and divide by one plus that number (0.04008 / 1.04008 = 3.85%, which is also 1 / 26, as presented in the chapter). For a more detailed approach to the calculations, see Bayes's theorem in any introductory statistics book. Many people overlook the false positive rate when assessing the validity of a test. For example, experts in corporate fraud detection have developed fraud detection questionnaires solely on the basis of the positive hit rate. See M. Romney, W. Albrecht, and D. Cherrington, "Auditors and the Detection of Fraud," *Journal of Accountancy* 149 (May 1980): 63.

8. For example, five hundred FBI employees with access to intelligence information were given lie detector tests after the arrest of alleged spy Robert Hanssen in 2001. All outside applicants for FBI jobs have been required to take lie detector tests since 1994. See D. Eggen and D. Vise, "500 FBI Employees Will Be Given Lie Detector Tests," *Springfield (MA) Sunday Republican*, March 25, 2001, p. A5.

9. R. Libby, *Accounting and Human Information Processing: Theory and*

Applications (Englewood Cliffs, NJ: Prentice-Hall, 1981), p. 56. While it is difficult to assess the definitive true and false positive rates of lie detector tests (e.g., screening for general truthfulness vs. truthfulness concerning a specific crime may yield different results), research suggests that overall error rates can be as high as 50 percent (see http://antipolygraph.org/read.shtml).

10. T. Kida, "The Effect of Causality and Specificity on Data Use," *Journal of Accounting Research* 22 (1984): 145. Remember our desire to find causes? Interestingly, if the base rate fits into a causal schema, auditors will pay more attention to it. For example, the study also found that when the base rate related to firms with similar cash flows (a causal variable), the auditors' average judgment (39 percent) was closer to the correct probability.

11. Representativeness may cause us to ignore regression to the mean because when we predict something about the future, we often base our prediction on some similar measure. For example, if a student received an exceptionally high score on the first test taken in a class, we tend to think she will be exceptionally high on the second.

12. And, if Woods isn't making many birdies now, it's more likely he will make them later in the game, given that he typically shoots under par.

13. Tversky and Kahneman, "Judgment under Uncertainty," p. 1124.

14. This example is from D. Kahneman and A. Tversky, "Subjective Probability: A Judgment of Representativeness," *Cognitive Psychology* 3, no. 3 (1972): 430.

15. This has been termed belief in the law of small numbers, where we think that the law of large numbers applies equally to small samples. See A. Tversky and D. Kahneman, "Belief in the Law of Small Numbers," *Psychological Bulletin* 76 (1971): 105.

16. Sutherland, *Irrationality*, p. 213.

17. Decision problem is from A. Tversky and D. Kahneman, "Judgments of and by Representativeness," in D. Kahneman, P. Slovic, and A. Tversky, *Judgment under Uncertainty: Heuristics and Biases* (Cambridge, England: Cambridge University Press, 1982).

18. S. Plous, *The Psychology of Judgment and Decision Making* (New York: McGraw-Hill, 1993), p. 112.

19. In a similar fashion, the United States and Russia can go to war for reasons other than the actions of a third country, so A must be more likely than B in that scenario also.

20. Plous, *The Psychology of Judgment and Decision Making*, p. 112.

21. Like representativeness, stereotypes concern similarity, but with stereotyping we consider a person to be part of a group, and then attribute a number of characteristics to the person given our preconceived notion of what the group is like.

22. H. Tajfel et al., "Social Categorization and Intergroup Behaviors," *European Journal of Social Psychology* 1 (1971): 149.

23. "Death Odds," *Newsweek*, September 24, 1990, p. 10.

24. B. Combs and P. Slovic, "Newspaper Coverage of Causes of Death," *Journalism Quarterly* 56 (1979): 837.

25. Women in their forties think that the chances of dying from breast cancer are one in ten, while the real odds are more like one in two hundred fifty. See B. Glassner, *The Culture of Fear* (New York: Basic Books, 1999), p. xvi.

26. A. Tversky and D. Kahneman, "Availability: A Heuristic for Judging Frequency and Probability," *Cognitive Psychology* 5 (1973): 207. As another example, subjects were given lists of people and asked to judge if there were more males than females. In one group, well-known personalities on the list were male, while in the other group the well-known personalities were female. In each case, subjects erroneously thought there were more males (females) if the familiar personalities were male (female).

27. National Safety Council, *Accident Facts*, 1990 ed. (Chicago, 1990); Stanovich, *How to Think Straight about Psychology*, p. 64.

28. A. MacDonald, "Parents Fear Wrong Things, Survey Suggests," *Ann Arbor News*, October 3, 1990, Stanovich, *How to Think Straight about Psychology*, p. 64. Many of us flock to convenience stores to buy power ball tickets, thinking the ticket could change our lives for the better. But as psychologist David Myers points out, if you drive ten miles to buy the ticket, you're actually sixteen times more likely to die in a car crash than you are to win the lottery. See D. Myers, *Intuition: Its Powers and Perils* (New Haven, CT: Yale University Press, 2002), p. 224.

29. K. Dunn, "Fibbing: The Lies the Good Guys Tell," *Toronto Globe and Mail*, July 10, 1993; Stanovich, *How to Think Straight about Psychology*, p. 64.

30. Glassner, *The Culture of Fear*, p. 133.

31. D. Fan, "News Media Framing Sets Public Opinion That Drugs Is the Country's Most Important Problem," *Substance Use and Misuse* 31 (1996): 1413; Glassner, *The Culture of Fear*, p. 133.

32. Ibid., p. 134; C. Reinarman and H. Levine, "The Crack Attack: America's Latest Drug Scare, 1986–1992," in *Images of Issues: Typifying Contemporary Social Problems* (New York: Aldine De Gruyter, 1995), p. 155.

33. Glassner, *The Culture of Fear*, p. 134.

34. Ibid., p. 136.

35. Consider the stringent regulations put in place after the World Trade Center tragedy. Airports did not allow their restaurants to use plastic forks (and yet you could get them on the plane). Nail clippers and other similar personal

items were being confiscated. The observation floor of the John Hancock tower in Boston was closed—the authorities said not temporarily, but permanently.

36. This decision scenario and data are based upon E. Joyce and G. Biddle, "Anchoring and Adjustment in Probabilistic Inference in Auditing," *Journal of Accounting Research* 19 (1981): 120.

37. Tversky and Kahneman, "Judgment under Uncertainty," p. 1124.

38. Ibid.

39. G. Whyte and J. Sebenius, "The Effect of Multiple Anchors on Anchoring in Individual and Group Judgment," *Organizational Behavior and Human Decision Processes* 69, no. 1 (1997): 75.

40. G. Northcraft and M. Neale, "Experts, Amateurs and Real Estate: An Anchoring and Adjustment Perspective on Property Pricing Decisions," *Organizational Behavior and Human Decision Processes* 39 (1987): 84.

41. G. Belsky and T. Gilovich, *Why Smart People Make Big Money Mistakes* (New York: Simon and Schuster, 1999), p. 143.

42. J. Greenberg, K. Williams, and M. O'Brien, "Considering the Harshest Verdict First: Biasing Effects on Mock Juror Verdicts," *Personality and Social Psychology Bulletin* 12, no. 1 (1986): 41.

43. J. Smith and T. Kida, "Heuristics and Biases: Expertise and Task Realism in Auditing," *Psychological Bulletin* 109, no. 3 (1991): 472.

CHAPTER 10: FRAMING AND OTHER DECISION SNAGS

1. This example is from A. Tversky and D. Kahneman, "The Framing of Decisions and the Psychology of Choice," *Science* 211 (1981): 453.

2. K. Sullivan, "Corporate Managers' Risky Behavior: Risk Taking or Avoiding?" *Journal of Financial and Strategic Decision Making* 10, no. 3 (1977): 63. See also K. Sullivan and T. Kida, "The Effect of Multiple Reference Points and Prior Gains and Losses on Managers' Risky Decision Making," *Organizational Behavior and Human Decision Processes* (October 1995): 76.

3. B. McNeil et al., "On the Elicitation of Preferences for Alternative Therapies," *New England Journal of Medicine* 306 (1982): 1259.

4. T. Odean, "Are Investors Reluctant to Realize Their Losses?" *Journal of Finance* 53, no. 5 (1998): 1775; G. Belsky and T. Gilovich, *Why Smart People Make Big Money Mistakes* (New York: Simon and Schuster, 1999), p. 62. Of course, a stock's price is likely to both rise and fall over time. The issue here is the timing of the sale. We are often quicker to sell a stock that is rising, as opposed to a stock that is falling.

5. Decision is based upon similar scenarios investigating the endowment effect. See, for example, Belsky and Gilovich, *Why Smart People Make Big Money Mistakes*, p. 94; D. Kahneman, J. Knetsch, and R. Thaler, "Experimental Tests of the Endowment Effect and the Coase Theorem," *Journal of Political Economy* (December 1990): 1325; and D. Kahneman, J. Knetsch, and R. Thaler, "Anomalies: The Endowment Effect, Loss Aversion, and Status Quo Bias," *Journal of Economic Perspectives* 5, no. 1 (1991): 193.

6. It's known as the endowment effect because we think the value of something is greater when it's part of our own personal endowment.

7. R. Thaler, "Toward a Positive Theory of Consumer Choice," *Journal of Economic Behavior and Organization* 1 (1980): 39.

8. Kahneman, Knetsch, and Thaler, "Anomalies: The Endowment Effect."

9. Thaler, "Toward a Positive Theory of Consumer Choice."

10. G. Quattrone and A. Tversky, "Contrasting Rational and Psychological Analyses of Political Choice," *American Political Science Review* 82 (1988): 719.

11. Tversky and Kahneman, "The Framing of Decisions and the Psychology of Choice."

12. See also C. Heath and J. Soll, "Mental Budgeting and Consumer Decisions," *Journal of Consumer Research* 23 (1996): 40.

13. Much of the discussion on mental accounts is based on the excellent book by Belsky and Gilovich, *Why Smart People Make Big Money Mistakes*. I would recommend it to anyone interested in refining their financial decision making.

14. Ibid., p. 36. One factor that may come into play is the size of the refund. Smaller refunds are typically blown, while larger refunds are often stashed away in the bank—which is funny since we typically can afford to spend more money if we get a larger refund.

15. This decision is based upon similar scenarios investigating mental accounts. See, for example, ibid., p. 37; R. Thaler, "Anomalies: Saving, Fungibility, and Mental Accounts," *Journal of Economic Perspectives* 4, no. 1 (1990): 193; and R. Thaler, "Mental Accounting and Consumer Choice," *Marketing Science* 4, no. 3 (1985): 199.

16. In a similar vein, F. Leclerc, B. Schmitt, and L. Dube, "Waiting Time and Decision Making: Is Time Like Money?" *Journal of Consumer Research* 22 (1995), asked people how much they would pay to avoid standing in a ticket line for forty-five minutes. People would pay twice as much to avoid waiting if the ticket price was $45 as opposed to $15.

17. D. Prelec and D. Simester, "Always Leave Home without It: A Further

Investigation of the Credit-Card Effect on Willingness to Pay," *Marketing Letters* 12, no. 1 (2001): 5; Belsky and Gilovich, *Why Smart People Make Big Money Mistakes*, p. 43.

18. To calculate the expected value, multiply the probabilities and the outcomes, then add them together (50% X \$2 million gain, plus 50% X \$1 million loss, equals a \$500,000 gain).

19. Thaler, "Anomalies: Saving, Fungibility, and Mental Accounts."

20. Belsky and Gilovich, *Why Smart People Make Big Money Mistakes*, p. 47.

21. Ibid., p. 127.

22. J. Entine, *Taboo: Why Black Athletes Dominate Sports and Why We Are Afraid to Talk about It* (New York: Public Affairs, 2000), pp. 202–203; Shermer, "Blood, Sweat and Fears," *Skeptic* 8, no. 1 (2000): 47.

23. Ibid., p. 47.

24. B. Fischhoff, "Hindsight ≠ Foresight: The Effect of Outcome Knowledge on Judgment under Uncertainty," *Journal of Experimental Psychology: Human Perception and Performance* 1 (1975).

25. This hindsight bias leads many to question the value of research because, after research results are known, we look back and say, "We knew it all along." But would the results be so obvious without knowledge of the research's outcome?

26. P. Slovic and B. Fischhoff, "On the Psychology of Experimental Surprises," *Journal of Experimental Psychology: Human Perception and Performance* 3 (1977): 544.

27. See S. Sutherland, *Irrationality: Why We Don't Think Straight* (New Brunswick, NJ: Rutgers University Press, 1992), pp. 240–44. Also see S. Lichenstein and B. Fischhoff, "Do Those Who Know More Also Know More about How Much They Know?" *Organizational Behavior and Human Decision Processes* 20, no. 2 (1977): 159; O. Svenson, "Are We All Less Risky and More Skillful Than Our Fellow Drivers?" *Acta Psychologica* 47 (1981): 143; S. Lichenstein, B. Fischhoff, and L. D. Phillips, "Calibration of Probabilities: The State of the Art," in *Decision Making and Change in Human Affairs: Proceedings of the Fifth Research Conference on Subjective Probability, Utility, and Decision Making* (Dordrecht, Holland: D. Reidel, 1975), p. 275; Belsky and Gilovich, *Why Smart People Make Big Money Mistakes*, p. 155.

28. R. Buehler, D. Griffin, and M. Ross, "Exploring the 'Planning Fallacy': Why People Underestimate Their Task Completion Times," *Journal of Personality and Social Psychology* 67, no. 3 (1994): 366; Belsky and Gilovich, *Why Smart People Make Big Money Mistakes*, p. 157.

29. Of course, sometimes planners deliberately lowball figures to get their projects passed.

30. S. Oskamp, "Overconfidence in Case Study Judgments," *Journal of Consulting Psychology* 29 (1965): 261.

31. E. Loftus, *Eyewitness Testimony* (Cambridge, MA: Harvard University Press, 1979), p. 101. Also see K. Deffenbacher, "Eyewitness Accuracy and Confidence," *Law and Human Behavior* 4 (1980): 243.

32. L. Goldberg, "The Effectiveness of Clinicians' Judgments: The Diagnosis of Organic Brain Damage from the Bender-Gestalt Test," *Journal of Consulting Psychology* 23 (1959): 25; R. Centor, H. Dalton, and J. Yates, "Are Physicians Probability Estimates Better or Worse Than Regression Model Estimates?" Sixth Annual Meeting of the Society for Medical Decision Making, Bethesda, MD, 1984; and J. Christensen-Szalanski and J. Bushyhead, "Physicians' Use of Probabilistic Information in a Real Clinical Setting," *Journal of Experimental Psychology: Human Perception and Performance* 7 (1981): 928.

33. E. Langer and J. Roth, "Heads I Win, Tails It's Chance: The Illusion of Control as a Function of the Sequence of Outcomes in a Purely Chance Task," *Journal of Personality and Social Psychology* 32 (1975): 951.

34. R. Dawes, *House of Cards, Psychology and Psychotherapy Built on Myth* (New York: Free Press, 1994), pp. 82–105.

35. One study compared the performance of students at the University of Texas medical school at Houston. Since the state legislature required the university to increase its entering class, they accepted applicants that their admissions committee interviewers said were at the bottom of the applicant pool. It turned out there was no difference in the performance of these students and the students that the interviewers said were at the top. R. Milstein et al., "Admission Decisions and Performance during Medical School," *Journal of Medical Education* 56 (1981): 77; N. Schmitt, "Social and Situational Determinants of Interview Decisions: Implications for the Employment Interview," *Personnel Psychology* 29 (1976): 79; and Sutherland, *Irrationality*, p. 285.

36. Other variables, such as a student's written statement, can also be given numerical evaluations and then considered along with the other data. These variables are typically standardized to make them more comparable before they are added together. Other more advanced statistical techniques, like regression analysis, are also available and produce more accurate judgments than intuitive assessments. With these techniques, each bit of information is multiplied by a coefficient and then summed to form an overall prediction. See P. Meehl, *Clinical versus Statistical Prediction: A Theoretical Analysis and Review of the Literature* (Minneapolis: University of Minnesota Press, 1954).

37. Meehl, *Clinical versus Statistical Prediction*; J. Sawyer, "Measurement and Prediction, Clinical and Statistical," *Psychological Bulletin* 66 (1966): 178; and Sutherland, *Irrationality*, p. 275.

38. R. Dawes, "A Case Study of Graduate Admissions: Application of Three Principles of Human Decision Making," *American Psychologist* 26, no. 2 (1971): 180; R. Dawes and B. Corrigan, "Linear Models in Decision Making," *Psychological Bulletin* 81 (1974): 98. Of course, it's difficult to evaluate the members' judgments completely because we don't know how rejected candidates would have performed. However, we can evaluate the members' judgments for those students accepted by comparing the students' performance toward the end of their program with the committee's initial assessments.

39. Not only would judgments be more accurate, a tremendous cost savings would accrue if people relied more on statistical data. R. Dawes, "A Case Study of Graduate Admissions," noted that millions of dollars a year would be saved if graduate schools in the United States used statistical methods instead of intuitive judgments to make their admissions decisions.

40. J. Carroll et al., "Evaluation, Diagnosis, and Prediction in Parole Decision Making," *Law and Society Review* 17 (1988): 199; Dawes, *House of Cards,* p. 89. The correlation was 0.06 for the interviewer and 0.22 for the statistical model.

41. H. Einhorn, "Expert Measurement and Mechanical Combination," *Organizational Behaviour and Human Performance* 7 (1972): 86; Sutherland, *Irrationality*, p. 286.

42. Sutherland, *Irrationality*, p. 287.

43. I. Goldberg, "Man versus Model of Man: A Rationale, Plus Some Evidence for a Method of Improving on Clinical Inferences," *Psychological Bulletin* 73 (1970): 422.

44. Sutherland, *Irrationality*, p. 288. This doesn't mean that the human element is not important in decision making. Many decisions are unique, and statistical models are therefore difficult to develop. Also, research indicates that humans are good at selecting the important variables to be considered in a decision. After those variables are measured, however, it's typically better to have a statistical model combine the information to form the final prediction when a model is available.

45. This is problematic, since clinical psychology has relied heavily on anecdotal data, and, in some segments, has harbored a number of different pseudosciences, such as facilitated communication and the use of the Rorschach inkblot test.

46. Paul Meehl, a noted clinical researcher, indicated that if clinical psychologists don't start taking a scientific approach to their profession, they run the risk of becoming nothing more than "well-paid soothsayers." See P. Meehl, "Philosophy of Science: Help or Hindrance," *Psychological Reports* 72 (1993): 707; K.

Stanovich, *How to Think Straight about Psychology* (Boston: Allyn and Bacon, 2001), p. 211. In fact, Tana Dineen goes so far as to say that "psychotherapy has no effective agent, but people . . . buy it, believe in it, and insist that it works because it makes them feel better about themselves for a while. This change, if it can be called that, may well be derived from nothing more than the expression of concern and caring, and not from specialized treatment worthy of payment." See T. Dineen, "Psychotherapy: The Snake Oil of the 90s?" *Skeptic* 6, no. 3 (1998): 55. While the efficacy of psychotherapy is debatable, there is no doubt that there has been tremendous growth in the number of people who seek help from various forms of psychologists. In the 1960s, only 14 percent of US citizens received psychological services. By 1976 the estimate rose to 26 percent, and was 46 percent in 1995. See Dineen, "Psychotherapy," p. 56. The *Diagnostic and Statistical Manual of Mental Disorders*, the Bible of the American Psychiatric Association, lists more than 300 mental syndromes. About twenty years ago, there were only 106.

47. A. Christensen and N. Jacobson, "Who (or What) Can Do Psychotherapy: The Status and Challenge of Nonprofessional Therapies," *Psychological Science* 5 (1994): 8; J. Landman and R. Dawes, "Psychotherapy Outcome," *American Psychologist* 37 (1982): 504.

48. Dawes, *House of Cards*, p. 5; Stanovich, *How to Think Straight about Psychology*, p. 210. See Dawes, *House of Cards,* for a discussion of the research supporting this assertion.

49. Stanovich, *How to Think Straight about Psychology*, p. 210.

50. Dawes, *House of Cards,* p. vii.

51. Some people have attacked psychology for its inability to predict an individual's behavior, but that's like saying we shouldn't bother with medicine because it doesn't help everyone. When medical science finds that a certain drug is effective in curing disease, that doesn't mean it will work for everyone. Knowledge of general statistics can be quite important, whether we can predict what will happen to an individual or not. We know that smoking causes lung cancer, but that doesn't allow us to predict whether a certain smoker will die from lung cancer. It means you have a greater likelihood of contracting that illness. More smokers will die from lung cancer than a similar group of nonsmokers—very important information—but we don't know which ones will die. Of course, there will always be someone who smokes heavily and still lives a long and healthy life. George Burns lived to around 100, and smoked cigars every day of his adult life. But these people are in the tails of the distribution—they represent the extreme cases. The fact is, of the men who make it to age 85, only 5 percent are smokers. When we use anecdotal evidence to argue against

hard statistical data that's based upon thousands, if not millions, of cases, we're making inappropriate judgments.

CHAPTER 11: FAULTY MEMORIES

1. E. Loftus and G. Loftus, "On the Permanence of Stored Information in the Human Brain," *American Psychologist* 35, no. 5 (1980): 410.

2. E. Loftus and K. Ketcham, *Witness for the Defense: The Accused, the Eyewitness, and the Expert Who Puts Memory on Trial* (New York: St. Martin's, 1991), p. 20.

3. I. Hunter, *Memory* (Middlesex, UK: Penguin Books, 1964); S. Plous, *The Psychology of Judgment and Decision Making* (New York: McGraw-Hill, 1993), p. 37.

4. U. Neisser and N. Harsch, "Phantom Flashbulbs: False Recollections about Hearing the News about the Challenger," in *Affect and Accuracy in Recall: Studies of "Flashbulb" Memories*, ed. E. Winograd and U. Neisser (New York: Cambridge University Press, 1992), p. 9.

5. See also E. Loftus and K. Ketcham, *The Myth of Repressed Memory: False Memories and Allegations of Sexual Abuse* (New York: St. Martin's, 1994).

6. D. Schacter, *Searching for Memory* (New York: Basic Books, 1996), pp. 111–12. The quote is from the "Hearings before the Select Committee on Presidential Campaign Activities of the United States Senate," 1973, p. 957.

7. Loftus and Ketcham, *The Myth of Repressed Memory*, pp. 1–2. Many of the reports of repressed memory discussed here are based upon the work of Loftus and Ketcham.

8. Ibid., p. 7.

9. E. Bass and L. Davis, *The Courage to Heal: A Guide for Women Survivors of Child Sexual Abuse* (New York: Perennial Library, 1988). Also see Loftus and Ketchum, *The Myth of Repressed Memory*, p. 140.

10. M. Orne, "The Use and Misuse of Hypnosis in Court," *International Journal of Clinical and Experimental Hypnosis* 27, no. 4 (1979): 311.

11. N. Spanos et al., "Secondary Identity Enactments during Hypnotic Past-Life Regression: A Sociocognitive Perspective," *Journal of Personality and Social Psychology* 61 (1991): 308; Loftus and Ketcham, *The Myth of Repressed Memory*, p. 79.

12. Loftus and Ketcham, *The Myth of Repressed Memory*, p. 229.

13. Ibid., p. 232. Also see C. Sagan, *The Demon-Haunted World* (New York: Random House, 1995), p. 162.

14. Schacter, *Searching for Memory*, p. 130.

15. Loftus and Ketcham, *The Myth of Repressed Memory*, pp. 250, 256 58. False confessions may be more common than we think. S. Kassin and L. Wrightsman, "Coerced Confessions, Judicial Instruction, and Mock Juror Verdicts," *Journal of Applied Social Psychology* 11 (1981): 489, had college students type a series of spoken letters. They were told not to press the ALT key because it would crash the program. None of the students hit that key, but they were accused of doing so. After initially denying they did, some of the students heard a "confederate" witness say they saw them do it. About 70 percent of the students eventually signed a false confession.

16. Loftus and Ketcham, *The Myth of Repressed Memory*, p. 261.

17. Associated Press, "Woman's Kin Awarded $5 Million in False Memory Syndrome Case," *Springfield (MA) Sunday Republican*, March 18, 2001.

18. E. Loftus, J. Feldman, and R. Dashiell, "The Reality of Illusory Memories," in *Memory Distortion*, ed. D. Schacter (Cambridge, MA: Harvard University Press, 1995), p. 63; I. Hyman, T. Husband, and F. Billings, "False Memories of Childhood Experiences," *Applied Cognitive Psychology* 9, no. 3 (1995): 181; I. Hyman Jr. and F. Billings, "Individual Differences and the Creation of False Childhood Memories," *Memory* 6, no. 1 (1998): 1; and S. Porter, J. Yuille, and D. Lehman, "The Nature of Real, Implanted, and Fabricated Memories for Emotional Childhood Events: Implications for the Recovered Memory Debate," *Law and Human Behavior* 23, no. 5 (1999): 517. Memories can also be implanted in very young children, which is particularly troubling since many therapists believe that children would not make up such stories. See Schacter, *The Seven Sins of Memory*, pp. 130–37.

19. E. Loftus and J. Palmer, "Reconstruction of Automobile Destruction: An Example of the Interaction between Language and Memory," *Journal of Verbal Learning and Verbal Behavior* 13 (1974): 111.

20. Ibid.

21. E. Loftus, D. Miller, and H. Burns, "Semantic Integration of Verbal Information into a Visual Memory," *Journal of Experimental Psychology: Human Learning and Memory* 4, no. 1 (1978): 19. In another experiment, individuals observed a series of slides depicting an auto-pedestrian accident. One of the slides showed a green car driving past the accident scene. Half of the subjects were asked, "Did the 'blue' car that drove past the accident have a ski rack on the roof?" The control subjects were asked the same question with the word 'blue' deleted. The results revealed that 28 percent of the control subjects accurately identified the color of the car, while only 8 percent of the subjects that saw the word *blue* in the question responded accurately. Overall, subjects who saw *blue*

tended to shift their color identification toward the blue end of the color spectrum. See E. Loftus, "Shifting Human Color Memory," *Memory and Cognition* 5, no. 6 (1977): 696.

22. H. Crombag, W. Wagenaar, and P. Van Koppen, "Crashing Memories and the Problem of 'Source Monitoring,'" *Applied Cognitive Psychology* 10, no. 2 (1996): 95.

23. D. Schacter, *The Seven Sins of Memory*, p. 88.

24. E. Loftus, J. Feldman, and R. Dashiell, "The Reality of Illusory Memories," in *Memory Distortion*, ed. D. Schacter (Cambridge, MA: Harvard University Press, 1995), p. 63.

25. Loftus and Ketcham, *The Myth of Repressed Memory*, p. 93.

26. See Loftus and Ketcham, *Witness for the Defense*, for a more detailed discussion of this case.

27. E. Aronson, *The Social Animal* (New York: W. H. Freeman, 1995), p. 148.

28. D. Ross et al., "Unconscious Transference and Mistaken Identity: When a Witness Misidentifies a Familiar but Innocent Person," *Journal of Applied Psychology* 79 (1994): 918; Schacter, *The Seven Sins of Memory*, p. 92. Experiments also document false identification. For example, one study had student "witnesses" view "criminals" for a period of time. Since witnesses often don't know they have to pay close attention to a potential criminal, the subjects did not think they would have to remember the criminals. They looked at mug shots two to three days later, and viewed lineups four to five days after the mug shot viewing. Eighteen percent of the "innocent" people in the lineups were mistakenly identified, while 29 percent were identified from the mug shot book. See E. Brown, K. Deffenbacher, and W. Sturgill, "Memory for Faces and the Circumstances of Encounter," *Journal of Applied Psychology* 62, no. 3 (1977): 311.

29. Loftus and Ketcham, *Witness for the Defense*, p. 21.

30. D. Schacter, "The Psychology of Memory," in *Mind and Brain: Dialogues in Cognitive Neuroscience*, ed. J. Ledoux and W. Hirst (Cambridge, MA: Cambridge University Press, 1986), p. 197.

31. M. Reinitz, J. Morrisey, and J. Demb, "The Role of Attention in Face Encoding," *Journal of Experimental Psychology: Learning, Memory, and Cognition* 20 (1994): 161; S. Rubin et al., "Memory Conjunction Errors in Younger and Older Adults: Event Related Potential and Neuropsychological Data," *Cognitive Neuropsychology* 16 (1999): 459; and Schacter, *The Seven Sins of Memory*, p. 97. It's interesting to note that some memory problems have been directly associated with certain parts of the brain. For example, neurobiological research has demonstrated that people with damage to their hippocampus make more memory conjunction errors. In addition, the hippocampus is needed in order to acquire and

store new memory traces. If your hippocampus was damaged five years ago, you would not have any memories after that date, but would remember what occurred before that date. This supports the modular view of the brain discussed earlier. Memory traces are not stored in the hippocampus, but it is needed to lay down a new memory. See V. S. Ramachandran and S. Blakeslee, *Phantoms in the Brain* (New York: Quill-William Morrow, 1998), p. 17. For example, neuroscientist Ramachandran reported meeting a patient who could intelligently discuss philosophy and mathematics. When Ramachandran left the room for a few minutes, and later returned, the patient had no memory of ever seeing or talking with him.

32. G. Wells et al., "Eyewitness Identification Procedures: Recommendations for Lineups and Photospreads," *Law and Human Behavior* 22 (1998): 603; G. Wells et al., "From the Lab to the Police Station: A Successful Application of Eyewitness Research," *American Psychologist* 55 (2000): 581; and Schacter, *The Seven Sins of Memory*, p. 97.

33. Schacter, *The Seven Sins of Memory*, p. 116.

34. T. Schick and L. Vaughn, *How to Think about Weird Things* (New York: McGraw-Hill, 2002), p. 47.

35. Schacter, *The Seven Sins of Memory*, p. 129.

36. See Schacter, *The Seven Sins of Memory*, for a more detailed discussion of memory errors.

CHAPTER 12: THE INFLUENCE OF OTHERS

1. S. Milgram, "Behavioral Study of Obedience," *Journal of Abnormal and Social Psychology* 67 (1963): 371; S. Milgram, "Some Conditions of Obedience and Disobedience to Authority," *Human Relations* 18, no. 1 (1965): 57; and S. Milgram, *Obedience to Authority: An Experimental View* (New York: Harper and Row, 1974).

2. See E. Aronson, *The Social Animal* (New York: W. H. Freeman, 1995), p. 42, for a review of this research. Our willingness to obey can be affected by other factors, such as the ability to actually see the pain we're inflicting. For example, when subjects saw the person in the other room, 40 percent continued to shock to the end, as compared to 62 percent when the person couldn't be seen. While a significant drop, many people still went all the way.

3. C. Hofling et al., "An Experimental Study in Nurse-Physician Relationships," *Journal of Nervous and Mental Disease* 143 (1966): 171.

4. Of course, that doesn't mean that the consensus view will always be right. Science is constantly advancing our knowledge of the world, and, every

now and then, a single scientist, such as Einstein, will propose a new and revolutionary theory that ultimately proves to be a better explanation of the workings of our universe. Since science wants to see evidence for a claim, it may take time for the general scientific community to embrace a new theory. In general, however, going with the consensus view of qualified experts is more likely to result in the most informed beliefs given our current state of knowledge.

5. S. Asch, "Effects of Group Pressure upon the Modification and Distortion of Judgment," in *Groups, Leadership and Men*, ed. H. Guetzknow (Pittsburgh: Carnegie Press, 1951), p. 177; S. Asch, "Opinions and Social Pressure," *Scientific American* (November 1955): 31; and S. Asch "Studies of Independence and Conformity: A Minority of One against a Unanimous Majority," *Psychological Monographs* 70, no. 416 (1956).

6. R. Crutchfield, "Conformity and Character," *American Psychologist* 10 (1995): 191.

7. G. Belsky and T. Gilovich, *Why Smart People Make Big Money Mistakes* (New York: Simon and Schuster, 1999), p. 176.

8. N. Humphrey, *Leaps of Faith* (New York: Basic Books, 1996), p. 181.

9. S. Plous, *The Psychology of Judgment and Decision Making* (New York: McGraw-Hill, 1993), p. 194.

10. B. Latane and J. Darley, *The Unresponsive Bystander: Why Doesn't He Help?* (Englewood Cliffs, NJ: Prentice Hall, 1970); Plous, *The Psychology of Judgment and Decision Making*, p. 196.

11. B. Latane and J. Dabbs Jr., "Sex, Group Size, and Helping in Three Cities," *Sociometry* 38 (1975): 180; B. Latane and S. Nida, "Ten Years of Research on Group Size and Helping," *Psychological Bulletin* 89 (1981): 308.

12. Study conducted by Ringelmann, reported in Plous, *The Psychology of Judgment and Decision Making*, p. 193. Also see A. Ingham et al., "The Ringelmann Effect: Studies of Group Size and Group Performance," *Journal of Experimental Social Psychology* 10 (1974): 371.

13. R. Zajonc, "Social Facilitation," *Science* 149 (1965): 269; J. Michaels et al., "Social Facilitation and Inhibition in a Natural Setting," *Replication in Social Psychology* 2 (1982): 21; C. Bond Jr. and L. Titus, "Social Facilitation: A Meta-Analysis of 241 Studies," *Psychological Bulletin* 94 (1983): 265; and Plous, *The Psychology of Judgment and Decision Making*, p. 192.

14. P. Tetlock, "Accountability and Complexity of Thought," *Journal of Personality and Social Psychology* 45 (1983): 74; P. Tetlock and J. Kim, "Accountability and Judgment Processes in a Personality Prediction Task," *Journal of Personality and Social Psychology* 52 (1987): 700; and P. Tetlock, L. Skitka, and R. Boettger, "Social and Cognitive Strategies for Coping with

Accountability: Conformity, Complexity and Bolstering," *Journal of Personality and Social Psychology* 57 (1989): 632.

15. R. Ashton, "Effects of Justification and a Mechanical Aid on Judgment Performance," *Organizational Behavior and Human Decision Processes* 52 (1992): 292.

16. See Tetlock, "Accountability and Complexity of Thought"; and Tetlock, Skitka, and Boettger, "Social and Cognitive Strategies for Coping with Accountability."

17. T. Gilovich, *How We Know What Isn't So* (New York: Free Press, 1991), p. 112. We also tend to exaggerate the extent to which we think others hold the beliefs we do. A false-consensus effect has been found, where our own beliefs and values bias our estimates of how many other people share those views. For example, L. Ross, D. Greene, and P. House, "The False Consensus Effect: An Egocentric Bias in Social Perception and Attribution Processes," *Journal of Experimental Social Psychology* 13 (1977): 279, asked students if they would walk around campus wearing a large sign that said "Repent." Those that would said 60 percent of other students also would wear the sign, while those that wouldn't estimated only 27 percent.

18. C. Sagan, *The Demon-Haunted World* (New York: Random House, 1995); K. Stanovich, *How to Think Straight about Psychology* (Boston: Allyn and Bacon, 2001).

19. Gilovich, *How We Know What Isn't So*, p. 99.

20. The quotes are by Oprah Winfrey, *USA Today*, and a member of the president's AIDS commission, respectively, in M. Fumento, *The Myth of Heterosexual AIDS* (New York: Basic Books, 1990), pp. 3, 249, 324. Also see Gilovich, *How We Know What Isn't So*, p. 107.

21. Gilovich, *How We Know What Isn't So*, p. 109.

22. I. Janis, *Groupthink: Psychological Studies of Policy Decisions and Fiascoes*, 2nd ed. (Boston: Houghton Mifflin, 1982), p. 9.

23. Ibid; Plous, *The Psychology of Judgment and Decision Making*, p. 19.

24. Janis, *Groupthink*, p. 16.

25. J. Esser and J. Lindoerfer, "Groupthink and the Space Shuttle Challenger Accident: Toward a Quantitative Case Analysis," *Journal of Behavioral Decision Making* 2 (1989): 167.

26. J. Dean, *Worse Than Watergate: The Secret Presidency of George W. Bush* (New York: Little, Brown and Company, 2004).

27. B. Woodward, *Plan of Attack* (New York: Simon and Schuster, 2004).

28. Plous, *The Psychology of Judgment and Decision Making*, p. 203; J. Russo and P. Schoemaker, *Decision Traps: Ten Barriers to Brilliant Decision*

Making and How to Overcome Them (New York: Simon and Schuster, 1989), p. 152.

29. See N. Kogan and M. Wallach, *Risk Taking: A Study in Cognition and Personality* (New York: Holt, Reinhart, and Winston, 1964); and Plous, *The Psychology of Judgment and Decision Making*, p. 208. My friend George faced an almost identical decision as this one.

30. J. Stoner, "A Comparison of Individual and Group Decisions Involving Risk" (master's thesis, Massachusetts Institute of Technology, 1961).

31. D. Myers and G. Bishop, "Discussion Effects on Racial Attitudes," *Science* 169 (1970): 778.

32. D. Myers and M. Kaplan, "Group Induced Polarization in Simulated Juries," *Personality and Social Psychology Bulletin* 2 (1976): 63; Plous, *The Psychology of Judgment and Decision Making*, p. 209.

33. Groups may also exacerbate some of the biases that exist from using simplifying heuristics. See, for example, L. Argote, M. Seabright, and L. Dyer, "Individual versus Group Use of Base-Rate and Individuating Information," *Organizational Behavior and Human Decision Processes* 38 (1986): 65.

34. The problem and data are from N. Maier and A. Solem, "The Contribution of a Discussion Leader to the Quality of Group Thinking: The Effective Use of Minority Opinions," *Human Relations* 5 (1952): 277.

35. R. Hastie, "Review Essay: Experimental Evidence on Group Accuracy," in *Information Pooling and Group Decision Making: Proceedings of the Second University of California, Irvine, Conference on Political Economy*, ed. B. Grofman and G. Owens (Greenwich, CT: Jai Press, 1986); G. Hill, "Group versus Individual Performance: Are N+1 Heads Better Than One?" *Psychological Bulletin* 91 (1982): 517.

EPILOGUE: SOME FINAL THOUGHTS

1. A. Mander, *Logic for the Millions* (New York: Philosophical Library, 1947), p. vii.

2. T. Schick and L. Vaughn, *How to Think about Weird Things* (New York: McGraw-Hill, 2002), p. 251.

3. T. Gilovich, *How We Know What Isn't So* (New York: Free Press, 1991), p. 109.

Index